This is the book for you if you are a student or young adult trying to figure out what to do with your life.

You want a career that fits you perfectly. A career where:

- You look forward to going to work most of the time
- You are extremely successful and productive because you are doing what comes naturally to you
- Your work is a natural expression of your talents and personality, so you fit with your work like a duck fits in a pond
- A day on the job leaves you feeling energized, not burned out
- You are proud of what you do
- Work often feels more like play
- You are highly respected at work because you are so good at what you do
- You do not have to pretend to be someone else at work
- The environment you work in brings out your best efforts
- You are on a winning team that is having a great time getting the job done

ALSO BY NICHOLAS LORE

The Pathfinder:
How to Choose or Change Your Career for
a Lifetime of Satisfaction and Success

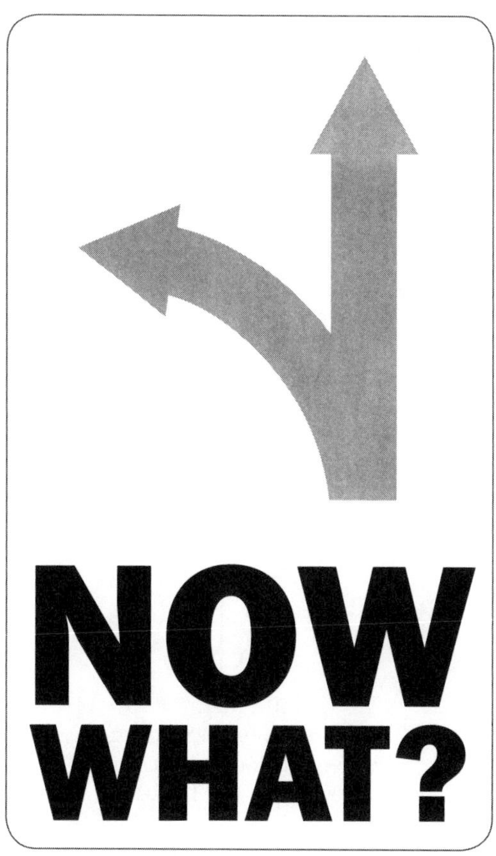

THE YOUNG PERSON'S GUIDE TO CHOOSING THE PERFECT CAREER

NICHOLAS LORE

with Anthony Spadafore

A FIRESIDE BOOK

Published by Simon & Schuster

New York London Toronto Sydney

For Erin, Newsha, Neema, Kyle, and Maia

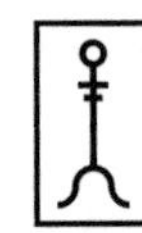

FIRESIDE
A Division of Simon & Schuster, Inc.
1230 Avenue of the Americas
New York, NY 10020

First Fireside trade paperback edition May 2008

FIRESIDE and colophon are registered trademarks of Simon & Schuster, Inc.

For information about special discounts for bulk purchases, please contact Simon & Schuster Special Sales at 1-800-456-6798 or business@simonandschuster.com.

Designed by Ruth Lee-Mui

Manufactured in the United States of America

1 3 5 7 9 10 8 6 4 2

ISBN-13: 978-0-7432-6630-7
ISBN-10: 0-7432-6630-7

Tell me, what is it you plan to do with your one wild and precious life?

—MARY OLIVER

CONTENTS

PART 1: HOW TO CHOOSE THE PERFECT CAREER

How to Choose the Perfect Career

SECTION 1

The Hero's Journey

You have just opened the last career book you'll need. You may have some idea where you are going, or you may be completely clueless about your future. Either way, this book was written for you.

This book is about choosing the perfect career for you, a career where you wake up in the morning looking forward to the coming day, where you're getting paid to do something you are really good at and very much enjoy.

You may have noticed that many people get up in the morning reluctantly. They get up because they have to, not because they want to. They hit the snooze button for a few more moments of oblivion before facing reality. They have to get up or terrible things will happen, like living under a bridge and pushing around a grocery cart with all their worldly possessions. They are slaves, wage slaves. They go to work because they have to, not because they want to. They are doing their best to get by in a life that is filled with struggle, toil, and trouble. You don't want to wind up like them. And you don't have to.

This book was written for a wide range of people and situations, basically people ages seventeen to thirty choosing their career direction for the first time. You may be a student or someone already out in the working world looking for the right direction. Whatever your situation, this guidebook can take you all the way to the point where you have decided on your future career.

CHAPTER 1

THIS IS AN ADVENTURE

Behold the turtle. He makes progress only when he sticks his neck out.

—James Bryant Conant

The greatest adventure is living life fully. What makes it such an extraordinary adventure is that it continues all through life, turning you into the main character in your own long and interesting novel. If you live your life fully day after day, you will never run out of enjoyable things to do. Since you will spend more of your life working than doing anything else, why not make your career part of your lifelong adventure? For most people, working is anything but interesting, enjoyable, rewarding, and fulfilling.

"We know that 55 percent of all U.S. employees are not engaged at work. They are basically in a holding pattern. They feel their capabilities aren't being tapped into and utilized, and therefore they really don't have a psychological connection to the organization," says the Gallup Organization, the experts in large-scale surveys. I know, just another statistic, but what if you turn out to be part of that 55 percent? Here's another statistic: only something like 30 percent of college-educated professionals say they like or love their work. The rest range from neutral to the deepest depths of career hell.

In the face of overwhelming (70 percent) odds that you will not land in the perfect career for you, you need expert coaching. This book will show you how to choose a career direction that fits you perfectly, a career that is not a compromise. I will supply the powerful and effective methods. You bring the commitment not to settle for anything less than spending your day in a career where you are successful, happy, and fulfilled—doing work you are proud to do, that is rewarding and challenging, with a big dose of self-expression, passion, fun, and the joy of making your dreams come true.

You may be still in school or you may have already experienced that slide from new-career delight to "Uh-oh, I have a bad feeling about this." Wherever you are, this book will save you time, money (wasted in studying the wrong thing for you), and worry.

WHY BOTHER

I have been coaching people for more than twenty-five years—thousands of people who have been in the wrong career for only a few years or as long as thirty years. I've seen them "before" and "after." I know the advantages of choosing a career that fits you perfectly.

Success

Success comes naturally when your career fits you well. Many people think they can guarantee their success by choosing a big-money career such as investment banking, medicine, or law. Money is definitely one way to measure success. Prestige is another.

Here's the dirty little secret no one mentions: if you are not happy to hop out of bed in the morning to go to work, the money or prestige will never be enough. I have clients who make six or seven figures. They will tell you it's not enough. It's never enough. My clients have included stockbrokers, doctors, lawyers, Hollywood movie producers, and CEOs of various kinds. Engrave this on your mind: no matter how much money or prestige you earn, you are not successful if you are miserable or not fully engaged in your work.

On the other hand, if making a lot of money is important to you, you are much more likely to reach that goal if you pick a career that both fits your talents and holds the potential for above-average earnings. Being good at what you do, you compete more effectively in the marketplace. Enjoying what you do, you bring an appetite and enthusiasm to your work that usually pays off.

Enjoyment

Having a career that fits feels better. It's as simple as that. When you're young, however, several things can obscure how badly a career fits: new experiences and the fun of trying your wings provide excitement, helped by powerful hormones that lend a rock-and-roll edge to life. When the novelty and chemicals taper off, however, you're left to your own devices. Watch the over-thirty crowd on their way to work. See how many look resigned, bored, angry, stressed, or sad. Contrast that with people whose eyes sparkle with pleasure, satisfaction, and interest in their work.

Personal Attractiveness

Speaking of eyes sparkling, being satisfied and fulfilled makes you more attractive to others. People love to be around people who glow with life, joy, and self-expression, whether or not they were born beautiful.

Good Relationships

Healthy people choose friends who make them feel good about themselves. They want friends who lift their spirits, who are fun to be around. Imagine, on the other hand, what it's like to live with someone who comes home exhausted and unhappy at the end of each workday. To enjoy great relationships, live a great life.

Self-expression

We all have innate abilities that want expression in the world. When we express them, we are most likely to make a contribution. If we do not express them, we sense that something is missing. All creatures except human beings express themselves naturally. We human beings are the only critters who are smart enough to talk ourselves into the wrong careers.

Self-esteem

Self-esteem is the reputation you have with yourself. Self-esteem never hovers. It is either rising or falling, based mostly on what is occurring in your life. It usually rises when you win, when you are satisfied with yourself and the progress you are making in your life. It falls when you lose regularly, when life is a constant struggle, when your confidence is eroded, when you feel no connection between you and the world around you. Your work profoundly influences your self-esteem. People who change paths in midcareer nearly always report that their ill-fitting careers had damaged their self-esteem. Create a future you will be proud of, and your self-esteem will take care of itself.

Health and Vitality

Many scientific studies show that the wrong career can actually make you seriously ill. People under significant stress at work have more than double the average number of colds. Their compromised immune systems cannot defend against illnesses, even life-threatening ones such as cancer. New research also shows that a lot of stress at work makes people age faster and die younger. People whose work uses their talents fully live longer and enjoy better health and, as a result, more vitality and well-being in all aspects of their lives.

THIS IS AN ADVENTURE, NOT JUST A BOOK TO READ

You can write yourself into this book as the hero in your own life, on a quest, a high adventure to find a career you love. As with any great adventure, you don't know how it will turn out, but you know there will be exhilarating moments, scary moments, and times when you want to turn back. That's the nature of an adventure. You don't go into the woods alone, however. Heroes have mentors to encourage them over the rough spots and a sidekick or two to offer moral support along the way. Start looking around for people who have your best interests at heart.

As the author of this book, I offer myself to you as a mentor. For more than twenty-five years I have scouted the woods of career choice. I know them like the back of my hand. Most important, I know where the pitfalls are.

Let's say you and a group of friends gather in a clearing in the wilderness to play a game, the winners being the first people to find their way back to civilization. The game starts. Off you go. Now suppose that you are the only person playing who has a map. Everyone else just wanders around, trusting to luck, hoping for the best. Some of your fellow players are confident they will do well. Others have big doubts. None of that matters because they don't have a map. You do. You have a huge advantage over your fellows who are just blindly bashing around in the woods. That's half the battle. The other half is committed action. If you just stay in the clearing and study the map, you won't win, no matter how good the map is. With a good map and committed action, you will win the game, which in this case means having career success and a life you love.

You and the Map

You are holding the map in your hands. I designed it specifically for you. Almost all career books and counselors are well-meaning but not capable of actually guiding you through the process of choosing the perfect career. Several years ago, frustrated because there was no really excellent career guidebook I could use with my career change clients, I wrote that book: *The Pathfinder: How to Choose or Change Your Career for a Lifetime of Satisfaction and Success.* It has been used by hundreds of thousands of people to design their careers and their lives. People like it because it works. Many people say it was the only book that got them to their career choice goal. But I wrote it mostly for midcareer people who are ready for a change, people who made a mistake early on and then want to correct it years later. This one is for you.

I am passionately committed to making sure that doesn't happen to you. What I care about is your having a life you love. I'm not particularly interested in whether you like me or not, at least not enough to suck up to you. This is not a kids' book. I promise you I will not pull any punches with you. I am almost certainly older than you, but I will not insult you by talking down to you or trying to sound "cool."

This may not be the right book for you. This one was written for people who want to live an extraordinary life and are willing to kick their own butt in the direction of that goal until they get there. If that isn't you, if you just want to dream about the future or complain about the present, then this book will only upset you.

I will suggest some other resources, other books, some additional testing of your talents, and so forth. But for the most part, this book is a complete guide. It won't leave you stranded in the middle of the woods. It will guide you through to your goal, step by step.

This is not a book to just read. It is a guide to use, to keep nearby and refer to all the way through the process of choosing your direction. Don't try to read it all now. Read the first few chapters and then decide how best to use it as the guide to creating a truly exceptional future for yourself.

Inquiry 1-1 **WHAT DO YOU WANT?**

Inside the front cover I said this book is for people who want certain things in their work life. Let's take a look at which of those are important to you. Check all the statements that apply to what you want your life to be like. This inquiry is about what you really want, not about what you think you can achieve.

___ I enjoy going to work because what I do is interesting and challenging.
___ My work is a natural expression of my talents and personality.
___ Success comes easily to me because I am so good at what I do.
___ I am proud of what I do and enjoy telling other people about it.
___ Work is often so enjoyable it feels more like play.
___ I don't have to pretend to be someone else at work because my personality suits my work.
___ I'm paid to make use of my own best and most natural forms of creative expression.
___ My work environment brings out my best efforts.
___ My job fits my most important values and allows me to fulfill my goals in terms of personal growth and achievement goals, income, stability, and so on.
___ I'm personally interested in what I do.
___ The result of my efforts makes a contribution that personally matters to me.
___ My job allows plenty of time for friends, family, and fun outside of work.
___ I like the people I work with.
___ I am on a winning team that is having a great time getting the job done.
___ A day on the job leaves me feeling energized, not burned out.

This book asks a lot of you! It will teach you to climb a tall mountain, one that requires more skill, dedication, and energy than anything you have done in your life. But the view from the top is worth the climb.

CHAPTER

2

REALITY 101

Don't believe everything you think.

—Bumper sticker

We all get our notions of reality from some pretty unreliable sources: television, movies, our friends' holding forth on life and love, and how we interpret what we think we see and hear. You're going to have to do better than that if you want to make good choices. There are some things you need to know before you begin the journey of designing your future career. You need to take a hard look at what it's really like out there and what obstacles you will face. If you don't get clear about this stuff now, it will haunt you later. So let's take a brief look at reality.

THE PLACE OF WORK IN YOUR LIFE

Of all you will do throughout the course of your life, you will work more than you do anything else, including sleep. The average American works nine hours a day and commutes a half hour each way. We're up to ten hours already. Add another hour for making yourself presentable (a shower, sure, but factor in picking up your clothes from the cleaner, polishing your shoes, and all the rest). That adds up to eleven hours a day, every day, forever. If you decide to become a doctor, lawyer, or corporate executive, add another two hours a day. I'm basing these figures on the supposition you are doing work you like. If you work in a career that is stressful and ill-fitting, get ready to spend the rest of your waking hours trying to recover from your crappy workday.

Given that, how much time does that leave to do the stuff you really want to do? After the eleven hours occupied by work and getting ready for work, you have thirteen hours left. Subtract eight hours for sleep and you're down to five. Subtract time for shopping, haircuts, clipping toenails, getting gas, finding your keys, visiting your tarot card reader, praying for help, cleaning up, washing the dog, helping your brother, mowing the lawn, answering your mother's questions about the new person you are seeing, and all the hundreds of other things people have to do, and you are left with maybe a couple of hours to do what you want each day. Unless you decide to have kids, in which case forget about having any time at all for yourself.

Okay, let reality pour over you like a big bucket of ice water: most of your life will be spent working. Please, don't jump off the roof yet. It's bad news only if you hate your job. If you love your work, you will spend your life having a great time. If you decide to create your own future, a future of high-level fulfillment and success, you can truly have the kind of life you dream about. What if you could have the kind of life described in the following quote?

> The master in the art of living draws no distinction between his work and his play, his labor and his leisure, his education and his recreation, his love and his religion. He hardly knows which is which. He simply pursues his vision of excellence through whatever he is doing and leaves it to others to determine whether he is working or playing. To himself, he is always doing both.
>
> —*Susan Fowler Woodring*

How well your work fits affects every other part of your life. Everything in your life is related. Think about times when you are in an especially good mood. Doesn't everything seem to turn out well? You find yourself singing in the shower, smelling the flowers. You can even forgive the cat for messing on your pillow. On the other hand, what about times when you've got the blues, when you are grouchy or bored? Nothing seems to go well, and even if it did, you wouldn't enjoy it anyway. Since you spend more time working than doing anything else, how well your career fits has an enormous impact on your entire life.

WHAT IT'S REALLY LIKE OUT THERE

In the first chapter we briefly mentioned that only 30 percent of educated people like their work. What effect does their level of career satisfaction have on the rest of their lives, their confidence, their health, and their relationships? Check out the Career Satisfaction Chart on the next page, the result of a study we did at Rockport Institute. This isn't some theoretical construct. This is reality. It is a description of the rest of your life depending on how well you design your future.

Notice how much workplace satisfaction affects the rest of life. There are rare exceptions, but we can say overall that the level of commitment and energy you are willing to give to choosing, preparing for, and working in a career that fits you perfectly will be paid back a thousandfold in the quality of all parts of your life.

Career Satisfaction Scale

0 to 10 scale	Estimated % of population	General Description	Effect on Personal Life	Contribution to Workplace
10	10 %	WORK OCCURS AS PASSIONATE PLAY Looks forward to going to work; sees work as vehicle for full self-expression, fun and pleasure; difficulties interpreted as positive challenges; considerable personal growth and contribution to self-esteem linked to work; little distinction between work and rest of life; sense of purpose and making a difference; uses talents fully; work fits personality.	Self-actuated lifestyle, generous with self—often participates in "service" to others; loves life, goes for the gusto, playful; high level of personal integrity; self-esteem is rarely an issue; very significant increase in longevity and disease resistance.	Work is an expression of a clear personal purpose; self-generating does not need supervision; very trustworthy—will persist until objective is reached; almost always contributes and is appropriate; takes correction as an opportunity; the presence of a person living at this level raises colleagues to a higher level.
8	20 %	POSITIVE Enjoys work most of the time; satisfaction dependent on circumstances, basic enjoyment of work tempered by difficulties; feels useful; usually has a sense of purpose or meaning regarding his or her job; career meets perceived needs, contributes to positive self-esteem; good fit between work, talents, and personality; high level of competence; value appreciated by others; would say work is "pretty good. I like my job."	Satisfying career enhances other areas of life: often has success in relationships, family and projects, positive self-esteem, increased longevity, increased resistance to disease; enjoys life much of the time.	Usually makes a positive contribution to the organization and other people; effective worker, fairly flexible; needs a minimum of supervision but not fully self-generating; handles responsibility well; decision making usually based on what's needed rather than personal agenda.
6	30 %	NEUTRAL Often accepts work situation without struggle; can appear to be a valued worker in a procedure-driven organization. This is the typical employee of a government agency or large, stable corporation. Some may say they like their work, others may grouse. If so, complaining is often simple socializing in an environment where complaining is a preference mode of communication.	Leads a life that has no real positive effect on the community, but usually has no significant negative effect either. Relationships and other aspects of life outside work may be "normal" but narrow.	May produce quality results in repetitive tasks; contributions are mechanical; little potential for real leadership, initiative, or creativity; resists change; at best, furthers own ends; would always hire the person with the best résumé rather than the best candidate; destructive when placed in a position beyond grasp.

Scale	%	Description	Effect on person	Effect on workplace
4				
	30 %	NEGATIVE Goes to work because forced by circumstances to do so; actively dislikes significant parts of job; daily routine marked by struggle, suffering, clock-watching, resentment, resignation; areas of life other than work may be satisfying; work either doesn't use abilities fully or requires talents not possessed; may be clash between personality or values and environment; complains about job; fear of job loss; may actively attempt to improve lot; may accept some personal responsibility for the situation.	Even though other areas of life may be healthy, career stress usually has negative effect on relationships, health, and longevity. May spend considerable portion of spare time recovering from work. Some erosion of self-esteem contributes to resignation or feelings of powerlessness in other areas.	Destructive to the workplace. Even if lack of satisfaction is hidden, it spreads to other employees; contributions, even when well meant, are outweighed by liabilities; is not really effective because usually wants to be somewhere else; motivated by need rather than choice. Needs supervision to produce consistent high-quality results.
2				
	10 %	CAREER HELL Work is a constant struggle, takes an act of will to go to work each day; strong sense of resentment, deep suffering; major clash between talents or personality or values and requirements of the job; symptoms similar to people between 2 and 4 on this scale except that here the dissatisfactions are more intense and the person feels completely trapped; each day at work erodes self-esteem; profound negative effect on other areas of life.	Because work is so enervating, little psychological room to do more than survive; reduced capacity to support others; difficulty in maintaining healthy relationships; marked hostility or resignation toward workplace; life shortened by several years; diminished immune system.	Dangerous and very destructive to environment; liability to self, others, and workplace; resistance (may be passive) to supervision, poor concentration, agenda is always at odds with organization's purpose; feels vindicated by the failure of others; completely untrustworthy; actively enrolls others in own agenda. Needs constant watching.

THE USUAL METHODS OF DECIDING DON'T WORK

Let's suppose that out of all the times you took your car to the repair shop, 70 percent of the time it came back still broken. Would you say the people at the garage knew what they were doing? Of course not. So if 70 percent of educated people are not enthusiastic about the work they do, that's the measure of how well the standard, old-fashioned career-choosing methods work. The bottom line: you are unlikely to have a life you love or live up to your full potential if you follow the standard methods.

You've got to give up the trusting, passive attitude some of your friends have. They think the common, everyday methods nearly everyone uses to pick their future direction will help them make good choices leading to a fulfilling life. Well, think again, dude and dudette. It isn't going to happen. That's the best way to make sure you spend your life doing something that doesn't fit.

The everyday method goes something like this. During your last years of high school, your parents and your guidance counselor ask you to "start thinking about what you may want to do." You, having no experience in this sort of thing, may come up with some possible careers, or you may not. The ideas most people come up with at this point are based on almost no evidence and not enough self-knowledge to think of anything suitable. Often their ideas are based on what seems cool at the time. You would be amazed at how many lawyers decide on their careers because of some movie or TV show, which bears no resemblance to the real practice of law. No wonder so many hate their jobs.

In college, you find yourself faced with choosing a major without much more clarity than you had in high school. By the time you reach the head of the line you have to decide, so you do.

THE TRUTH ABOUT COLLEGE

At college graduation, the real speech should be: "Congratulations! Most of you have just spent four years and a small fortune studying something you will never use or, if you do use it, you will hate. Have a nice life."

Most educated adults work in jobs that have nothing to do with what they studied in college. Many others who do work in their area of study dislike it but stick it out. Either way, college becomes a big waste of time, effort, and money. Don't rely on most college career centers to guide you in choosing a career direction. Some are very good at helping you learn how to job-hunt, write a resume, interview, and so forth. But what's the use of learning how to land a job in a field that's wrong for you? To make sure you don't wind up like so many of these students, make full use of the tools in this book to point yourself in the right direction. Then you will find it much easier to pick the best major—a major that leads to a career you will love.

After twenty-five years, I can say without hesitation that the single most critical element in career satisfaction—and the element colleges could address but don't—is the match between your innate abilities and the functions you perform at work each day, every day. When I say "innate abilities," I mean that complex combination of talents, abilities, and aptitudes that makes each of us naturally gifted at certain activities and less gifted at others. This goes way beyond personality and interests. Let's take a closer look at this critical area.

Your innate abilities make you a unique individual. People who are both very successful and satisfied with their careers nearly always have found a way to combine these abilities so that they are using them all day long in their work. They are doing what comes naturally. Understanding your own natural gifts and abilities is obviously one of the most important things you need to do in order to pick the perfect career.

You probably know much less about these abilities of yours than you think. Everything you know about what you do naturally well is based on experiences in the past, heavily colored by what people have told you all your life, the culture you were raised in, your beliefs about yourself, and a lot of other things. Using solid knowledge about your natural talents rather than ideas about yourself may mean the difference between success and failure, between a life of fulfillment and one of suffering. The question is where to acquire such knowledge.

You can go through a testing process that uncovers all these abilities and teaches you how they work, how they fit together, and which careers might suit you best. Most colleges don't provide this kind of testing. If you ask them if they have career testing, they may say yes because they mistakenly think that testing personality and interests provides all that's necessary. That's like your doctor's saying he has a stethoscope, so he doesn't need to see X-rays of your broken leg. (Actually, given the testing sophistication of colleges, it's more like his saying, "What's an X-ray?")

People who raise puppies for search and rescue, as guide dogs for the blind, and for other demanding doggy professions put puppies through a series of eleven puppy aptitude tests that sort out which dogs excel at those functions and which would make better family pets. They care about the dogs' success. They want the dog to match its owner so that both are happy and get what is best for them. I find this a troubling question: which group offers more guidance for the youngsters they are supposedly helping to train and educate to succeed, colleges or dog breeders?

For the most part, colleges don't care if you are not naturally talented in whatever career your major is supposed to prepare you for. They would let a duck major in piano without a single word of caution. They will rarely make it clear to the person considering majoring in Polynesian philosophy that there are no jobs in that field. They are not going to help you figure out what to do with your life. I am deeply sorry to say that it's going to be completely up to you to figure out what field to study. If you are reading this book as a part of a career choice process or class at your school, consider yourself fortunate: Your school is way ahead of the curve in being accountable for useful guidance. Most of you will have to do it without their help.

Want to start a revolution? Raise hell with your school about its low level of commitment to its students' lives and futures. Make the school take responsibility for initiating career guidance that works!

PARENTS

What about parents? Your parents love you and want the best for you, but they have no training in career coaching. If you were a passenger in a little airplane and the pilot suddenly died, would you call your parents to guide you through landing the plane? Of course not. If they are wise, they support you as you figure out how to make a great choice yourself. Maybe they even bought you this book. But they also have certain hopes and wishes apart from your concerns.

Every human has his own personal agenda built into his point of view. All parents are human. They are going to have more bragging rights if you become a famous brain surgeon instead of a taxidermist who specializes in stuffing mice in ferocious poses.

Your parents want life to turn out well for you. They also have had years of practice telling you what to do. So naturally they want to offer all sorts of counsel and advice. Listen to what they say—it might be wonderfully wise—but at the end of the day you are the one who has to live your life in your skin. Part of growing up includes learning to separate your own voice from the voices of your parents. This project, choosing your life's direction, is a good time to do that. This is something you have to do yourself. It is your life, and it's your choice.

YOURSELF

Should you trust yourself to make the best choices? The answer is both yes and no. You may know just enough about yourself, the world around you, and how the two may fit together to be a dangerous influence on yourself. Without much experience, mistaken ideas may interfere with good judgment. A friend of mine has the perfect natural talents and personality to be a doctor. She grew up wanting to be a doctor. Her sister is a doctor. But then she read a book by Dr. Christian Barnard, the guy who did the world's first heart transplant surgery. She says he talked about how he took strays home from the dog pound and performed heart transplants on these cute doggies in his garage. This grossed her out so much that she decided she didn't want to be a doctor after all. Does this make sense? Not really. There isn't any real connection between Dr. Barnard's autobiography and the actual practice of medicine. We all think in this slightly twisted way without knowing it. We all make inaccurate assumptions and decisions based on too little knowledge.

Then again, only you can make these decisions for your future. You can do it well, even brilliantly, if you know how to go about it. The first step, however, is to acknowledge that you don't have a clue about how to have a life you love. The truth will set you free, but first it very likely will piss you off. Face this and you are free from the illusions that hamper discovery. If you can admit you don't know, then you can learn. Then you can become more skilled at planning and directing your life than most of the people you know.

> You've got to jump off cliffs all the time and build your wings on the way down.
>
> —*Ray Bradbury*

SKIMP NOW, PAY LATER

Choosing work that will give you a successful and satisfying life involves taking on a major project, most likely the biggest and most important project you have ever done. That doesn't mean it has to be difficult. It doesn't have to be solemn. If someone gave you $10,000 and said you had to spend it all on a two-week vacation, think how much you would enjoy figuring out where to go and what to do. That's essentially what you will be doing in designing your career, except it's not a vacation we're talking about—it's your entire life, and nobody is going to give you $10,000. So enjoy this project. Get excited about it. And go all the way. Do it fully, as if your life depended on it. It does. Life is too short to have the wrong career. If you do not choose wisely in the beginning, you will pay later.

How difficult is it to design a career that fits you perfectly? Do you remember a college course that you enjoyed yet was challenging and a lot of work? It will take at least that amount of work and energy to do this well. Plus it will take extensive research. Unfortunately, there is no quick and easy way to do this that actually works. The quicker and easier the method, the less likely you will have a life you love and the kind of success and fulfillment you want. There are plenty of books that provide a quick and easy approach. This isn't one of them.

Doing it the right way only looks like a lot of effort because of how little energy your friends put into deciding what to do with their lives. Most people spend more time deciding which house or car to buy than they do choosing their career. You get what you give.

> Too often we enjoy the comfort of opinion without the discomfort of thought.
>
> —*John F. Kennedy*

HOW COME SOME PEOPLE PICK THE RIGHT CAREER WITHOUT ALL THIS EXPLORATION?

One well-known professional female bassoonist, when asked why she had chosen that instrument, said that when the school music teacher asked who wanted to play the bassoon, she raised her hand because she thought the teacher had asked who wanted to play the *kazoo*. She was too embarrassed to admit she didn't know what a bassoon was, so she learned it and found she not only liked it but was very good at it. Like her, some folks are just lucky. Other people have a knack for knowing what will fit them well. Neither of these is likely to apply to you. The odds are overwhelmingly against it. So, here's the bottom line: The cavalry isn't coming. Nobody is going to rescue you or do this for you. You are going to have to find a way to do it yourself. The good news is that you are the only person who can make the best choice for yourself. How? Read on.

> Security is mostly a superstition. It does not exist in nature, nor do the children of men as a whole experience it. Avoiding danger is no safer in the long run than outright exposure. Life is a daring adventure or nothing.
>
> —*Helen Keller*

CHAPTER 3

HOW TO USE THIS BOOK

Please read this very important note: The first principle in using this book is not to believe anything I tell you! Don't believe what other people tell you either. Sometimes you would be wise to question what you tell yourself. In order to make any decision about your future, you've got to see it with your own eyes, feel it in your bones, know it through your own thinking, and research it after having checked it out with many other resources. Everything in this book is just one man's opinion, not the truth.

COACHING

> If you always do what you've always done, then you'll always get what you've always got.
>
> —*Sign on convenience-store cash register*

In this book I will serve as a mentor and guide. A more apt designation might be "coach." If you aim to compete in the Olympics, for example, you need a coach to provide expertise, support, and encouragement. Without a great coach, forget it. You don't know enough, for one thing. Plus, to paraphrase Tom Landry, former coach of the Dallas Cowboys, a coach's job is to get you to do what you don't want to do so you can be the kind of player you always wanted to be.

If you take on a coaching relationship, whether in some athletic endeavor or in anything else, the best way to get results is to follow the instructions. That's called being coachable. How coachable you are remains to be seen. In the film *The Karate Kid,* the coach, Mr. Miyagi, has the kid wax a yard full of cars ("wax on, wax off"). The kid's mental resistance is massive. He has big doubts. He wonders if the coach is manipulating him, using him. But he waxes the cars anyway, because his commitment is bigger than his doubts. And that's when he first enters the arena of being committed and coachable. If you haven't seen this movie, or if you don't have a really vivid memory of this scene, please watch it now. Put this book down immediately and come back after you have seen it.

YOUR COACH

Before taking anyone on as your coach, you should know a lot about that person. Otherwise, how can you trust your guide when your mind is telling you there's no relationship between wax and karate?

My name is Nick Lore. When I was your age, it was the 1960s, and I lived in Greenwich Village, which in that short moment in time was the center of one of the greatest explosions of new possibilities and music in human history. My fellow Villagers were people such as Jimi Hendrix and Bob Dylan. Some of my closest friends had become rock stars, successful writers, scientists, and entrepreneurs. I was sure I wasn't going to be a rock star (not enough talent and no desire), but when it came to my future career, I wasn't too sure of much else. Since I had no idea what to do with my life, I just did what seemed like a good idea at the time.

My first job was as a paperboy at age eleven. Later on I was a lead singer and rhythm guitarist, then a researcher in psychology, then later still a CEO and an entrepreneur. I wound up living on the coast of Maine participating in the formative days of the green revolution, teaching organic farming and running an energy conservation company. After a while it became just as boring and repetitive as all my previous jobs. My office looked out over a beautiful harbor. I had great people working for me. But still, every day I watched the hands of the clock and hoped they would move a little faster toward quitting time, so I could get out of there and begin my real life. Eventually, I tried to find a career counselor to help me figure out what to do with my life. I was shocked to discover that their methods were so old-fashioned as to be completely useless. After working with one of my mentors, the great futurist R. Buckminster Fuller (the fellow who designed the big, spherical dome at Epcot Center), I decided to dedicate my life to reinventing the field of career counseling, to create ways people could choose careers they love.

In 1981, I founded Rockport Institute (www.rockportinstitute.com), an organization dedicated to helping people like you make the best possible career decisions and to creating powerful and effective methods to make that possible. Over the years we have helped many thousands of clients choose the perfect career—more, I think, than any other organization in human history. I created the profession and the term "career coaching." In old-fashioned career counseling, a counselor gave you some tests and advised you on what careers might fit you. Primitive stuff, totally ineffective, and still how it is done in most college career centers. I based career coaching on the model of athletic coaching: clients (that's you) are the players on the field, doing the work, progressing toward the goal of choosing a fitting career, while the coach makes sure they get there.

I wrote this book for you, with a lot of help from many friends your age. But reading a book and having good coaching are just two pieces of a bigger pie. The biggest, most important piece is your commitment. You have to decide to take this on, to make a project out of making sure you wind up with a great career and a life you love.

This isn't one of those start-at-the-beginning-and-go-until-the-end books. It is a guide, so there may be parts you read multiple times and others you don't read at all. It is actually two books in one.

PART 1: HOW TO CHOOSE THE PERFECT CAREER

"How to Choose the Perfect Career" is similar to the manual your flight instructor would give you if you wanted to learn to fly. It contains most of what you need to master to be successful in choosing your future career. Like a student pilot, you may wonder, "Why do I have to go through the pilot's flight manual? Why can't I just do the flying part, up in the air?" Like me, your flight instructor would answer, "Because you would crash and burn." It is not about doing what is entertaining or feels good. It is 100 percent about doing what works, what keeps the plane in the air, no matter what. Here's what is in Part 1:

- **Why only 10 percent of your friends will wind up in careers they love.** The traditional methods most of us use to choose what to do with our lives are useless, incapable of guiding you to your goal—that is, if your goal is to have a career that gives you a life you love.
- **What makes a career fit perfectly? What are the important pieces of the puzzle?** If you know what makes a career fit, you can design one that fits you. If you don't, you can't.
- **How to move a project from beginning to end with power.** Career design is a big project, possibly the biggest project you have ever taken on, and one of the most important ones you will ever undertake. Having mastery in working projects from an idea to a final, successful completion is a skill that gives you enormous power to have the kind of life you most want to live.
- **How to design the perfect career.** Einstein said, "Make everything as simple as possible, but not simpler." That's the goal of this book. This stuff isn't simple, and it demands more of you than people usually put into career choice. The best-selling student pilot's flight manual is 440 pages, and if you want to fly, you've got to nail most of it. Luckily for you, the first part of this book is much shorter.
- **How to deal with obstacles that keep people from having what they want.** A flight manual will tell you things like "Do your preflight inspection carefully" and "Don't fly under bridges." This book does the same thing in preparing you to succeed in this project. You will understand just what obstacles you face and how to deal with them.
- **How to get what you want.** Everyone wants to have more skill at getting what they want. Now you will.
- **How to put the pieces together and make the final decision.** Yes!

PART 2: THE CAREER DESIGN TOOLKIT

In this part you actually get the plane up in the air and do some flying. "The Career Design Toolkit" provides inquiries and exercises that give you new ways to look into every important aspect of yourself that you will use to design the perfect career. These exercises allow you to take your own measure the way a custom tailor does to ensure that a suit fits perfectly. Over the course of several chapters, you investigate three major areas:

- **Who you are.** What are your natural talents and important personality characteristics?
- **Why you work.** Nobody wants to spend his or her life doing meaningless work. This part of the book explores the importance of doing work where you enjoy the subject matter or feel you are making some special contribution.
- **Where you work.** Would you be at your best in a busy, competitive environment or a laid-back, cooperative, low-stress place? Find out what environment would be the perfect fit for you.

Once you've narrowed down the who, why, and where, this book will help you explore possible careers and narrow them down to a final choice. There is also a third part, the Career Finder—a systematic way of identifying some careers that fit your talents and personality.

USE THIS BOOK IN A WAY THAT WORKS FOR YOU

When we coach clients through designing their careers at Rockport Institute, we custom-design the process for each individual. People think, learn, and decide differently; plus, they all begin the program at different stages of their life's journey. Maybe you don't usually think much about your unique qualities, or maybe you have thought about them quite a bit. You may learn best by doing rather than through "book learning," or you may read everything you can find before venturing out. You may be facing this issue seriously for the first time, or you may have already made some career decisions. You may feel you can take your time, or you may feel an urgency to decide soon because, for you, college is a trade school where you need to learn a specific discipline in depth. The best way for you to design your future career won't match the best way for another person.

At Rockport, we are constantly experimenting to create new and better ways to help people design their lives. To ensure you have access to our latest techniques, and to keep this book from being five hundred pages long, you can find recommendations at www.rockportinstitute.com for applying the tools in this book to your own specific personality and situation. You may not need to do all the inquiries in Part 2.

If for some reason that doesn't work for you, here is a generic method that can work for many people: Read and do Part 1 of this book, "How to Choose the Perfect Career." Don't do the inquiries. Just read. Then come back and reread the parts that you think are most applicable to you and your own unique situation. Make sure you really understand the career design process. Then move on to Part 2, "The Career Design Toolkit," and begin to do the inquiries. As you do these exercises, you will generate clues about important elements of your future career. Work these clues like a detective. Keep working them until you can decide whether or not a specific clue will definitely be an important element of your future career. Keep turning clues into commitments.

WHAT DO I NEED BESIDES THIS BOOK?

I have done my best to include everything you could possibly need to go through the process of choosing your future career. The one thing no book can do is test and assess your natural abilities. The single most critical part of choosing a career is matching it to your talents and personality. (When we say each person is a unique individual, we're not talking about your purple Mohawk.) Each of us is born with a unique profile of natural gifts and personality traits, the gift of our ancestors transmitted to us through DNA. Knowing the hand dealt to you by Mother Nature is extremely useful in making the best possible career decisions. People who report both success and fulfillment in their work have an elegant and complete fit between their natural abilities and what they do all day.

You can access all the other pieces of the puzzle through the exercises in this book. Chapter 16 of this book, "Natural Talents," helps you evaluate your natural talents. If you are able to get absolutely crystal clear about them through the inquiries in that section, terrific. That may be all you need. I would be less than honest to say that this section of the book works as well as high-quality testing. Programs that test you and teach you how to understand and combine your natural abilities are very different, and much more powerful, than the kinds of self-assessment tests you may have done in school, with a career counselor, or online. Good abilities testing can give you a definite edge in making an excellent career decision.

Natural talents and abilities testing is such a powerful tool that we use it with all of our career decision-making clients. Time after time, clients express amazement that they can learn so much about themselves from a series of tests. People making a first-time career choice say that they finally understand which careers would fit them best and why. This kind of testing is not cheap. A good testing program can cost $500 to $600, but given what people spend to go through college—and then to go *back* to college after their first career doesn't work out—it is well worth the cost.

A young woman called us a few years ago who said she had a master's degree in English but didn't want to teach. Before I could respond, she said that after the master's, she had gone to law school. (*Oh,* I thought, *another lawyer.*) But no. She said she had a law degree but decided she didn't want to take the bar, and she was now completing an acupuncture certificate. She took a breath and dropped the final bomb: she now realized she didn't want to practice acupuncture either, and she was $80,000 in debt. After that, I stopped being shy about telling people about testing for fear that they would think I was trying to talk money out of their pockets.

The only reason people try to decide on their career by themselves is that they have always done it that way. It is a cultural habit. A century ago, there were only about a hundred different careers. Now there are more like ten thousand. In the old days, people didn't expect to like their work. They just wanted to make a good living. Now that we want satisfaction and the highest possible level of success, making the best choice takes more than a good guess. If you broke your arm, you wouldn't set it yourself. You would find a doctor. If you were sued, you wouldn't defend yourself. You would hire a lawyer. If you want to know more about getting your natural abilities tested, you can find contact information in the back of the book. Rockport offers testing programs worldwide. Many of our affiliates and various other organizations also offer this kind of testing program. Find us at www.rockport institute.com, and call or write for more information and sources.

Various organizations, including Rockport Institute, also have programs that personally coach clients through the career design process. This is the best possible way to design your future. Every college and university should offer this sort of program. We're encouraging them to do so, but so far most schools have not taken up the challenge of helping their students choose their life's direction. This book may be all you need. But I suggest that, if possible, you do natural ability testing or take an in-depth career design program. Here's a list of different approaches you might select to take you through the career choice process, listed from most effective to least effective.

- A complete, coached career choice program such as the Rockport Career Design Program, or a similar program with natural-talent testing, using this book and a couple of others as reading material.
- An in-depth, practical college course in career design including natural-talent testing and this book or an equivalent as the text, or a similar intensive career design program by an enlightened college career center.
- Natural talent testing with this book or an equivalent as your career coach.
- A group of friends supporting each other and meeting regularly to work through this book. (Dialogue is always better than monologue.)
- Using this book on your own.
- Making use of a career counselor using traditional methods.
- A typical college career center.
- Dive into some career that seems like a good idea now.
- Flip a coin.

I know you thought you'd just pony up a few bucks to buy this book and that would be the end of it. But after creating the field of career coaching and working with more than twelve thousand career clients, I can tell you for sure that, like everything else in life, you get the best results with the best methods.

> Twenty years from now you will be more disappointed by the things you didn't do than by the ones you did do.
>
> —*Mark Twain*

CHAPTER 4 HOW LONG WILL IT TAKE?

You may be wondering how long the process of choosing the perfect career will take, but there is no one answer that fits all. Some of you are thinking about your future seriously for the first time. Others are ready to make that final choice now. The problem is that many young people lack enough experience or self-knowledge to make a good career decision. This book is designed to remedy that situation as much as possible, especially in the realm of self-understanding, and to give you a head start on research in a way that reduces the need for experience.

Career design is a process, not a linear problem you can just sit down and solve in a few days or weeks. It will take time—several months at the least, several years for some of you. When we at Rockport Institute work with midcareer people seeking a change, they go through the career design process quickly, in three months or so, because they have to make a decision *now,* and they have enough experience of the world to make things go faster. People in their undergrad years sometimes take a couple of years to go through the same process.

Some people, mostly techie types, have already discovered a matching talent and passion because computers and other tech stuff is so much a part of our everyday lives. Most other young people have no idea what sort of career would fit best. Making the best choice involves a combination of commitment to having an excellent life, going through a competent career design process, and the passage of time. For most people, the best advice is to take your time working your way through this book. Don't rush. Do some inquiries in the second part of this book and then let what you have learned bubble away in the back of your brain for a while. Give yourself time to absorb what you have learned.

Remember, you aren't going to sort this out all at once. For most people the best way to do it is to make a choice in a general area first and then narrow it down as the career design process continues. For example:

General	More Specific	Very Specific
Science	Medicine	Research physician
Business	Marketing	Technical sales
Hands-on trade	Electrical	Own electrical contracting company
High tech	Software engineering	Robotics
Music	Jug band	Kazoo and washtub bass

Let's break down the "How long will it take?" question into categories by age. Remember, these general guidelines may not fit your unique situation precisely.

SEVENTEEN TO TWENTY-ONE

At the younger end of this age group, most people are just starting to think about their future. Do as much of this book as you can by age eighteen or nineteen so that by then you know enough about yourself to make some reasonably competent decisions and sort out your general direction.

By the time you have to declare a major, you may know enough to make a generalized choice. Start wide; narrow down later. For example, if you decide that the business world is right for you, head in that direction and tighten up your choice over the next couple of years. If you haven't decided on your general direction and you have to pick a major, don't pick some narrow area because it seems attractive right now. It would be wiser to pick a wider, more general area where you will learn things that will be useful throughout your life, no matter what you decide to do. Most forty-year-olds say they don't use and don't remember much of anything they learned in their undergrad years, so don't feel you have to make a narrow choice if you aren't ready.

Once you know the general area, you can use the exercises in this book to narrow further. Don't rely too heavily on courses at school to help you decide. Most college courses are nothing like the real world. In other words, studying something is not the same as working in the field. As you take courses, however, you can pick up some strong clues about where you have some natural talent and what you like to do. For example, if you love science courses, treat your taste for science like a good clue rather than an arrow pointing directly to a career. Don't assume that because you like science courses, a career in science is right for you. Don't rush to decide. The exception to that rule is a career that requires you to specialize during your undergraduate years. If you are a natural techie, for instance, and committed to a high-tech career, it behooves you to push your career design forward as far and as fast as you can. For you, college is more like a trade school than for most people your age.

If you are not planning to go to college, the same plan applies: choose a wide, general area and keep narrowing down, refining your direction as time passes. You still have to learn how to do what you want to do. That might mean your educating yourself, learning on the job, or taking on an apprenticeship or some other sort of educational alternative to college.

Strange as it may seem, living in your parents' basement, smoking pot, and hanging out with your friends does not constitute career exploration. Taking a few courses to please the parental units does not equal a commitment to choosing a career you will love. Just remember: given the low percentage of people who love their jobs, you would be well advised to become actively engaged in designing your life.

TWENTY-ONE TO TWENTY-FIVE

Now you are either headed for grad school or out in the real world. Don't rush into grad school if you don't know where you are headed. Spend a year or two sorting out your direction. Grad school is trade school for a specific career, so don't go to grad school to postpone choosing. If you think you need a break to mature a little, spend a year swinging from vines in some tropical paradise. If there is a field you think may be right for you, work in it, try it out. The shortsighted hiring policies of some corporations generate a lot of fears for people in this age group, fears like "If I don't get started early, I will be left behind." Well, that may be true. But what's wrong with being left behind on a trip you really don't want to take anyway? Don't let them scare you. If you feel pressured, use the pressure to push forward harder in your career design process.

If you are already out in the real world in a job that is not your final career choice, read the next section.

TWENTY-FIVE TO THIRTY

Now you are probably out of school unless you are in med school, a PhD program, or an extended educational experience to avoid reality. You are most likely in some sort of career field that isn't right for you or you wouldn't be reading this. You are actually at a great point in your life to design the perfect career because you have experienced something most younger people have not—an ice-cold dose of reality. This isn't theoretical to you. You have seen the future, and it looks grim. You probably feel more urgency to dive into this design process than someone with less real-world experience.

If you haven't decided on your specific career, don't worry. It's likely that most of your friends are in careers they aren't too excited about anyway. But it is time to get serious. Don't hang back. Well, I suppose you can. But then, you are choosing the career of no career, which is fine if that's what you really want. But most people do want to be engaged in something they love that is challenging and also pays the bills. So don't make up tales that all is well if it really isn't. Start right now. Work through this book. Do some natural abilities testing. Promise yourself that you *will* have a career you love.

THIS IS A LIFETIME PROJECT

It used to be that a person chose a career, prepared for it, and did it for the rest of his or her life. Back in 1880, as a farmer, a teacher, or a storekeeper, you just stumped through a lifetime of predictability. In today's fast-moving world, you will most likely need your *Now What?* career design skills again and again. There are several reasons for this:

- The world moves so fast that the career that fits you today may no longer fit in the future. Teaching, medicine, and book publishing, to name only three, are very different now than they were twenty or thirty years ago.
- Many careers contain a hierarchy of increasingly complex roles, providing more opportunities as well as challenges as the fields evolve over time.
- People want personal growth and development.
- Often, as you grow and develop, you discover your horizons expanding and your interests changing.

Many of us grow and develop throughout our lives. A friend of mine is the perfect example. In high school, as a somewhat typical computer science geek, he envisioned a career as a project manager for a typical computer software company. In college he discovered a talent for creating innovative solutions and found that he enjoyed bringing excitement to presentations of complex material for people. He became the Microsoft representative on campus.

He took off his junior year and backpacked around Asia alone, avoiding the tourist areas and getting to know local people and their cultures. He would often wander into a small village where the local people would take him in, teach him their language, and treat him with warmth and respect. Among many other things, this taught him courage. Previously, a small cut was a major upset. After this year out adventuring, a nasty wound became just a minor annoyance.

He became even more dedicated to living a life he loved. He knew the technical side of things wasn't enough for him. He also wanted to make a difference in the quality of people's lives. He studied human-computer interaction in grad school. There he was amazed to learn that students who were more technically brilliant than he was looked to him as a natural leader to create the "big-picture" solution that the supertechs could then develop. He began submitting technical papers alongside his professors, seeing himself as someone valued by the senior people in his field. Now he works for a huge computer company in their idea lab on the other side of the world, inventing educational solutions that help people in developing countries live better lives. This is just the current step in an evolving career. He sees his life as an ongoing journey of growth and development, both personally and professionally. Through the years he has learned more about himself and developed skills that make fuller use of what comes naturally to him. He says the only constant is change.

For most people, change may not be quite so dramatic. But even the solid, seemingly fixed careers, such as dentistry or auto mechanics, keep changing, and people often grow out of one role and want to expand or shift their direction. The skills you learn here will be useful throughout your life. Even though you have a specific goal—choosing the perfect career—you would be smart to consider this an ongoing, lifetime project. The skills you use to make the best career choice now can be useful the rest of your life.

CHAPTER 5

A CAREER THAT FITS YOU

There is only one success—to be able to spend your life in your own way.

—*Christopher Morley*

Why is it that some people absolutely love their work, while for others a day at the job is pure torture? How come some people are still energized at the end of a long day, while many others look like they need a long vacation? It's mostly a matter of how well people's careers fit who they are. So let's begin to take a closer look at you.

IT'S ALL ABOUT YOU

You are a unique, one-of-a-kind individual, not exactly like anyone else. To have a career that gives you the highest possible level of success as well as satisfaction and enjoyment, you need to design it yourself, piece by piece, so it fits *you* perfectly.

That's why it makes no sense to choose a career only because it's "hot"—or "cool"—or because Uncle Louie said the pay was great or because some people you know are going to do it. The first principle of choosing a fitting career is to focus your attention on yourself and figure out what comes naturally to you, so you can pick work that fits you instead of trying to squeeze into a job that doesn't.

WHAT MAKES A CAREER FIT?

Great question! Knowing the answer could have a huge impact on the quality of your entire life.

The answer is so simple that it is hard for most people to understand. *What makes a career fit is that it fits you naturally.* It uses your natural inborn talents fully. It fits your personality. You find the subject matter interesting and the work personally meaningful. The position fulfills your goals. Your work environment nurtures and rewards your best efforts. You enjoy what you do, and it stays interesting and challenging as the years roll by.

Jamming yourself into a career that is not a great fit is like swimming upstream. At first you may think of it as a challenge, something to conquer. But after a while, constantly fighting the current makes you feel drained. It becomes a struggle; then resignation and boredom set in. Plus, if you watch the trees along the bank, you notice you are not getting very far very fast. That's what work is like for many people, including plenty of extremely smart people who went to the best schools.

Sometimes they get tired of the struggle and find an eddy in their career's river. An eddy is a little place in a river that's out of the main current. In the working world it is a job where you can relax, a peaceful little spot where not much is happening and not much is expected of you. Eddies are terrific if you are kayaking upstream and want to take a break. But spending your life that way gets dull. You never get anywhere. The scenery never changes.

> The only difference between a rut and a grave are the dimensions.
>
> —*Ann Landers*

Now, imagine that you are back swimming in the river again. But this time you are swimming in the same direction as the current. Every stroke takes you a good, satisfying distance downstream. You are moving quickly, getting somewhere. Putting in a big effort is not a struggle but a powerful move in the direction you want to move. You know your efforts are paying off. Like swimming downstream, a career that fits you naturally is much more satisfying and fun.

Every species except human beings spends every day doing what comes naturally. They know what fits and what doesn't. You don't have to train a duck to paddle. Drop him in a pond, and he instantly begins his perfect occupation. Drop a chicken in that same pond and listen to the frantic squawks of protest. Drop a human being into the pond and five years later you can still hear him muttering as he paddles around: "Why is this so difficult? Maybe I should take more courses in pondology. Maybe I should move to a different pond."

We humans are so smart and adaptable that we can do many different things with reasonable competence. Our fabulous ability for complex reasoning has a downside: we can talk ourselves into things instead of paying attention to the subtle signs that the careers we are considering might not fit us that well.

THE ELEMENTS OF A PERFECT, NATURAL FIT

> Be faithful to that which exists nowhere but in yourself.
>
> —*Andre Gide*

Natural Talents and Innate Abilities

Everyone is born with a unique group of talents that are as individual as a fingerprint. These talents give each person a special ability to do certain kinds of tasks easily and happily, yet also make other tasks seem like pure torture. Can you imagine your favorite stand-up comedian working as an accountant? Talents are completely different from acquired knowledge, skills, and interests. Your interests can change. You can learn new skills and knowledge. Your natural, inherited talents remain with you for your entire life. They are the hand you have been dealt by Mother Nature. You can't change them. You can, however, learn to play brilliantly the hand you have been dealt to your best advantage. This is the foundation of choosing a career that fits you like a custom-made suit.

The Work Matches Your Personality Traits and Temperament

Imagine a teacher who would rather spend time alone, a surgeon who hates the sight of blood, a shy salesperson. You want a career that gives you a chance to be yourself, that fits your personality, that makes you feel at home. Many people are engaged in careers that require them to suppress themselves while at the job. An elegant fit between you and your work supports your self-expression. Telltale signs that a career doesn't fit your personality include needing to assume a different personality at work or a suspicion that the people you work with may be aliens from another planet.

Rewards Fit Your Values

Like the biscuit you give the dog, rewards are the motivators that help keep you happily performing your tricks at work. Some rewards mean more to you than others. That is because they are linked with your values. If recognition for doing something well is important to you, then it may also be a necessary reward to motivate you to keep performing well. Doing without adequate recognition will slowly erode your well-being on the job as will the lack of reward for any other important value.

You Fulfill Your Goals

To have something to shoot for is an important part of the joy of working. A custom-designed career supports you to fulfill your life goals and gives you a sense of challenge on the job.

Your Work Is Interesting and Meaningful

People engaged in something they care about are proud of what they do and feel they are making a contribution. Their work fascinates them. They may need to go to work to pay the bills, but that is not what gets them out of bed in the morning.

You Find the Workplace Environment Compatible

Each person flourishes in some work environments and finds others stressful or otherwise inappropriate. "Environment" includes geographical area, company style, and corporate personality, as well as the physicality and mood of the work setting and your relationships with others including your supervisor, fellow employees, and clients or customers.

• • •

Obviously, you are not just your interests or personality or any other single factor. You are made up of many different elements. The trick to choosing a career that fits you is to find a way to express all of your unique self, with nothing important left out.

HOW YOU GOT TO BE THE WAY YOU ARE

Nature

Families have long recognized the genetic basis of various traits because they "run in the family": things like a strong chin, dimples, a stubborn streak, creativity, good looks, and so on.

Some of the most telling studies have involved sets of identical twins separated at birth and adopted by different families. These sets of twins grew up amazingly alike, even though they had no contact with each other. One pair of separated-at-birth twins left school early at the same age, met their husbands at the same age and in the same setting, miscarried, and then each went on to have two boys and a girl. Both had the same odd little personal habits. They both used the palms of their hands to push their noses up, which they both called by the same made-up name, "squidging." They both laughed the same odd way, dyed their hair the same shade, drank their coffee cold, feared heights, and experienced discomfort around blood. They scored the same in psychological and IQ tests, used the same brands of personal care products, and had the same thyroid problems, heart murmurs, and allergies. After they discovered each other, they sent each other identical birthday gifts, and when they met for the first time they were wearing nearly identical clothes. This pair of twins is an especially dramatic example of what the studies revealed.

The point is that genetics determines much more of our personalities and talents than we sometimes think. Much of who you are came preformed from the factory. You know that the most beautiful girl and most handsome guy in school didn't create themselves that way. Their good looks are a happy accident, the gift of their genetic heritage. If they also naturally learn quickly, they didn't plan that either. So if you daydream in class, or talk too much or not enough, or your left zorch is too small or your hair sticks up, it is not your fault. If you came out cool or hot or sweet, you didn't do that either. It is all a part of the package the stork delivered.

Nurture

Simpler critters, like reptiles, arrive with their software fully programmed. A newborn snake knows all it needs to know to get by in life without lessons from Mom. It is for the most part a miniature adult, ready to fend for itself. That may be why there aren't any snake training schools in your town. You just can't train a snake to do anything it isn't programmed to do.

Other animals, including most mammals, are more complicated. Their parents teach them how to survive. Although you may think you learn much more these days than when you were little, quite the opposite is true. By the time you were six years old, you had learned the vast majority of what you will ever know, including all the basics, such as walking and talking, and a good chunk of your basic personal strategy and attitude about life.

Throughout our lives we learn from the influences around us: parents, friends, television, the "tribes" we belong to, our culture and society, our experiences, our decisions and mistakes. Zoologists call us "tribal primates," just like our hunter-gatherer ancestors. In ancient times, each of us belonged to one tribe. Now we belong to and are influenced by the wisdom, values, and rules of multiple tribes. Each of your tribes contributes to your personality, no matter how much of an independent-thinking person you consider yourself to be.

We absorb most of this without thinking about it. Mostly we don't know there *is* anything to think about. We tend to take our point of view for granted, as if it's a universal truth and not the product of our upbringing and genetic heritage.

You Are an Accident That Already Happened

Scientists are still arguing about how much of you comes from your ancestors and how much from your environment. In terms of figuring out what to do with your life, it doesn't really matter. The basic structure of your talents and personality will not likely change very much no matter what their original source. You will master new skills. You may develop and expand your personality and your abilities. But you are not going to become a different person. Who you are now is a lot like who you will be years from now.

When you combine all you have been given by nature with all you have learned through nurture, you get this marvelously complicated and completely unique creature: you. There is no one just like you out of all the billions of people alive. Nobody has the same mix of talents, personality traits, and history.

What does all of this have to do with choosing your career? It obviously makes sense to design a career that fits who you are, not someone else, and not some fantasy character you wish you were. If you are a quiet, private person, you may wish you were the life of the party. But it would be a mistake to pick a career that fits the fantasy instead of who you really are. That doesn't mean you can't grow, improve, and learn to be more outgoing. But you would be smart to pick a career that fits the real you rather than some imaginary character. You turned out exactly as you are now. You are perfectly designed to be the best possible you. That's why it is so important to get to know as much as you can about yourself, your talents, and your personality.

THE HUMAN SPIRIT

Right now you might be wondering: "Are you saying I'm just some animal or elegant, complicated machine without freedom of choice and self-determination?" No, not at all. What we have been talking about is just one side of human nature. There is another part that changes everything.

Nature and nurture cannot explain the totality of what it means to be human. Yes, there are things we cannot change. At five foot two as an adult, you will not be scouted by the NBA. That's the way it goes. It would be wise to consider a career other than basketball.

Where we humans surpass every other creature on earth is our ability to imagine a possible future that isn't going to happen automatically, to create a commitment to that future, and then to make it real. I'm not just talking about our human capacity to plan. I'm talking about the ability to invent a future we desire, even one that seems nearly impossible, and make it happen. That is the power of the human spirit. It is the ability to create.

When John F. Kennedy was president, he created a possibility, a vision for the future: the United States could land a man on the moon within ten years. Even though such an accomplishment seemed nearly impossible, Kennedy created a commitment to that possible future, convinced the American people to share his commitment, and then generated a project to make it happen. Many experts said it was impossible to predict whether we could actually pull it off. We went ahead anyway, and, as we all know, it was a brilliant success. Against all odds, we did it.

Human history is filled with stories of people doing what others considered impossible: Hannibal crossed the Alps with his elephants; the Wright brothers flew; a small group of American colonists created a vision for a brand of democracy that had never existed on the planet before. Vision alone, however, was insufficient. Next, they turned this vision into a commitment, even with all their doubts and fears about whether or not they could fulfill their dream. Then, in the case of the colonists, they declared that commitment to the world through an extraordinary document called the Declaration of Independence. They essentially said: "This is how it is going to be. We stake our lives on fulfilling this dream."

Vision, commitment, and declaration are not sufficient either, however. Those colonists also had to do all the hard work necessary to make the dream a reality, including hammering out agreements with each other and the part we call the American Revolution. The project of making this dream come true is still one of the major themes of American politics.

So What Does This Have to Do with Me?

Everything. You have the ability to turn dreams into reality every bit as much as Kennedy, Hannibal, the Wright brothers, and James Madison did. It is built into you. I have seen many thousands of people who shaped their own lives, often far beyond what they thought was possible, once they discovered the degree of power they had to create a new and extraordinary future for themselves.

We are all potential inventors, creators, artists, authors, entrepreneurs, and discoverers—not necessarily in the traditional ways, but in our own lives. We have the power to invent our own individual futures, create a vision of the kind of life we most want to live, and then find a way, against all odds, to make it happen.

SECTION 2

Gearing Up for Your Career Design Project

CHAPTER 6

HOW TO GET WHAT YOU WANT

This chapter contains some of the most powerful secrets for having your life turn out well. I know that sounds like a big claim, but let me explain. Most of this chapter is based on the distilled wisdom of humanity, drawn from the advice of hundreds of people, some living today and some long gone, who have been extraordinarily successful and who have had a huge impact on the world—the people who created the most successful companies, changed society for the better, made big breakthroughs in science, business, the arts, and the understanding of human nature, the great creators and thinkers in all fields. You will use these skills throughout your journey through this book. And you can use them in every part of your life. Like the rest of this book, these are things to practice, not just read and learn about. Master these skills to get your hands on the wheel of your life to steer through the obstacles to a rewarding future.

CREATE A FUTURE FOR YOURSELF THAT WASN'T GOING TO HAPPEN AUTOMATICALLY

We can predict the likely outcome of projects taken on by the guy who charges into things like a mad bull or the overly cautious person who avoids making decisions. Their usual way of operating makes certain results likely. Even with the unforeseen advantages of luck, what they get is usually consistent with how they go about doing whatever it is they are trying to accomplish.

Some people produce extraordinary results without any apparent luck whatsoever. How do they get what they want and achieve what they say they will? Most of us think they must have some special talent that the rest of us don't possess. But if you ask these especially accomplished people to reveal the secret of their success, they will tell you that they are ordinary people like you and me. They may be ordinary in a lot of respects, but in one way they are extraordinary: they have mastered projects.

PROJECTS

Whenever you are participating in something that has a goal and requires concerted effort, you are involved in a project. Projects all have the same series of steps, whether it's a big project such as ending world hunger, a medium-sized one such as having a life you love, or a little one such as making a sandwich. We can call this series of steps an "accomplishment cycle."

Accomplishment Cycles

Everything in life is part of a cycle, including the twenty-four-hour day, the seasons, and your life. Everything has a beginning, middle, and end. If you can master accomplishment cycles, you will gain tremendous power in moving your life forward, and in having a life you love.

Look over this summary of the accomplishment cycle as it applies to projects. This may look familiar, and if something looks familiar, we think we know everything about it. Big mistake. *Huge* mistake. This section is so critical that we have to sneak up on it. We'll look first at an example of an easy project. In the next chapters you will dive deeply into each step, including the pitfalls. Do not skip anything.

1. **Formulate a goal.** What goal do you want to achieve? A two-week vacation in Europe this summer? A career that gives you both maximum success and satisfaction? Learn to climb mountains? How about a peanut-butter-and-jelly sandwich?
2. **Commit to reaching the goal.** Wishing has no place here. The signers of the Declaration of Independence pledged their lives, fortunes, and "sacred honor." And they did it publicly. That's commitment.
3. **Plan how to get to the goal.** Fortunately, much of the planning for choosing a career you love is built into this book.
4. **Get in action.** This is the "work your plan" part. Deal with obstacles. Move it forward. Most projects are 90 percent action phase.
5. **Persist, problem-solve, adjust.** Once in action, you'll find roadblocks and the unexpected (both help and hindrance), so you need to keep updating your plan and adjusting your actions. At this stage you have to remember to act consistent with your commitment even if the road gets rough.
6. **Declare the project complete and celebrate!** After all that, you deserve a party.

Mastering the Steps of the Accomplishment Cycle

This example of an easy project follows the same accomplishment cycle. Let's say the project is a peanut-butter-and-jelly sandwich.

1. **Formulate a goal.** You're sitting on the couch watching TV. You notice a familiar call from your midsection: *Send food now!* Your preference mechanisms refine that request to: *PBJ.* (You may have performed some complex reasoning in an instant: your taste buds really want pizza, but between the choices of pizza later and PBJ now, now wins.)
2. **Commit to reaching your goal.** This commitment is much simpler than bringing forth a new nation so you skip the public declarations. Most likely, you commit to the PBJ without even thinking about it. (In this case, your stomach mainly drives the commitment.)
3. **Plan how to get to the goal.** Simple plan for a simple project: Get out bread, chunky peanut butter, jelly. Find knife. Spread stuff on bread.
4. **Get in action.** Make the sandwich.
5. **Persist, problem-solve, adjust.** You persist even if the peanut butter tears the bread. You consider starting over, maybe heating the peanut butter first to soften it up, then decide to just fold the bread over and forget about it. You have no commitment to aesthetics.
6. **Declare the project complete and celebrate!** When the project is a sandwich, this is the part where you gobble it down. This step might naturally flow into your formulating another project. Now that your immediate hunger has been satisfied, you might consider that longer-term goal of pizza.

You have already mastered the accomplishment cycle at the level of sandwiches. You did that when you were a little kid. With a big project such as designing your career, you need to approach it with a lot more conscious intention. The steps demand more of you. If you cut corners in an accomplishment cycle, you crash and burn. This is one difference between the people we call amazing and the rest of us: they honor each step, and we justify blowing off one or more.

Let's take one step as an example, one that most people slide over: commit to reaching the goal. You have to bring forth a commitment that matches the importance of the project. If you treat designing a great life the same way you approach designing a sandwich—casually, based on how your stomach feels—your commitment won't carry you anyplace close to the goal. It won't see you through more than one obstacle in the persistence stage. Then, like most people, you can complain about how obstacles kept you from achieving your dreams.

Here are a few more likely scenarios from cutting corners in the accomplishment cycle:

- Afraid you won't formulate the "right" goals, you don't formulate any and live a random life. What you need to realize is that there are no "right" goals. Stick with this book, however, and you'll become more and more clear about what goals may be right for you.
- Without a coherent, well-thought-out plan, your actions will be reactions, hit or miss. It's one way some people invite failure.

- Without getting in action you are only pretending to have a project. Some people never get beyond talking about all the great things they are going to do.
- If you don't persist and deal with obstacles (and there are *always* obstacles; that's life), you will never arrive at the destination. Some people become attached to continually working on the same obstacles, which is another way of never arriving.
- Without declaring the project complete and checking out what worked and what didn't, you rob yourself of both triumphs and lessons for the next project.

POWER

This whole chapter is really about power, what it is and how to get it. Considering power the domain of corporate big shots, generals, politicians, or weight lifters limits the notion of power. The kind of power I'm talking about is personal power, the power to get what you want, make things happen, have your dreams come true. This doesn't require dominating others or working out seven days a week.

You measure this kind of power by how quickly and effectively you move through cycles. Let's say you work for a corporation and you set a goal to jump up a couple of levels in the corporate structure. Getting there in a few months exhibits a lot of personal power. Moving up two notches over the course of several years exhibits less power. If you take on a project to buy a new car and it takes you twenty years to get it, you have very little power. If it takes you an hour, you are exhibiting a higher level of power.

Personal power isn't just for the wealthy and famous. You make your life more or less powerful with every choice you make. The more you master accomplishment cycles and the quicker you move through your projects, the more powerful you will be. I recommend that you practice this series of steps often, even when it doesn't seem necessary. You might be amazed at how much of your life is actually one project after another: decide on career, go out to dinner, visit your grandmother, run for office, vacation in Tibet, get better grades, find love, help your friend, buy a cabin in the woods, learn Thai cooking, make the team, become enlightened, lose weight, pass the test, move to the city, get a better job, decide what to do this weekend, write a poem, plan a prank, get married, sky-dive. For some of us, even taking a shower can be a project.

Make projects a conscious part of life. Take on some bigger ones than you're used to, projects that are not a slam-dunk for you. Convert the information in this book from words on a page to a powerful set of tools in your real life by regularly working your way through the steps of the accomplishment cycle with the focus on continually improving the results you achieve, until getting extraordinary results becomes routine. Fail a lot. If you don't, it means you aren't taking on projects big enough to really stretch you out into new territory.

Remember when you first learned to drive? At first you had to give it all your attention, so you wouldn't hit little old ladies or wrap the car around a tree. The more you drove, however, the easier it became. With practice it became almost automatic, so you could drive without thinking about it at all, and without leaving a trail of the dead and wounded behind you.

That's mastery. If you make a habit of turning your goals into projects and running them through the accomplishment cycle, you will become truly dangerous—in a good way.

CHAPTER 7

FORMULATE A GOAL (STEP 1)

You can begin to formulate goals in several ways. One is to ask "What do I want?" or "What do I need?" or "What does the situation need?" Another is to have someone tell you what your goals should be. Right now, let's look at wanting. People often confuse wanting with committing.

WANTING IS AUTOMATIC

We want to do well, be highly thought of, have some bigger or smaller body parts, live a life we love, make a difference, or get some special thing. Without conscious thought on our part, wanting just happens. Many times what we want comes directly from the values of the tribes we belong to, the culture we're born into. In the 1960s, most college students' number one goal was to live a meaningful life. Today 70 percent of college students say that above all else they want to make a lot of money. Our tribes' values change with the times, and we go along without even thinking about it.

WANTING NEVER STOPS

Here's something so obvious it is easy to miss: We all want what we don't have. Since we can never have everything, our list of wants never runs out. It's like a list of movie credits that scrolls forever. If you get some of the things on your list, new wants pop up. Ask anyone who has acquired real wealth. The more money they get, the more they want. Once they buy the yacht they wanted, they want a bigger one. On a more down-to-earth level, you don't even get your new computer out of the box before another item waves to you from your want list.

WANTING DOESN'T MAKE THINGS HAPPEN

You can want and hope and dream until your wishbone is worn out, and nothing will happen unless you act. If a friend says, "I really want to backpack through Asia next year," and another friend says, "I'm backpacking through Asia next year, no matter what," you might think these two should get together. In fact, they may not be on the same page at all. One is expressing a wish, a want—not much different from wanting to meet Elvis. The other friend's message is something completely different: *I'm definitely committed to backpacking in Asia next year. You can count on it!*

WANTING IS NOT COMMITTING

With the latest brain-imaging techniques, we now know that wanting and committing light up different parts of the brain. If you listen carefully to your friends, you may notice that talk about the future is 98 percent wanting and 2 percent committing. Sometimes wants translate directly into action, but only when it comes to habits. Addicted smokers go directly from desire to their hand reaching for a cigarette.

It is important to know what you really want. It's one way to start creating commitments. This chapter gives you an opportunity to see what you want most in your life and work. I would like to distinguish this as active or conscious wanting, on the path to making commitments, which is different from automatic or casual wanting. If right now you are thinking you don't know what you want, that's fine. Helping you figure that out is what this book is about.

We are now leaving the flight manual for a little while and doing some real flying. The active part of your career design process begins right here. What follows in this chapter are inquiries to help you firm up what you want in your work life. Please spend the time necessary to engage with these inquiries to the point where you are satisfied with the result.

Inquiry 7-1 **WHAT I WANT**

1. What do you want to get from this project, this book? What is your goal? Be specific. Be completely honest with yourself. What is the real goal? Why are you doing this? Here are a few ideas. If none of them fits, fill in your own.

   __ I want to design my future career to the point where I know exactly what I will do. I don't know how long it will take or how difficult it will be, but that's the result I want.

   __ I want to move toward designing my future career, but I'm not ready to go all the way. I want to decide on some parts of the design and leave others open for now.

__ I'm not ready to design my career now. I want to use this process to learn more about myself and begin to explore career issues.

__ I'm reading this because I'm supposed to, expected to, or have to.

__ ____

__ ____

2. Make a list of what you want in your future career and your life as it relates to your career. You want this written down somewhere. For the time being, you could just use your computer or a piece of paper. Later on you will be setting up a notebook you will use throughout your career design process. (If you want to get started with your notebook now, one option that's easier than setting up your own is to download your notebook from the Rockport Institute Web site: www.rockportinstitute.com. We have created notebooks in different formats to save you the work of creating one yourself. Many people enjoy using one of these predesigned notebooks in addition to using word-processing documents or a handwritten notebook.)

Write down everything you want regarding your future career—your wildest dreams as well as the practical stuff. Don't stop until you have at least some of both. If it arises in your mind as a career-oriented desire, wish, hope, or dream, put it on the list, even if it seems impossible to achieve or beyond what you think you are capable of achieving. Don't try to do it all at once. Write down everything you can think of now. Then come back and give it another go in a day or two.

People often ask, "How do I know what I want?" That's easy. If you want something, you know it. If you don't know if you want something, you don't. Wants are like hairs. They are right on the surface, not buried somewhere in the deep Freudian recesses of your mind. When people have difficulty answering this question it is usually because they are asking a different question, such as "What is most important to me?" or "What am I committed to?"

Here are some ideas to get you started. Use them as examples, but don't just check off items in the list and leave it at that. Designing a life that fits you perfectly is never quite as simple as ordering from a restaurant menu.

__ I want to be successful. To me, being successful means ______________________

__ I want to be extremely successful, one of the top people in my chosen field.

__ I want to make lots of money. I want to be wealthy.

__ I want to feel satisfied and fulfilled in my career.

__ I want my work to be a natural expression of my talents and personality.

__ I want a career where I am doing things that come easily to me and that I enjoy.

__ I want to enjoy my work, so it often feels more like play than work.

__ I want to be on a winning team that has a great time getting the job done.

__ I want a job that does not take over my entire life. I want to have plenty of time for friends, family, and fun outside of work.

__ I want my work to include adventure and danger.
__ I don't really want to work. My life outside of work is what really matters to me. I want a career that doesn't leave me burned out at the end of the day and gives me plenty of time for my real life.
__ I want to work for a small, creative company that treats its employees like family.
__ I want to be highly respected at work because I'm so good at what I do.
__ I want to make a contribution that personally matters to me. I want to feel I am doing something that makes a difference.
__ I want to be an expert in some specialty.
__ I want to spend the majority of my time working by myself.
__ I want to struggle and have a good reason to exercise my hobby of complaining.
__ I want to work in an environment that rewards me for what I accomplish, rather than how well I play office politics.
__ I want to be self-employed or an entrepreneur.
__ ____
__ ____
__ ____

3. Go through the list you made and number a few items, starting with what you want most as number one. You are not committing to anything at this time. You are just identifying the big wants, the most important wants, the things you might consider committing to later.
4. Look at the list of what you want. For each item, ask yourself: "Do I really want this, or do I want it because I'm supposed to want it or because somebody else wants me to want it?" Cross off the stuff *you* don't really want. Are there things you want but didn't put down because you thought they would be unacceptable to someone? Are there any dreams you once had but gave up on? If so, please resurrect them and put them on your wants list.

HOW TO FIGURE OUT WHAT YOU REALLY WANT

One of the best ways to explore wants is to ask, "What's in it for me?" In other words, why do you want that? What's the appeal? Say you want to go to the beach. Why? To have fun? Get a tan? Go wild? Swim? Relax? Explore a new place? Show off? Party? Get away? Meet new people? Study fish? If you know why you want to go to the beach, you can think up other ways to satisfy that desire. Then you have more choices besides beach or no beach. You have more power to have what you *really* want.

Many Americans put money somewhere near the top of their wants list. It is almost automatic. Let's look at what can come of going with the automatic. We'll call the hero of this scenario Leo. Leo decides early on that whatever he does, it has to give him a high income, in the top 10 percent of Americans. He dreams of a big house in the right suburb, luxury cars, and great toys. He works hard in college to get into a top law school, which leads to a job in the right law firm.

As a hardworking lawyer, he wakes up at 5:30 A.M. for a quick breakfast, hops into his cushy, high-performance car, and sits in rush-hour traffic for an hour, trying to suppress feelings of rage and hopelessness. He drops off the car at the parking garage, where the attendants take the car screaming into the bowels of the building. This cranks up the rage a notch or two, but Leo barely notices. For the next eleven hours, he throws himself into making sure his clients win whether or not he thinks they deserve it. He hates having to argue with other lawyers. He hates trying to come up with a huge number of billable hours, which means, among other things, working sixty-hour weeks.

After another battle with rush-hour traffic, he gets home at 8:00 P.M., needing a couple of stiff drinks to blunt the day's irritations. He doesn't want to talk to anyone. His wife tells the kids not to bother Daddy. He sits in his favorite, very expensive chair watching the news on his giant state-of-the-art TV and worrying about his investments. His stomach hurts, and he wonders if he's a candidate for a heart attack. He realizes he's going to have to put in at least ten hours over the weekend to get everything done.

If you'd asked Leo way back when he was deciding on a career, he might have told you that he chose law because he wanted to make lots of money so he would be successful and happy. If you asked him what he meant by success, he might have said a certain status in the community. If you asked why having that status was important, he might have said he wanted to feel good about himself. Uh-oh. Too bad for Leo that no one pressed him to carefully consider what he really wanted instead of going with the knee-jerk answer.

There have been major studies of income and happiness showing that when people make less money than a schoolteacher, it negatively affects their happiness and satisfaction. Making more money than a schoolteacher, however, has no effect on happiness. In other words, billionaires are no happier than schoolteachers. Hard to believe, but true. A word to the wise: If your goal is to be happy, making a lot of money is unlikely to fulfill it. No matter how much cash you pile up, it will not fulfill the real goal behind the surface goal. That's why it is useful to ask these questions. What you think you want may not lead to what you really want.

Inquiry 7-2 **WHAT DO I *REALLY* WANT?**

The point of this inquiry is to fine-tune your wants by looking under the surface. Everyone wants what they want for a reason. You want new running shoes? Why? It might be that you want to look sharp, want to run faster, want people to think you care about running fast, want to sport blinking lights on your shoes. It is rarely as simple as "I want new shoes because I want new shoes." Ask yourself:

- Why do I want to be who I want to be?
- Why do I want to do what I want to do?
- Why do I want to have what I want to have?
- What is it going to give me? What is the big benefit?

For example:

I want to make a lot of money.
Why?
I want to live in the right part of town.
Why do you want to live in the right part of town?
To be comfortable and respected.

In this case, the real goals are comfort and respect. Those may not take as much money as you thought. You might be able to gain respect more certainly in other ways than living high on the hog. There is nothing wrong with going after money to reach other goals. The point here is that if you can dig down and sort out the real goals under the surface wants, you have more choices. And you are more likely to get what you really want.

Go over your wants list in the previous inquiry. Ask: "Why do I want this? What big benefit would I get?" Write that down. Spend some time considering the answers that pop up. Then it might be appropriate to make some changes to your wants list to reflect any new insights.

WHAT IS POSSIBLE?

If you want to have an extraordinary life, you want to develop some skill in creating new possibilities. Options are limited to what seems realistic or available to us. The options that occur to us are narrow and restrict us from having the juicy and extraordinary lives we could live. People who have developed a skill for creating new possibilities aren't bound by the same constraints that limit other people's choices. If you can create new possibilities, your horizons are endless, you have more choices, and you can shape your actions more powerfully. Let's look at some examples so you know what we're talking about.

- A young woman with a talent for engineering and a love of art felt torn between the two. Her parents pushed for engineering. She knew she could never be fully expressed without art. One night, she sat down and asked, "What might be possible? Could I be an engineer and an artist at the same time?" Out of creating this new possibility, she decided to specialize as an engineer designing beautiful, sculptural, practical things for people's homes.
- Steve Jobs, one of the two founders of Apple Computer, created tornadoes of possibilities: the Mac computer, the iPod, brilliant, award-winning animated films, and more. All of these amazing

successes started as possibilities Jobs created and then turned into projects that ended as extraordinary contributions to our culture.

All breakthrough ideas, all the ways our civilization has moved forward, start with someone creating a new possibility. Somebody asks, "What might be possible?" and takes action to make it so. At one point God must have said, "Sure would be nice to have some stuff around here. Maybe I could create a universe." You are not going to create anything new in your life unless you first imagine it as possible. Without creating new possibilities, you'll only have something new by happy accident. All that will be available to you will be the same old options you have now.

In previous chapters I talked about the limitations of human beings, the mechanical parts of life. The skill of creating takes us beyond those existing options. It is one thing that distinguishes us from the rest of nature. Our ability to create new possibilities is one of the big reasons we don't still live in caves. When you ask "What is possible?" you open yourself up to designing your future instead of just picking from a limited menu of the predictable.

HOW TO CREATE NEW POSSIBILITIES

Asking "What do I want? What is my goal?" is the first step of any project. But if that is the only question you ask at that point, you will be limited to what you already want and think you can achieve. When you also ask "What might be possible?" you are taking the "What do I want" question out into new territory.

I put this possibility section at the end of this chapter because I wanted you to ask "What do I want?" in the usual way first. If you are totally satisfied with the answers you came up with, you can just skip this possibility stuff. But if you are not sure that your stated wants are big enough or interesting enough to lead to a life you love, then I suggest you look at your future from the viewpoint of what might be possible.

Inquiry 7-3 **WHAT'S POSSIBLE?**

Take a moment and imagine you are walking down the street one day and—blam—you get run over by a truck. You wake up in heaven with a concerned-looking angel wringing his hands and apologizing. He tells you that you were run over by mistake, and you will be sent back to earth. As compensation for the error, you get to choose the kind of life you will have, the kind of work you will do, where you will live, and so forth. The only limitation is that you will be the same you who got run over, so if you can't sing, you can't pick "rock star" as a career. If you are four feet tall, you can't pick "NBA star." What would you choose? What sort of work? What sort of life? Would it be different from what you said you wanted earlier in this chapter? In other words, are you selling yourself short, looking at what is only *probable*? If you could have exactly what you wanted, what would that be? Feel free to add any of this to your wants list.

The simple, straightforward way of creating new possibilities is to ask "What's possible?" I do it all the time. I have a daily discipline of creating new possibilities and opportunities instead of just dealing with what life throws at me. If I'm going into a meeting, instead of just hoping it turns out well, I ask, "What could be possible?" and make up some really juicy outcome. And I commit to that outcome, commit to having it turn out that way. Every morning, instead of being stuck in whatever mood I wake up with, I ask, "What's possible today? How good can I stand it?" And then I invent a day for myself and promise myself something that stretches me out into new territory. The commitment and promising part is in the next chapter, so don't worry about that now. Just consider whether you are willing to create some new possibilities for yourself. Try this out in your day-to-day life. Start interceding in your day by creating new possibilities.

THREE WAYS TO DEAL WITH WANTS

There are just a few ways to handle the endless wanting we all experience:

- **Become deeply resigned** about life and just go after the little stuff, the stuff that seems reasonable, easily attainable. Don't stretch. Don't expect much. Sigh deeply.
- **Give up your attachment to wanting.** Buddhist monks are trained to just watch the endless parade of thoughts, emotions, and wants march down their mental Main Street, welcome all of it, but not automatically act on those thoughts and emotions. You probably don't want to be a Buddhist monk, though, or you would be reading a different book.
- **Learn to make powerful promises.** This is the one I recommend. Commit to getting what you want the most. Practice sticking to those commitments until they are fulfilled.

This third option is the most important skill a person can learn. This next chapter presents the most potent element of the accomplishment cycle—one ability we humans possess that separates us from the other beasts.

CHAPTER

8

COMMIT TO REACHING YOUR GOAL (STEP 2)

When you think about the automatic nature of wanting, it's curious how seriously we take our wants, as if they are the most important things in the world. We spend much more time wishing, dreaming, hoping, wanting, yearning, craving, coveting, and longing for what we don't have than we do in asking, "What am I committed to making happen?"

Please understand: there is nothing wrong with wanting. Wanting can get you started on the path to commitment. But it does not make anything important happen. You want a career that fits you well? So what? So does everyone else. Wanting a great career and five bucks will get you a nice big (excuse me, *grande*) cup of coffee at Starbucks.

Gaining some mastery with commitment can completely transform the quality of your life. If you can learn to make big promises, commitments that take you out of your comfort zone and point you toward achieving what you most want, and then persist until you reach the goal even though you may have some failures along the way, you will be truly powerful. Here's an example.

Not long ago I met an extraordinary woman named Jody Williams. She has a dream to end the horror of land mines. All over the world, warring countries bury countless thousands of antipersonnel mines a few inches underground. They remain active for years after the end of the conflict. They kill or dismember people indiscriminately: enemy soldiers, farmers, tourists, children. In Cambodia alone, more than thirty thousand innocent people have had legs amputated because of them.

Lots of people believed land mines were wrong. They shook their heads. They discussed. Jody instead created a project to ban land mines worldwide. Starting alone at her computer, she convinced a growing number of people to participate in her project. Over the course of several years, as chief strategist and spokesperson for the International Campaign to Ban Landmines (ICBL), she built a coalition of more than thirteen hundred organizations around the world. Her efforts bore fruit when more than 130 countries (but not the United States) ratified the Mine Ban Treaty. In 1997 Jody was awarded the Nobel Peace Prize. *Forbes* magazine named her as one of the 100 most powerful women in the world.

Jody was not born with magical powers. She simply put two commitments first: one, the banning of land mines, and two, being unstoppable in fulfilling that objective. You and I have the same power. Unlike Jody, however, we usually pay more attention to our automatically scrolling wants or excuses than to our commitments.

It doesn't have to be that way. All it takes is practice.

Most of us have spent our lives practicing doing what we feel like doing (which—ask any baby—doesn't really need practice). We have less practice simply doing what we said we would do.

You get to say which mode of operation you will empower:

Doing what you feel like doing.

or

Doing what you say you will do.

Here's a common scenario. Let's say you decide to get up in the morning and go for a run, so you set your alarm. When it goes off, two competing voices in your head have different advice. One says, "Rise and shine! Pull on those stinky old sneakers and get out there. Honor your commitment to your health and vitality." The other voice says, "Go back to sleep. You need your rest. You can run tomorrow. It doesn't matter if you don't do it today."

Essentially, one voice says you are someone with the power to say, "This shall be," and it is so. The other voice says you are someone who gives in to automatic urges and feelings. ("Hey," the second voice whispers, "comfort is good. Why knock yourself out?")

Why indeed? Only one reason: to have the personal power to design and live a great life. Otherwise you'll just get whatever the wind blows in. Feelings are part of what the wind blows in; they're as changeable as the weather. When people say, "It just seems like nothing much matters," they may have been buffeted by the wind too long.

> I don't wait for moods. You do nothing if you do that. Your mind must know it has got to get down to earth.
>
> —*Pearl S. Buck*

Empowering that first voice takes practice. The second voice is automatic and points to our default mode: We want our inner weather to be 75 degrees, sunny, with a light breeze and puffy white clouds in a blue sky. We are fully committed to what every animal wants—comfort and ease. That's fine for ordering in a restaurant, but it's not sufficient for designing our lives or producing something extraordinary.

Here's another way of looking at this. At any moment you can run your life in proactive mode or automatic mode. Other creatures operate in automatic mode all the time. As animals ourselves, we also run on automatic most of the time. But all important human creations—including the United States, works of art, and the polio vaccine—are products of the proactive mode.

Creating definite commitments is the one step in the accomplishment cycle that separates us from the rest of nature. In the process, we define who we are. When you stretch to do everything you can to fulfill promises no matter what, without caving in to your reasons, excuses, circumstances, and obstacles, you are exercising a uniquely human capacity. You are saying, "I am the captain of my ship, not just a passenger. I am the author of my life, not a character in someone else's story."

Making and keeping promises outside your comfort zone takes practice, and you can begin practicing where you are. If you have never been on time for anything in your life, start keeping your word in that arena. You will fail from time to time. But you will build capacity, just as weight lifters start with a few pounds beyond their comfort zone and add weights as they add muscle.

THE POWER OF A PROMISE

One of my clients, a forty-year-old single mother, wanted to create a life she loved now that her daughter was grown, and so she decided that she wanted to be a doctor. In college, she had majored in partying, so she didn't have much of an academic track record. She also didn't have the money for medical school. But she committed to being a doctor and became an unstoppable force of nature, successfully lobbying the people on the med school's admissions committee to accept her as a nontraditional student, taking remedial courses, raising money, and dealing with all the obstacles. She is now a doctor.

Most people with similar circumstances would never even think of trying to become a physician. If they did think of it, they would have sensible, logical reasons why it was impossible. They would just dump the dream into the "impossible goals" box and find something less challenging to pursue. My client, on the other hand, made a promise and took actions consistent with the promise. She made the promise superior to her thoughts, feelings, fears, and external circumstances.

I'm not suggesting that you will need to stretch yourself nearly this far to have a career that fits you perfectly. The point isn't the amount of stretch but the willingness to commit to having the kind of life you really want no matter what the obstacles. When you become willing to live a life of committed action, to take a stand for your future, you are automatically elevated to playing on the big kids' team.

> You can run with the big dogs or sit on the porch and bark.
>
> —*Wallace Arnold*

BUT I HAVE A PROBLEM WITH COMMITMENT

Do we really have commitment problems? When a woman complains that her guy has a commitment problem, all that means is that he is not committed to what she wants. He may be committed to not being committed, to being free, or something else. He doesn't have a "commitment problem"; she does. She has a problem with what he is committed to.

We are all committed, all the time. To see what people are committed to, watch how they spend their time. When you see one guy throwing back a few cold ones and complaining about how hard calculus is, it's easy to conclude he is committed to bitching or at least to avoiding calculus. If another guy spends that same time getting coached in calculus or doing his homework, it's obvious he's committed to something else. Two guys, same amount of time, both committed, different commitments.

We human beings are 100 percent committed every waking moment of our lives. That's one of the things that distinguish us from the rest of the natural world. Dogs are never late. Only humans are late. We are late when we make a promise to show up somewhere at a specific time and don't get there when we said we would. If you haven't made a definite promise to be there at the appointed time, you aren't late. We confuse commitment with obligation. If you are supposed to be at work at nine and usually show up fifteen minutes late, you are screwing around with an obligation, a rule, an expectation, and perhaps you're flirting with getting fired, but you aren't necessarily breaking a promise. Folks who habitually show up late are committed to something else. It could be to giving the finger to authority, or to dealing with personal issues, or to their identity as slightly spaced out, or to any one of innumerable other things, but they are not committed to being on time.

Most of us think our lives would work better if we were more committed. The problem isn't our degree of commitment but what we are actually committed to. It may be very uncomfortable to admit that we are not always committed to what we know would be best for us, and to quit blaming circumstances, fate, parents, or some personal shortcoming.

WHAT EXACTLY IS A CREATED COMMITMENT?

Glad you asked. When you strip off all the crapola we have added to this ten-letter word, the meaning is simple: *a created commitment is a pledge to produce a specific result.* It is a promise to achieve some result that wouldn't have happened otherwise. You make it happen by promising and then taking actions consistent with your word.

If the promise is too loose and unspecific—"I will be successful," for instance—it provides no sense of how to get there. A good, solid commitment includes specific results toward which you can plot a course. You can tell whether or not you've reached the goal. A more powerful commitment would be: "I will reach my success goals by 2035. To me success means having a swimming pool twenty feet wide by forty feet long by eight feet deep filled to the top with hundred-dollar bills." With a commitment to a goal like this, you can measure the depth of bills in your pool, so at any time you can tell where you are in the process of fulfilling that goal. If, in the year 2025 you find you have only an inch of bills in the pool, you know you need to alter your strategy if you're going to make the target.

Personal power comes from exercising your ability to make big promises and then doing what you said you would do, even if the circumstances turn against you, you want to give up, you think it's too hard, and you don't want to do it anymore anyway. Here's a personal example of how sticking to your word gives you power to have your life go the way you most want.

Many years ago, I promised a mentor I would change the way Americans choose their careers so that their careers fit them so well that they loved their lives. As soon as I made that promise, my thoughts screamed that it was impossible, that I was just one little person, that I couldn't do it, and so forth. With great difficulty, I stuck with my promise rather than empower the endless objections. Even after developing extraordinarily successful career tools for people, I still had no idea how to reach people faster than one at a time. Every expert I consulted said I should write a book on the subject, and it would have to be powerful, well-written, and popular. More thoughts screaming: *You can't even write thank-you notes! What makes you think you can write a better book than all those you don't think are much good? Who do you think you are?* Once again I clung to my promise to be true to my word rather than my dark thoughts and hopeless feelings. For three years I got up early in the morning and wrote, never knowing if what I wrote was any good, fearing my publisher would reject my work, dealing with the daily barrage of critical thoughts. In the end, my publisher raved about the book, which became a best seller, and many people have said that it guided them to a career they loved.

CHAPTER 9

PLAN IT (STEP 3)

Planning gives you a path so you know you're on track. We will cover only the basics here. If you need more, get into one of the many project-planning books, Web resources, or software programs on the subject. If you use this book from beginning to end, the book itself acts as the basic plan. You still need more detailed planning for some parts of your journey to the perfect career in areas such as job hunting, further education, and achieving other big goals along the way. Hundreds of people have told me of years spent on an advanced degree only to discover that the degree did not prepare them for the career goal they hoped to pursue. Others came out of programs to find a dearth of jobs in the field they studied. Figuratively speaking, they were running off through the woods without a map. Careful planning, including research, would have warned them about the bear caves and quicksand.

Make the plan fit the project. The bigger the project, the bigger the plan. If the goal is to go to the movies, the plan can be short and sweet:

Step 1. Pick up Spike at 8:00 P.M.
Step 2. Go to movie.
Step 3. Watch.

If your goal is to become the Empress of the Universe, the plan is going to be complex and detailed, and no doubt will take years to execute.

PROJECT-PLANNING STEPS

State Your Intended Project Goal

If you have completed Steps 1 and 2 in the accomplishment cycle (see the previous two chapters), you have a specific goal to which you are fully committed. If you don't have that, you're like a blind man in a shooting gallery. Go back to the beginning of the cycle and work on those steps.

One of the big secrets of effective planning is specificity—the more specific the better. You want your goal as sharp as a laser beam, something like: "Gain admission to the Miskatonic University master's degree program in fiction writing. Get a book bought by a major publisher while still in the program." That's exactly what you want—laser-beam clarity and specificity.

Explore Possible Ways to Achieve the Goal

Now it's time to figure out how you are going to reach your goal, step by step. The way to come up with the best actionable tasks is to create and consider multiple possibilities. Brainstorm different ways of moving your project forward and reaching the goal. Instead of just mapping out the logical, obvious tasks, go wild—come up with as many ideas as possible. Think of both practical methods and outrageous ones, and consider actions that would stretch you into new territory. We all tend to favor actions within our comfort zone rather than the most effective ones. Introverted people may avoid calling people they don't know. Action-oriented extroverts may not be comfortable sitting down and planning. The most effective people do what works rather than only what feels good in the moment. In fact, whatever would be most challenging is probably worth considering. Imagine how people you respect for their ability to get difficult things done might take on the challenge you face. "How would ______________________ [Bill Gates, Gandhi, General Patton, or some other powerful real-life person] tackle this goal?"

Figure out the most important questions and ask them. Our aspiring writer might ask, "What do I have to do to get past the admissions committee? What are the admissions criteria? What would it take to become a candidate who was impossible to reject?" Ask the admissions people, current students in the program, anyone who knows. Then take those answers and see how you would need to upgrade yourself to meet the criteria. If you need to improve your writing samples, you might get a talented friend to coach you. Need recommendations? Ask past writing professors for really strong ones. Need more credentials? Get that great story published somewhere, even in a small publication.

You might have to step out of your comfort zone by asking professors for really strong recommendations. Like most of us, you might prefer to ask for less than what you really want rather than risk rejection. It's your choice: risk rejection (by the professors) now or ensure rejection later.

Pick the Action Steps You Will Use

After exploring the various methods and steps that might get you to your goal, you then decide on how you will do it. Break down the basic strategy into concrete steps from the first action to the last. An action is specific and measurable. You can tell if it is done or not.

"Walk ten miles today" is an action step. "Walk" is not. If the goal is a big one, get some advice from the most highly effective people you know, particularly if they have a special gift for or insight into the kind of thing you plan to do.

Create Milestones and Emergency Procedures for Each Part of Your Project

Oftentimes projects get bogged down, slowed down, or sidetracked. People usually don't notice right away when something is not happening, and they rarely plan what to do when the caca hits the fan. You want to make sure you keep things moving and that you know what to do if the project gets slowed down or compromised.

Guesstimate how long each action will take and pick a completion date for it. That completion date is a milestone. Before the days of cars with their odometers and GPS navigation systems, travelers depended on stones set alongside highways with a number carved into them corresponding to the distance from the beginning of the road. It was the only way to tell how far they had traveled. Milestones serve the same function in projects. They tell you how you are doing, if you are ahead or behind schedule, when to start a new action step. They are a wake-up call allowing you to go into emergency mode if the project begins to drag. Having specific milestones as targets allows you to manage with a level of power and precision that would be impossible otherwise. If you pay attention to your project milestones, you can enact corrective measures quickly, before things get worse.

You may also find it useful to come up with emergency procedures you will put into action if the project slows down, gets off course, or gets crushed by the fickle finger of fate. You may tend to do that already. "We're going to see *Son of Saw 3* tonight at seven. If the theater is too full to get good seats, we'll go over to Spike's place and have a little party." The advantage in setting up emergency procedures while planning your project is that these procedures are much more likely to be rational and effective if thought out ahead of time. Cruising sailors, people who might be hundreds of miles from land in a small sailboat when a big storm strikes, take this very seriously. They figure out exactly how they will deal with any type of emergency, knowing that this extra planning may make the difference between life and death. One mishandled small problem in raging seas and gale-force winds often cascades into multiple emergencies that are much more difficult to handle. So it is with your projects. What will you do if you don't get into the schools you thought would accept you? What if you have trouble getting through to people you need to talk with to find out about a career you are considering? What if your resume isn't attracting interviews? What if you find out that there are no jobs available for PhDs in sheep herding?

When people use the phrases "backup plan" and "plan B," they usually mean that reaching the original goal may not happen, so it is time to change direction. Most of the time, this is not necessary. We give up on our dreams too easily and hold on to our bad habits as if they were bags of treasure. Life is going to be a lot more fun if you do just the opposite: hold on to your *dreams* as if they were bags of treasure. Usually the best emergency procedures don't require you to change or abandon your goal. Instead, they get you back in the game, on track to achieving your goal and completing your project successfully no matter what gets in the way. Just because you didn't get into Carnegie Mellon or MIT doesn't mean you have to give up on your dream of becoming a master of robot technology. You might have to go to Billy Bob's Discount Drive-in Robot School. So what? Find a way to live your dream. Don't give up unless there is no other choice.

> First say to yourself what you would be; and then do what you have to do.
>
> —*Epictetus*

CHAPTER 10

ACTION: DESIGNING YOUR CAREER (STEP 4)

You can't build a reputation on what you're going to do.

—*Henry Ford*

Earlier in this book, I said that there are two absolutely vital groups of skills you need to practice and master if you are serious about choosing the perfect career for you. One involves projects, accomplishment cycles, creating commitments, and so forth. The other vital group of skills involves taking action. The title of this chapter says it all: the next pages are about the nuts and bolts of designing your future career.

This chapter is going to turn you into your own career coach, an expert in designing a life you will love, especially if you really absorb what this chapter has to say and take it on wholeheartedly as the method you use. Many very successful people say that they were not skilled at this when they made their own career decisions. So learning and using this technology will give you an enormous advantage. An eternity from now, when you are an ancient forty years old, thinking about how wonderfully well your life is working, you will look back and thank your lucky stars that you made the commitment to refuse to compromise on your life, and instead to put in the effort to master the art and science of career choice.

At Rockport Institute, we have spent more than twenty-five years creating and refining a very specific process that allows you to design your career step by step. What sets this method apart from the usual career choice methods is that it actually works. You will be using the most advanced, state-of-the-art methodology available anywhere.

This chapter in particular is one not to just read but also to master. You want to know this stuff as well as you know your name. Think about whatever it is you know more about than anything else. That's the level of familiarity that would serve you best to make use of this method. What follows, first of all, is a brief introduction to the Rockport Career Design Method. You will get a basic idea of how the process works. Then we'll take a deeper look at the whole process, piece by piece, and give some guidance on how to use it most effectively to design your future career.

INTRO TO THE ROCKPORT CAREER DESIGN METHOD

To design your future career, you'll be taking many measures of yourself (called *inquiries* in this book) so you can shape a custom-made career based on what fits you. The more accurate the measures, the better the career will fit.

With the Rockport Method, you'll actually design your future career from the ground up. There is one big question you keep asking all the way through this process: "What am I sure will definitely be some of the components of my future career?"

This question is the heart of the method. This is a much more difficult question than "What do I like?" or "What are some good careers out there?" because every time you answer this question you are making a choice, a commitment. You are adding a definite new element to the design of your career. You start with a blank canvas and add to it as you sort out elements of your future career. There are three different stages of this process and you will be taking on three different roles, wearing three different hats: Detective, Decider, and Designer.

You will be playing these three roles as you go through a series of exercises that make up the second part of this book. They will guide you through choosing your future career step by step, one piece at a time. We call these exercises *inquiries* because that's what you will be doing—inquiring into what would make a career fit you perfectly. These inquiries are all designed to help you come up with strong clues and play the three roles of Detective, Decider, and Designer as you go through the process of creating some definite commitments—little islands of certainty in the midst of the raging storm that is your mind. To make it easier, we break the process down into small, manageable pieces. You will have a chance to look into every area of your life that may be related to your future career.

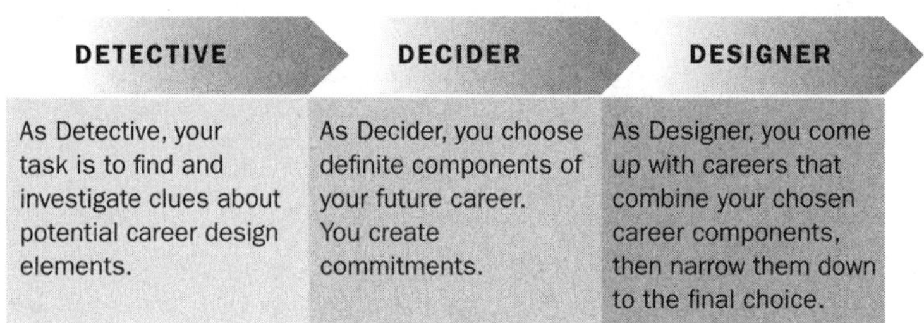

DETECTIVE
DECIDER
DESIGNER
As Detective, your task is to find and investigate clues about potential career design elements.
As Decider, you choose definite components of your future career. You create commitments.
As Designer, you come up with careers that combine your chosen career components, then narrow them down to the final choice.

You start the career choice process by putting on your invisible Detective hat and operating in Detective mode. Just like a police detective, you search for and gather clues, then work those clues by asking good questions, and sometimes do some investigating and research. A good clue may consist of any information or insight that helps you understand just what sort of work would fit you best.

For example, your friend tells you that you never get enough of talking with and doing things directly with people, face-to-face. This one hits you right between the ears as an accurate observation. So now you have a good clue.

The goal is to move each important clue in the direction of making a decision about it as a definite career design component. Once you have worked a clue thoroughly, you put on your second hat, that of the Decider. What you do in this role is make choices. You decide if a particular clue will definitely be a component of your future career.

Back to the example. After having this insight, based on your friend's observation, you start paying more attention to what you do naturally. You notice that your friend is accurate. You become more convinced that spending most of your time working with people may turn out to be an important career design component. You also look back at your past and realize that you are always happy dealing directly with people. Plus, you aren't all that good with mechanical things and get easily bored working with computers and data. This is so clear to you that you now put on your Decider hat. You decide that one major element of your future career will be that you will definitely spend most of your time working directly with people, face-to-face.

Once you have a sufficient number of definite pieces of the puzzle (definite career design components) decided, you move to the third mode, Designer. As Designer, you combine the career design components you're committed to and come up with specific careers that would fit them. Then you research the various careers, and as you learn about them, you narrow the list down, crossing off careers that, for some reason, don't fit you perfectly, coming ever closer to being able to choose your final and definite career.

Let's say you come up with the following definite components (in real life you will come up with a lot more than two definite components):

- I will spend most of my time at working directly with people, face-to-face.
- My work will combine teaching and problem solving as major daily elements.

After some head scratching, research, and asking other people, you come up with the following list of careers to explore: college professor, teaching AP courses in high school, corporate trainer, golf pro at a country club, seminar leader, and public speaker. They all fit the specifications. After doing a lot of research on what it would take to actually learn these professions, you choose to become a corporate trainer.

When you are in the midst of this design process, you wear all three of these hats at once. For example, once you start exploring specific careers, you discover that some don't fit you. That information provides more clues, which takes you back to your Detective role.

You do detective work, make decisions, and, after a while, explore specific careers all at once. (Remember, this example makes career design seem fast and easy. To do it right takes months, sometimes a year or more.)

Now it's time to take a more in-depth look at the Rockport Career Design Method.

NEW ROLES TO PLAY

Each of us unconsciously plays various roles in life, such as the one who's got it handled, the cool one, the one who's quiet and deep, rebel, nerd, athlete, wallflower, searcher, party animal, the one who's kind of confused, slacker, superachiever, and so forth. Taking on new roles can sometimes have a profound effect on your effectiveness and creativity.

Walt Disney built his empire using this technique. He had three completely different roles he played during different parts of his creative process: the dreamer, the realist, and the critic. He had a different physical office for each role. When it was time to play the dreamer, he stepped into the dreamer office, and he didn't plan or criticize; he just let his creativity soar. When he wanted to take a realistic look at what he'd dreamed up, he stepped into his realist office and operated in that mode. Each of these roles contributed to the many projects Disney created.

To do a brilliant job of designing your future, you'll get good at playing the roles in the Rockport Career Design Method: Detective, Decider, and Designer. Many people talk about playing roles as "wearing different hats." When you want to switch from Detective to Decider, you just mentally remove the Detective hat and put on the Decider hat. You might find it useful to get three real hats to represent the three roles, just as Disney did with his three different offices. World-class athletes and performers know that putting themselves in the right frame of mind for each task at hand contributes to their mastery. It takes practice, so use whatever works for you—props, visual displays, or notes to yourself.

THE DETECTIVE

In the Detective role, you investigate anything and everything that might be useful in learning what sorts of careers fit you. You search for clues to become sure about elements of your future career. In this case, real life is a lot like the movies. The dumb cop jumps to erroneous conclusions based on a few clues and an overabundance of self-righteous opinion. The hero keeps searching and working the clues until she or he can point a finger with confidence at the one who did the dastardly deed.

You need to take multiple steps in solving your career question, just as a good detective does in solving a crime. The first step is collecting as many potential clues as you can. At this stage you don't know what will ultimately be useful and what won't. Some clues, such as your natural talents and personality traits, will be as obvious as a bloody, fingerprint-covered dagger sticking out of the victim's back. Some will be more subtle, such as what you like to read or watch on TV. These might prove to be strong clues or they might not. Still, you make note of them. Any of them might turn out to be important. Others may take a lot of work to uncover. You need to be open-minded and thorough, leaving no stone unturned. You need to poke around anywhere there might be the slightest chance of finding a good, strong, juicy clue.

Clues

Any information or insight might be useful as a clue in your career design project:

- How you think
- How you behave in various situations
- What you do well or not so well
- What you learn about yourself from exercises in this book
- Subjects you enjoy or master easily
- Passions and interests
- Your positive or negative reactions to something you learn about a particular career
- Wants
- Goals
- Insights
- Dreams
- Fantasies
- The things you care about
- Your outlook on life
- What attracts or repels you
- Your quirks and idiosyncrasies
- What other people say about you
- Your natural talents
- Tasks you enjoy

Notice that the kinds of clues I just listed are all about *you*, not about what various careers might be like. In the early stages of the career design process, looking for clues means paying attention to yourself and how you function. That's because your objective is to choose a career that fits you, not one you can barely squeeze into. First you need to investigate the *you* that the career is supposed to fit. Start paying attention to your everyday life. What do you enjoy so much that you lose track of time? What do you enjoy that others think is difficult or a chore? What kinds of shows do you watch on TV? What do you talk about with your friends? Later on in your career design process, you will investigate careers in Detective mode, looking for clues about how well various careers might fit your specifications, commitments, measurements.

Most of the second half of this book is done in Detective mode, as you find and work clues about your natural talents, personality, what matters to you, what workplace environments fit you best, and so forth. The book provides a lot of assistance in both finding and working these clues. But don't depend on the inquiries in this book as your sole source of clues. They are designed to get you started paying attention to yourself, how you function, what are you attracted to, and so forth. Because we don't always see ourselves with clarity, you'll want to use some outside sources—friends, family, coworkers, teachers, bosses, and others who may be able to supply some useful observations.

Some clues will turn out to be useless. If you happen to be the average young American male, you may not find any useful clues in the fact that you watch sports and talk about sports, women, and technology toys. Those "clues" say something about one of the tribes you belong to, but not much about you as a unique individual. You have to keep a sharp eye peeled.

When I was going through the career design process years ago, I noticed that what I liked best about the Super Bowl was the ads—not just watching them for enjoyment but critiquing them, noticing which were effective. So, for me, the Super Bowl provided a useful clue. Once I investigated this clue (started watching myself), I discovered that I walk around all day critiquing everything. In restaurants, I critiqued the food and the service; in movies, I noticed every flaw; in talking with people, I always listened to what was going on below the surface.

I ended up designing my career so I would get to enjoy using my "positive critic" talent every day—coaching people, training professionals in my field, inventing new methods, even writing the words you are reading now. What started as something I noticed watching the Super Bowl became a powerful clue that turned into a huge design element of my career, and became one of the big reasons I love my work.

How to Work a Clue

After you have a collection of clues, pick the best, strongest ones and then work them. For a detective, this means choosing the clues most likely to lead to solving the crime, asking questions the clue suggests and investigating where that leads, what it signifies, how it fits together with other clues, and finally figuring out what conclusions it supports. That's exactly what you're going to be doing. When you're in Detective mode, you have a particular relationship with everything in your life: instead of just living it, you are, at the same time, checking out what's going on in a new way, from the perspective of a detective working on the biggest case of his or her life.

The chart on the next page shows how to work a clue:

DETECTIVE *Gather clues. Then investigate each important clue and move it toward consideration as a potential commitment.*			
Gather Clues	**Ask Questions**	**Research and Things to Do**	**Answers and Findings**
As Detective, your task is to find and investigate clues about possible career design elements.	What questions does this clue suggest? Get clear on the real questions.	How, specifically, can you answer this question? What do you need to do, learn, investigate?	Work this clue until you have sufficient definite answers and findings. What's the bottom line?

After gathering clues and picking the most likely ones, do what any detective would do—start to ask questions about that clue. These questions are all subsets of the big question you are working on answering: *What am I sure will definitely be some of the components of my future career?*

The strategy is to move each clue in the direction of making a choice about it as to whether or not it becomes a definite design element of your future career.

I thought my Super Bowl clue was worth investigating, so I started observing and asking questions such as:

What exactly is going on when I'm critiquing ads during the Super Bowl?
What natural talents am I using?
Where else do I do the same thing?
How often do I do it?
Is it fun whenever I do it?
Where is it useful? Where does it get me in trouble?
How can I find out more?

Once you have some good questions about a particular clue, you go on to the next step, asking: *How, specifically, can I answer this question?*

What do I need to do, learn, investigate?
How can I move this clue forward so I can decide if it will be a definite career design element?

Once you have worked the clue sufficiently and have some definite answers and findings, you can then switch roles from Detective to Decider and make a choice about the clue you have been working on. Will it be a definite career design element or not? More about this later.

Asking Razor-sharp Questions

Your most useful investigative tool is asking and answering questions. People whose job is to get high-quality answers—people such as scientists, real-life detectives, and journalists—know that half the battle in getting the best answers is asking the best possible questions. Usually we just ask whatever questions pop into our minds. But the quality of the answers we get is directly related to the quality of the questions we ask. Spend some time honing your questions to a sharp point. You want them as clear as a laser beam to help you move the clue toward making a definite decision about it.

Where to Find the Answers

One difficulty in answering questions is that we sometimes look for answers in the wrong places. Whenever you are operating in Detective mode and trying to answer a question, it is always smart to spend a few moments getting clear where the answers will come from. Fortunately, there are only three places to find answers: inside yourself, in the outside world, and if there is no answer either inside or out, you can always make up the answer.

It's also useful to know that each of us favors one of these locations. Some internally focused people look inside themselves to answer most questions. Others tend to look for answers in the world around them. Few of us have much practice creating or inventing answers to important questions even though it is often the most potent method.

Looking inside is where you will find answers to questions about your preferences, personality, wants, needs, hopes, dreams, ideals, requirements, experiences, and so on. "What do I enjoy most?" "What would I like to do this weekend?" "How much of the time do I enjoy computer work?" "How important is it for me to travel as part of my work?" "How do I feel about the current administration?" are all questions that can be answered only by looking inside yourself. You may discover that you already have some specific, definite requirements for your future career that you can access simply by asking yourself the right questions.

Looking out to the external world is where you will find answers that require research, such as: "Is physical therapy a growing field? How much can I expect to earn as a physical therapist? What are the subspecialties in this field? What education is required?"

Making up the answer is what you must do if you need answers and cannot find them anywhere else. Some people search endlessly for answers within themselves to no avail. They wind up tremendously frustrated because they believe that they are here on earth for some preordained purpose; somehow, after years of searching, the answer still eludes them. They are looking in all the wrong places, inside and outside. If the answers cannot be found in either of these places, the choices are to give up asking the question or to make up the answer yourself.

A really hot, juicy life comes from this third source of answers, the ability to invent answers. This is what scientists do when they create a theory. When a business chooses a particular marketing strategy, they have usually considered various alternatives. Even though they may have good insights based on personal experience (internal answer) and have done a lot of research on possible strategies (external answer), they really don't know for sure what strategy will be best. When they make a final choice, they are actually making up the answer. They usually don't know they are making up the answer. If the CEO asks why they picked a particular strategy, they can't tell the boss they made it up, so they'll explain how the answer was based on research. But in reality they are making up the answer.

When you write a paper in school where you are supposed to come up with your own interpretation of something, such as the meaning of your favorite song, a historical event, or whatever, what you are actually doing is making up an answer. All of us make up answers every day, but not usually in a conscious, useful, and powerful way. If you wave to your friend and the friend seems to give you a sour look, you will immediately make up an answer to "What's up with her?" Maybe, you imagine, your friend is having a bad day, has PMS, is upset with you, or was out too late last night.

If the only sources of answers were inside and outside, what would you do if you couldn't find a good answer in either place? You would be permanently stuck. You can find many of the answers you need inside or outside, but knowing you can make up the answer sets you free. It makes it possible to answer anything you need to know.

Here's an example: Many years ago when I was designing my present career, I knew that I passionately wanted my work dedicated to making a big difference in people's lives. That was an internal answer. But the external answer from nearly every source was, "It will never work. You will never make a living helping other people. Be practical." So I created my own answer: "I will have it all—the satisfaction of a life dedicated to making a difference and also financial success."

When you make up an answer, you are not just making a random selection. You are making a creative choice, a commitment. You are inventing your future. Notice that the choice I made in the above example was not at all logical or reasonable. It required me to make a big stretch into unknown territory to have the kind of career I most wanted. That's why making up the answer is such a powerful and useful tool. It gives you the ability to stretch yourself in ways you wouldn't if all you had was access to internal and external answers.

How to Know Where to Look for the Answer

First of all, decide if the answer can be found inside or outside. This is usually easy to figure out. If the question is "Am I willing to go back to school and get another degree?" the answer is obviously found internally. If the question is "How much do charter boat captains make in the Virgin Islands?" you will need to ask someone with experience.

People run into difficulty in determining if the answer is to be found internally or if they have to get creative and invent the answer themselves. This is actually easy to determine. First, look inside. Poke around and see if the answer is in there. If it is, it will appear. You may have to think about it seriously, meditate on the subject, give it a few days to bubble up, or wait for circumstances to develop. If you cannot come up with the answer within a few days, most likely you never will. You do not have some cave of answers hidden deep within yourself. Most of what is inside you is readily accessible. If you cannot find the answer inside yourself, it is probably hopeless to continue looking there. You have to make up the answer.

When you make up answers, you can pick anything you want. You can pick an answer that makes you feel safe and secure, even if you have to settle for less than you want. Or you can go for it and make up an answer that gives you everything you want. Making up answers is quite simple. Here's my favorite method. First figure out what you would most like the answer to be. For example, if the question you have been unable to resolve by looking in or out is "Am I willing to start my own company?" look to see what answer you would prefer if you had a choice. Which answer would move your life forward the most? Which answer do you have more passion for? The next step is simply to decide that the answer you lean toward is the one and only answer for you. Then commit to doing whatever it takes to make it happen. That's all there is to it, folks. Inventing an answer can be nothing more than selecting the most desired possibility and then hanging your star on it.

Sometimes the answer may involve looking in more than one place. For example, if you are trying to decide what sort of organization you want to be associated with, you may want to look for answers both inside and outside. Unless you are intimately familiar with a wide range of organizations, you need to do some research. Then you check out how you feel and what you think about what you uncovered in your external research.

THE DECIDER

Now that you have collected clues, worked the best ones, asked good questions, and answered them, you have reached the point where you know enough about a specific clue to be able to ask the big career design question: "What am I sure will definitely be some of the components of my future career?" When you make a definite decision about a clue, you are actually creating a part of the design of your future career.

When you have worked a clue to the point where you can say it is definitely going to be a part of your future career, it becomes a solid part of the design. When you decide an element won't be a part of your career, you are also adding to your design.

DECIDER *Turn clues into definite design components (commitments).*			
As Decider, your task is to make some definite commitments to specific components of your future career. Can you turn this clue into a definite career component?			Answers to the question "What am I sure will definitely be important components of my future career?"
No	Maybe	Yes	Definite Career Design Components

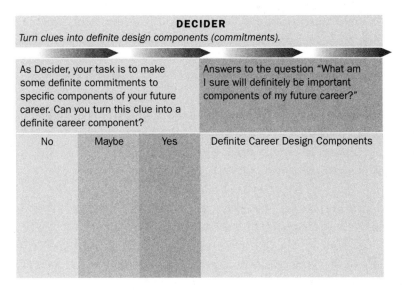

I suppose it might be possible to make a sculpture out of smoke or fog or clouds, like skywriting. But as soon as the wind blows (or you sneeze), the whole creation disappears. So, instead of trying to design your career from wishes, hopes, and maybes, you want to use solid elements you are sure of, elements you have decided must definitely be a part of your design.

Certainty is like pregnancy. It's either 100 percent or zero. You can't be 85 percent sure. Either you are sure or you're not sure. Imagine you were planning to walk down a road in a war-torn country and were told by trustworthy people that the road was 100 percent definitely free of land mines, that every day hundreds of people walked on that road and no one was ever injured by a mine. Wouldn't you feel confident traveling down that road? Now imagine that you were told that the experts were 85 percent sure that there were no land mines in that road. Walking down that road would be a completely different experience. That's the power of certainty.

Another example? Suppose you are trying to figure out your future career. And let's say you are really passionate about talking in front of groups of people and writing. That's a nice clue, but it falls into the category of a passion, an interest, not a definite commitment. So it doesn't have any real power in designing your future. You can't design with maybes. You also like ice cream, music, dark eyes, dancing, and Picasso. So what? Your passions and other clues have very little juice until you claim them as a definite part of the design of your future.

If you can get to the point where you are sure that presenting to groups of people and writing definitely will be major parts of your work, you have created some big and powerful pieces of your career design. The Decider role is one of the most powerful and compelling roles you can assume. You are not just the engineer driving the train. You are also the guy out in front laying track. Not only do you get to drive, but you also get to decide where the train is going.

So, how do you become the Decider in your own life? How do you go from being an average schlub who hopes for the best but feels like an ant lost in a giant, uncaring machine to someone laying your own track? We all do it every time we make any decision, but we usually don't think about what we are doing and how we are doing it. It is done by declaration, by saying what will be. We do it when we make a simple declaration such as "I will work out today," and we do it when we make the big decisions in our lives.

Most of us don't notice when we play this role. If someone asks why you are working out today, you probably give credit to your desires or circumstances: "I want to have giant biceps" or "I need to lose ten pounds." But lots of people want the biceps or weight loss and don't do anything about it. The real reason you are working out today is that you said so. You stepped into the Decider role and created a future that wasn't going to happen by itself.

All around you, in the wider culture we live in, are many who live this way. If you listen closely to interviews with some of the people you most admire and respect, you will find that they are out in front of their own train, laying new track. They may describe it differently, but that is what they are doing. They are declaring how it will be and then doing what is necessary to make it happen. And that is what you will do as you create your future career.

It doesn't take an extraordinary person to live this way. But it does take willingness, commitment, and persistence: the willingness to stand out and be a little different from the crowd, a commitment to a fully lived life, and the persistence to keep working on your design until it is fully shaped and becomes the life you are living every day.

So why doesn't everyone do this? How come most people seem to be just barely driving their train, let alone out there ahead of the train laying new track? Because it is harder than going with the flow; it takes thinking for yourself. You can't just jump on the train and hope it will arrive at the destination. You can't just declare how it will be and expect everything to magically fall into place. You have to be willing to do what it takes to forge your declaration into reality. After the Declaration of Independence, the rest of the world, particularly England, didn't just say, "What a jolly good idea. Let's get behind those Americans and support their big dream." The Americans had to fight to make their declaration real.

Fortunately, there is no universal law that says you will have to struggle every inch of the way. You just have to be willing to. You have to be more committed to having the kind of life you want than you are to the easier road of compromise. Here's a little secret. I have no idea how or why this works, but it does. Sometimes when people totally commit to creating something new in their lives to a degree that their word, their promise, becomes almost an unstoppable force of nature, the path smoothes out and the obstacles disappear. It almost seems as if the entire universe has turned in their favor. Now forget I told you that, so you won't slack off and just expect this to happen.

Making the Best Choices

One of the tools you will use to design your future career is decision making. It's a tool like any other: just as a hammer inserts nails in hard materials, so decision making moves you from not knowing to knowing, from wanting to a commitment, from thinking about something to having made the decision. Every carpenter knows that having high-quality tools makes a big difference in the quality of the final result. The same is true with decision making. So right now we're going to pull out your decision-making tool and check to see if it is up to the job of designing your life. If it isn't, get a new and better tool.

People have their own method for making decisions. Some go with their gut instinct; some are ruled by their feelings, or by logic and analysis, or by going with advice from other people. Most people use some combination of methods. At some earlier chapter of your life, most likely your early teens, you came up with your own method of making decisions, because it seemed to work for you. Then it became a habit. Now every time you have an important decision to make, you dump all the pertinent data into your decision-making machine, and after a while, out pops the decision. It's like a factory: in go the raw materials, some clues that go through a manufacturing process, and out pops a finished product, a decision. Everyone runs the thing to be decided through their own decision-making factory. The only problem with this method is that it was designed unconsciously by an eighth grader with limited knowledge of how to make the best decisions. You've trusted the way you make decisions up until now. Should you trust it to make big decisions, such as your life's direction, or might you want to make some improvements in the method to make sure that it is doing the best possible job for you?

You will most likely find that some decisions are relatively easy. The whole point of going through the various steps in playing the Detective role is to make pieces of the puzzle obvious and easy to turn into commitments. If you notice that you spend every possible minute working alone and solving logical puzzles, it won't take much to decide that these must be some big career design components. If you give 110 percent to the Detective phase, many decisions should be obvious enough to make without difficulty. Some decisions will be made easier by going back into Detective mode, asking better questions, and doing more research. Perhaps you don't have enough information, or you're trusting the wrong sources, or you don't have a clear picture of the situation. When in doubt, do more Detective work. If you are confident that your everyday decision-making method hits the bull's-eye every time, then by all means trust it. But if you aren't totally sure, don't.

If you have any doubt about the effectiveness of the way you make decisions, you may want to create a more useful decision-making method. The first step is to notice how you go about making decisions now. Most of us use more than one method in a certain fixed sequence. I start off with pure enthusiasm, imagining whatever is positive about the choice to be made. Then I start having doubts, begin to look at the situation logically, do extensive research, and wind up making an informed but mainly feeling-based decision. A close friend does the whole thing with logic using spreadsheets and factor analysis, then asks everyone she knows and respects, and finally returns to analysis to make the decision. Another friend seems to always go with his gut with a little research thrown into the mix. Here are the most common methods. Notice which ones you trust and use.

- **Logic, analysis, common sense.** People who use this method describe this approach as rational, sensible, prudent, moderate, and balanced. There are many versions. One common approach is to list the pros and cons of the careers you are considering, assign weighted values to them, and add up the scores. The career with the best pro/con ratio wins. You might just think things over logically and make the decision that way. The problem with this method is well represented by Mr. Spock in *Star Trek:* the decision makes perfect sense but misses the human element.
- **Feelings, desires, passions.** Some folks use their feelings, emotions, sentiments, impressions, and attitudes to make their decisions. Others just blindly follow their passions and desires. Living a passionate life is extraordinary, but being ruled by your passions means nobody is driving your train. It's running wild down the mountain with no brakes—a great servant but a poor master.
- **Romantic yearnings.** People fall in love with images of themselves in certain careers, just as they imagine themselves in a relationship with that magical someone. They float on a cloud of sweet dreams, envisioning themselves in the midst of a glorious future. They think people who try to talk some sense into them are trying to burst their bubble.
- **Gut instinct, intuition.** "I know it's right if it resonates with me." "I go with my gut." People who make decisions this way are usually a little vague about exactly how they know, but this is one of the more common decision-making methods. When I ask people where they feel this resonance, they aren't quite sure. When I ask how they know that this is the best decision, they say they just know. If it were a matter of life and death, would you still trust this method before all others?
- **External sources.** It's amazing how many people follow the recommendations of others—parents, experts, friends, the media, books, career counselors—to make the most important decisions of their lives. Whatever you do, don't become a doctor because it would make your mom happy. It's you, not your mom, who has to get up every morning and go to work. No one else can possibly know you as well as you can know yourself. No one will ever care as much as you do about how well your life works.
- **Compliance or rebellion.** Do you usually go with whatever is accepted as common practice or recommended by your tribe or the mainstream? Or do you usually do exactly opposite? If you

most often comply or rebel, you are completely controlled by outside forces. If someone wants you to sit down and you are a rebel, all that person has to do is tell you that you aren't allowed to sit down.

- **Random.** Go with the flow, take the job you are offered, roll the dice, choose the major with the shortest registration line.
- **Shoulds, shouldn'ts, and yeah-buts.** People are often propelled into doing all sorts of things they don't really want to do because of the little voice in their head that tells them what they should do and shouldn't do, or puts up a firestorm of objections about anything that appears risky.

Free Choice

The problem with all the above methods is that they all exclude one very important person in the final decision: you. This is obvious when you allow other people to make the decision. What is less obvious is that whichever of those methods you use, the decision is made by something other than you. If the method you use is logic, then the most logical option is selected. Logic makes the decision. If you trust your feelings, they do the deciding. There is nothing wrong with using whatever method you use. It probably works fine most of the time—but perhaps not always. When you have a difficult choice to make or you are not absolutely confident that your method will produce the best decisions, try free choice. What I mean by free choice is *to select freely without being ruled by conditioned thinking.* Or *to select freely after thoughtful deliberation.*

The whole concept of free choice is that *you*—not the circumstances, other people, or your usual, everyday decision-making method—make the final decision. With free choice, you check out the matter to be decided using whatever methods you usually trust, then you look into the matter using the methods you don't usually use. If you usually trust your gut, you would check out the potential decision using the other methods. You would ask other people for their opinions and guidance. You would work it out logically, which might mean asking a couple of highly logical friends for their take on the matter. You would pay attention to your feelings despite any yeah-buts that arise, and so forth. In other words, you would become a well-rounded expert on all sides of the question at hand. Then you make a selection freely yourself, kind of like pointing and declaring, "I'll have that one." This way you take into consideration all sorts of viewpoints that you might not usually give credence to. And *you,* not some reason, are the one making the final choice.

"But," you say, "what is this choice based on? It seems like I would be making a random selection this way, just pointing at something and saying, 'I'll have that one.' " Actually, just the opposite is true. This method is probably further from random than whatever you are using now. Random selection is like flipping a coin. Whatever answer comes up is completely uninformed, up to chance or luck. But free choice is totally different. Because you have checked out and considered the matter to be decided from every possible angle, you have become an expert and understand all sides of the question. You have done the research. You have become intimately familiar with everything that could influence the decision. You have sorted it out logically. You have explored your internal world. You have talked with other people. You have become fully aware of your passions and desires, talents and tendencies. You know what is important to you. Now that you have accomplished all that, you are in a perfect position to actually make the choice yourself. So when you point your finger and say, "I'll have that one!" it is a free choice illuminated or informed by your thoughtful deliberation into everything important. You decided yourself. What could be better than that?

Even if practicing free choice sounds a little unusual, there is a tremendous advantage to checking out various aspects of a potential decision in ways you usually don't bother with.

Inquiry 10-1 **PRACTICING FREE CHOICE**

1. **Pay attention to how you make decisions now.** Check out the different methods people use and sort out how you usually make big decisions. Before you can do it differently, you've got to know how you do it now.
2. **Learn all you can about the matter in question.** The secret of free choice is revealed in the second definition: to select freely, *after thoughtful deliberation*. Let's take this one step at a time. First let's deal with the "thoughtful deliberation" part. Later, we'll get to how to select freely.

   It is foolish to make important decisions without knowing everything you can about the matter in question. The more you know, the better off you will be. Thoughtful deliberation involves skillful detective work, rigorous research, discussion, study, reflection, meditation, speculation, calculation, and education. It includes looking into every nook and cranny that could have any bearing on what choice you make.

   What do you look into and thoughtfully deliberate about? Everything that might be important! Fortunately, you already have a full set of powerful research tools at your disposal. The conventional decision-making methods we discussed a few pages ago make the ideal set of research tools. Using them as part of your Detective role is completely different from relying on them to make the decision for you. As research tools, they provide you with everything you need to know: access to all the diverse aspects of your personality as well as practical information about the external world. If you usually go with your feelings, take an in-depth look at the practical and analytical side. If you tend toward a logical approach, delve more deeply into your feelings than usual. If you usually trust the outside world for answers, make sure to give special attention to internal voices, feelings, and insights as well. Explore all of it thoroughly. Look at your potential choices from as many perspectives and directions as you can. Here's how you can use some of the methods that usually dominate the decision-making process as allies to ensure that you make the best choices.

- **Logic, analysis, common sense.** Read everything appropriate. Find out all you can. Become an expert on the subject. Read a year or two of recent issues of the trade magazines of whatever fields you are considering. Read books. Make a list of all the important questions you need to answer to know enough to decide. Make lists of pros and cons. Ask your computer. Do some in-depth career testing to evaluate your talents and personality.
- **Feelings, passions, inclinations, preferences, resonance, romantic yearnings.** Notice how you feel about the different options before you. Which way do you lean? Which option are you trying to talk yourself into? If you are the sort of person who keeps falling in love with exciting new possibilities, you may not feel the same way next month. If something is a huge stretch for you, you may feel terrified. In this case, feeling scared may be a positive sign that you are on the right track. If you tend toward consistent, long-term passions, you may want to give these yearnings special significance. To have a strong natural liking for something is a powerful clue. But remember, just because you have been passionately interested in snakes for many years does not mean you have to become a charmer. Remember that it might be very different to do something all day, every day than it is to dream about it or have it as a hobby. In Maine, there are very few lobstermen who enjoy eating lobster.
- **External sources.** Ask everybody you can who knows anything about whatever you are considering. Find some experts. You need to speak with many of them to form your own opinion. Ask your friends and family.
- **Reaction, rebellion, compliance.** Strong negative feelings and reactions are powerful resources. It's a lot easier to find out how people really feel about things by asking what they don't like than it is to ask them what they do like. People are always crystal clear about what they don't like. Career coaches constantly hear new clients say, "I know what I don't want. But I don't know what I do want." If you have a rebellious streak, turn it into an ally. Many of the great leaps in human culture, art, and business were created by rebels with a cause. If you have a compliant streak, make sure to notice whether it pulls you in a particular direction. Is it fine with you if it makes your choices for you?
- **Shoulds and yeah-buts.** If you recognize the yeah-but voices in your head telling you what you should or shouldn't do as just more information and not necessarily the one and only truth, then you can enlist these noisy voices as allies. They will come up with everything that might possibly be wrong with whatever you are considering. Sometimes they offer practical, down-to-earth viewpoints that prove invaluable in accomplishing what they warn against.

3. **Make a choice.** After you have looked from every possible viewpoint at whatever you are trying to decide, you arrive at a cliff, the moment of choice. You can leap courageously into the unknown, or you can turn around, go back home, put your feet up, and take a nap. Okay, here's the part you have been waiting for, the part where you find out the secret of how to choose freely. A dramatic drumroll, please, maestro! Here's how you do it. You lay all the possible choices out before you.

If you are deciding whether to buy the conservative tie or the one decorated with mating rabbits on 3-D velvet with sequins, you can do this physically. Just point and say, "I pick this one." For choices with less physical substance, it helps to write down the different possible choices on a piece of paper. Next, you simply point to one of them and say, "I pick this one." That's all there is to it.

I know this sounds too simple, but give it a chance to sink in. How else can *you* make the choice? When you do it the usual ways, aren't you giving over the choice to the method you use? Isn't it your life? Then who should make the choices?

I'm not saying you should use this new method for deciding everything from now on. I decide what movie to see based on pure emotion, and I figure out how much income tax to send to Uncle Sam based on pure analysis.

Building Your List of Definite Commitments

Your answers to the question "What am I sure will definitely be components of my future career?" are the building blocks of your future career. Make them clear and strong and what you really mean. Here are some examples. If you find something that rings your bell, steal it.

- I will do work at which I will be appreciated and sought after for my talents, personality, and temperament. I will not have to pretend to be a different person to do the work well.
- I will be moving around on a typical day, not chained to a desk or computer.
- I will do work that changes the way people think about themselves.
- I will do work that focuses on real objects in the real world.
- I will work in a field that has new information being generated all the time. Being current and innovative will be important.
- I will do work that involves finding and using ideas and information from different fields and sources.
- My work will have a series of steps to follow—there will be some structure within which I will have plenty of room for invention, imagination, and innovation.
- I will not do work for a dysfunctional company that cares only for the bottom line and not for the quality of life of its employees.
- I will do work that involves explaining complex things in simple ways.
- I will manage a group of people.
- I will work in sales and/or marketing.
- I will be an artist, a sensualist, a creator of beauty.
- My work will let me live in a rural area somewhere in the Rocky Mountains.
- I will diagnose and fix organizational problems.

- I will do work that involves successfully solving problems every day.
- I will primarily design solutions rather than implement solutions.
- My career will fit in with my goal to have children.
- No boss looking over my shoulder.
- My career will make a big, positive difference in many people's lives.
- I will use my diagnostic problem-solving talent at least several times a day.
- I will build or repair physical systems—buildings, machines, or something similar.
- I will gather, compile, and analyze data 20 to 30 percent of the time.
- I will apply my favorite processes (researching problems by reading, finding underlying patterns, brainstorming solutions, discovering, designing, teaching, organizing, counseling) to a variety of content (whether it be different people, companies, or subject matter).
- My work will mainly involve short-term projects.
- Communicating with other people will be my central job function.
- My work will not involve drumming up business.
- I will work alone 50 percent of the time, unless I work with a partner I really like—then it could drop down to about 25 percent of the time.
- No more degrees. But I would take a few courses if necessary.
- I will do work that I am proud of and enjoy telling other people about.
- I will do work that I have a large degree of control over.
- I will do work that is good for the world.
- I will earn $250,000 a year or more.
- I will do work that does not require formal clothing more than one day a week. I will wear casual yet hip/fun clothes.
- My work environment will be casual, relaxed, friendly, fun.

THE DESIGNER

As Designer of your future career, you take the elements you declared as definite pieces of the puzzle and fit them together into a final masterpiece. Your role as Designer includes all of these synonyms: architect, artist, author, creator, director, engineer, inventor, master builder, planner, and prime mover. Everything around you—the building you are in, the art on your wall, this book, your computer, the clothes you are wearing, the ring on your finger—is the creation of someone playing the role of designer/artist/inventor/author. And that is exactly what you are going to do—craft your life, create your future.

For the American founding fathers, the Declaration of Independence began the creation of a new nation. The next step was designing the future United States, which included, among many other steps, drafting the Constitution. From that design flowed all the freedoms and opportunities that made it a unique and extraordinary place and provided a model

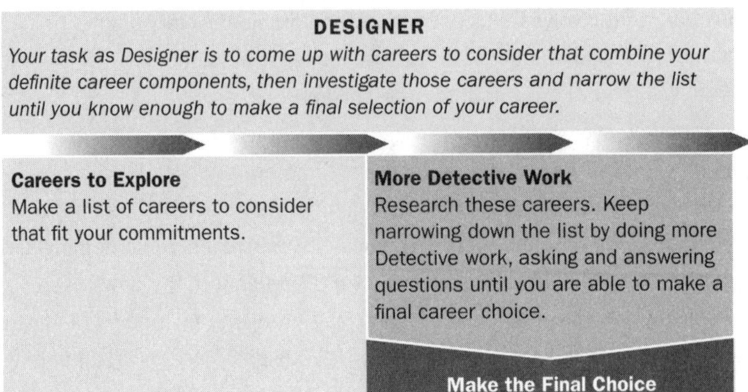

for other countries around the world. In the second half of this book, you will be doing the same thing with your own life.

DESIGNER
Your task as Designer is to come up with careers to consider that combine your definite career components, then investigate those careers and narrow the list until you know enough to make a final selection of your career.
Careers to Explore
Make a list of careers to consider that fit your commitments.
More Detective Work
Research these careers. Keep narrowing down the list by doing more Detective work, asking and answering questions until you are able to make a final career choice.
Make the Final Choice

In Designer mode, your task is to come up with careers to explore that combine your definite career components. Once you have a list of careers that seem to fit your specifications, you go back into Detective mode, investigating and researching each of these careers. Most of the work you have done previously has been speculative and centered on you, like a custom tailor taking measurements of a client as the first step in making a made-to-measure article of clothing. Now you will be looking outside yourself at real careers in the real world.

As you learn more about them, you will most likely find useful new clues you haven't considered before. These may lead to new commitments, new definite career design components. Nothing is more useful than the real world to help separate reality from fantasy. The first steps you took, understanding the *you* your career is supposed to fit, are absolutely essential, but because that part of the process is internally focused, it is almost impossible to avoid making naive and false assumptions about the real world. Now you will align the internal and external worlds. Researching actual careers provides practical data that may require you to change some of your career design specifications or recognize that to fulfill your commitments will ask more of you than you previously thought.

Some careers will sink to the bottom and get crossed off your list. Others will rise to the top. As you learn more about a career, you will learn more about yourself and what you need and want. As you narrow down, you will get closer and closer to making a final choice. Later parts of *Now What?* will guide you through this phase of your career design project. You will find useful inquiries and exercises as well as information on researching potential careers.

The success of this action phase depends on two skills we will talk about in the next chapter. The first is becoming skillful at paying attention to how your project is moving forward and adjusting your actions to correct your course. The second is persisting until you reach your goal no matter what gets in the way.

CHAPTER 11

PERSIST, PROBLEM-SOLVE, AND ADJUST

Once you are in action, you've got to keep the project moving forward until you reach the goal. Every year, many millions of projects get bogged down and eventually abandoned because of a lack of awareness and skill in persisting, problem solving, and adjusting actions to keep things moving forward.

PERSISTENCE

> When in doubt, gallop!
>
> —*Proverb of the French Foreign Legion*

Throughout history, men and women who have made extraordinary contributions have been asked the secret of their genius. The one thing that most of them agree on is the power of persistence:

- The best way out is always through. —Robert Frost
- Many of life's failures are people who did not realize how close they were to success when they gave up. —Thomas Alva Edison
- If you're going through hell, keep going. —Winston Churchill
- I know the price of success: dedication, hard work, and an unremitting devotion to the things you want to see happen. —Frank Lloyd Wright
- Let me tell you the secret that has led me to my goal: my strength lies solely in my tenacity. —Louis Pasteur
- Energy and persistence conquer all things. —Benjamin Franklin

So, which are you going to trust, the yeah-but thought in your head that tells you to abandon ship or Ben Franklin and Winston Churchill? These people weren't just making up pithy quotes. They knew the score, and they're talking directly to you. Edison didn't invent the lightbulb. Others got the glass globe part right before him. What Edison did was work on different filament materials until, after hundreds, he came up with one that lasted. So it is with most complex and difficult projects. If you keep moving forward and keep the momentum up, you will probably reach your goal. If you give up, you won't. No matter how brilliant your plan, without persistence your project is doomed.

Yes, there are people who are born with persistence built in. Fortunately for the rest of us, this is easier to master than it appears to be. The goal is to become like a force of nature, as unstoppable as the wind and rain. The method is simple:

If stopped, start.
If slowed, speed up.
If off course, adjust.

When we run into difficulties, we tend to make life complicated, either stopping to lick our wounds or going back to the drawing board to start over without figuring out what the problem really is. Either way, we wait too long to get back into action. It is usually better to keep moving forward when stopped, even if you don't know the best answer. Action generates forward movement, which supports better problem solving. Wringing your hands, trying to work out the best solution, is rarely as useful as doing something, even if that something isn't the perfect solution. It is like driving: you can't steer unless you are moving. The same applies when you find your project is moving too slowly. When progress is slow, speed up. Once again, there are no perfect solutions. There are only workable solutions, found by getting to work.

ADJUST

An endless parade of difficulties can kill your dreams, destroy your commitments, hinder your forward progress. Most of them can be dealt with. What usually kills people's dreams is not the difficult circumstances that arise but how they interact with them.

Another common tendency is to change the goal when obstacles arise, not noticing that what is actually happening is that you're abandoning the goal to chase comfort and ease. When you do this, you are training yourself to avoid obstacles instead of powering through difficult problems and building goal-fulfillment muscles. Adjust your actions instead of changing your goal. It may be difficult, but practice builds your skill and power to have what you want.

CHAPTER 12

COMPLETE YOUR PROJECT AND CELEBRATE

Since all projects are accomplishment cycles, each project and each section of a bigger project has a beginning, a middle, and an end. Each of us likes some parts of accomplishment cycles more than others. Some people love the early, creative phase, while others like the action in the middle of a project. Few of us have much skill at the final phase: completion.

We keep dragging our old projects along behind us, the failures as well as the successes. Think of how many things you never finished: that relationship that haunts you long after the person is gone, that project you began and abandoned, the guitar in the closet. Pulling the past along with you into the future is a huge power drain. It's like filling up your car with everything you use, including the old pizza boxes and the empty soda cans. When the car is full, you buy a trailer to pull along behind the car, and when that's full you buy another trailer and hitch it to the back of the first one. In a few years you have a long train of trailers filled with crap you don't need dragging along behind your (now straining) car. That's what most people's lives look like, except that the trailers and the trash are invisible. What you actually see are the piles of magazines they mean to read someday, the half-knit sweaters, the unstrung rackets, the clothes that don't fit, the unanswered e-mails.

When you carry the past along with you into the future, you lose power—a lot of power. Earlier we defined "power" as the ability to move through accomplishment cycles quickly. Nothing slows this down like a bunch of incomplete projects dragging along behind you, whether it is the long-dead relationship, the pile of magazines, or your career design project.

Do an experiment: Make a list of everything that is incomplete in your life, including everything in your past that nags at you. Get rid of the clothes you never wear, the piles of magazines, the boxes of stuff you never use. Get some strings on that racket (or give it to someone who actually likes tennis). Call up the person you had the disastrous relationship with and apologize and clean up the part you played in that catastrophe. When you have completed everything you've been dragging along behind you, don't be surprised if you suddenly feel you could take on the world. This is not magic. It is physics—dragging stuff along with you consumes energy.

Not only do the unfinished or abandoned projects rob power and energy; the successful but incomplete ones do also. One of our clients got into grad school with the generous assistance of the department head. She never really thanked him, and didn't do a couple of things he asked. Later on, she needed a letter of recommendation from him, and didn't ask him because she was embarrassed. She thinks this cost her a job she really wanted.

Completing a project does not happen automatically when you reach your goal. You got the result you wanted, but there may be loose ends. The human mind can find fault with anything, even a brilliant result. "Could it have turned out even better if I had done X instead of Y?" "It doesn't look exactly like I planned. Does that mean I failed?" Complete your projects, the successful ones as well as the failed ones. Pretty soon you will be whizzing along through life without dragging trailers full of the past along with you.

Sometimes there are projects inside of projects. Your career design project might involve smaller subprojects, like getting a certain degree or job or learning what you need to know to answer some important question. Completing subprojects allows you to keep moving on to the next part of your career design project with maximum power and energy available.

Inquiry 12-1

COMPLETING PROJECTS

The final phase of any accomplishment cycle is mostly a matter of acknowledging what you have and haven't achieved, perhaps taking some necessary actions, and then declaring the project complete.

1. **Assess how your project turned out.** Ask a few questions about your project:

   - Did you reach the goal?
   - Are you satisfied with the result?
   - If you got a result different from the original goal, does it still satisfy what you wanted in the first place?
   - Was your strategy effective?
   - What can be learned that will be useful next time?
   - Did you change goals in the middle? Did that work?
   - What were the breakthroughs? The breakdowns?
   - What difficulties arose? How did you face them?
   - What is left undone?
   - What promises are not yet fulfilled?
   - What do you need to do or say to complete the project?

2. **Do what you need to do.** You may need to take some actions to finish the project, to clean up afterward. There may be things you need to say to someone. Look and see what you need to do to leave the project squeaky clean with no junk dragged into your future.

3. **Complete the project.** This is done by declaring the project complete. Who is to say if the project is complete or not other than you? Nobody. It is your project and you get to say whether it is complete or not. Remember, we talked about the power of declaration before—how the United States was created by declaration—and since you are the one who decides what's what in your life, you might as well make those decisions consciously. In this case, you get to decide whether the project is complete or not. Make a little ceremony out of it: "I declare this relationship complete. I will not drag it along with me anymore." "I declare my formal education complete." That's all there is to it. This is important to do whether the project turned out the way you hoped it would or not.

CELEBRATE

Once you have completed your career design project, it will be time to celebrate and have a party. Don't hold back!

SECTION 3

Problems and Obstacles

CHAPTER 13

WHY PEOPLE DON'T GET WHAT THEY WANT

I suggest that you read this chapter now, and then come back to it and the following chapter when you are face-to-face with a situation where you need some assistance in dealing with a specific obstacle.

The reason most people do not get what they want goes beyond the endlessly scrolling wants list that never lets you be completely satisfied. There's something more fundamental: most people don't deal skillfully with what gets in the way, the obstacles that stand between them and having what they most want. If it weren't for problems and obstacles, you would not have to embark on a hero's quest to choose a career. You would simply do the inquiries in the second part of this book and shout "Done!"

First, I'm going to introduce you to the most dangerous beasts of the jungle, the essential, basic reasons people don't get what they want. Then, in the next chapter, we will talk about how to deal with the obstacles to having what you most want.

MEET JIMINY LIZARD

We have met the enemy and he is us.

—*Pogo*

When you look in the mirror, you see only one you staring back, unless you were misbehaving last night. But if you squint your eyes and look closely, you may see another you standing on your shoulder, whispering and sometimes jumping up and down and shouting in your ear. Is it Pinocchio's beloved Jiminy Cricket, his conscience who always advised him to do the right thing? Unfortunately, no. Meet Jiminy Lizard.

The everyday you is a twenty-first-century person navigating the complex postmodern world we inhabit, a person who wants to be happy and successful, someone who has benefited from thousands of years of social evolution and is skilled at all sorts of things that would baffle our ancient ancestors. Physically, however, we are exactly like these ancient people of 100,000 years ago. We share all the behavioral traits that allowed them to survive.

In the world we live in today, however, those automatic behaviors carried over from the ancient past are not always useful. In fact, they turn out to be the biggest reasons we don't get what we want.

Jiminy Lizard is my name for the ancient voices of survival programming that still speak to us and have much more control over our lives than we imagine. Jiminy is always standing on your shoulder directing your thoughts, decisions, and behaviors to help you survive in a world that no longer exists. Whenever you start thinking seriously about going after some goal that will stretch you into new territory, Jiminy makes a lot of noise telling you why it won't work and why you don't really want to do it anyway. His programming steers you away from anything that your brain thinks might be risky and unknown.

WHY YOU AREN'T JAMES BOND

Some people are unstoppable in the face of huge obstacles. Most of these people don't actually exist. They are fictional characters such as Indiana Jones and James Bond. In real life, we often get stopped by obstacles that stand between us and our dreams. Why is it so hard to dream big and then take action to fulfill the big dream? Could it be that there's some sort of mechanism built into all of us to keep everything the same, a mechanism that resists change?

Think of how a thermostat works. You set it to 70 degrees. When the temperature goes down, it turns the furnace on, and then turns it off when the temperature gets back to 70. It is a device that keeps things the same, at equilibrium. Nature works the same way. You work the same way. That's why your blood stays at 98.6 degrees. Your body is set for this temperature, just as the thermostat in your house is set for some specific temperature. Whenever your blood temperature starts to go up, this mechanism registers ERROR ERROR ERROR, and that turns on a whole bunch of behaviors, such as perspiring, designed to get your temperature back to normal. If you fall into a lake in the middle of the winter, your blood temperature will start to drop. This sets off another set of error messages that turn on other behaviors, such as shivering, to get your temperature up to 98.6 degrees. If that doesn't work and your blood temperature keeps dropping, the system turns on more radical behaviors, such as shutting down blood flow to your extremities, which is why fingers, toes, and noses get frostbitten first.

This ability to react to keep everything the same is called homeostasis. Here's the formal definition: homeostasis is the property of living organisms to regulate their internal environment to maintain a stable, constant condition of equilibrium. This isn't just a human phenomenon; it is a big part of how all animals function. The frog doesn't jump in the pond when you walk too close because it thinks you look French and might like a nice plate of frog legs for dinner. What happens is that the frog is happily sitting there at perfect equilibrium, and when you show up an alarm is set off—ERROR DANGER DIVE—and it jumps in the pond. This prehuman survival system is concerned with having their bodies survive. Each of us has all the survival systems of earlier prehuman creatures.

Let's say you are an experienced mountaineer. You come across a hundred-foot cliff you would need to descend in order to get to McBurger's to have that triple-decker with cheese you're dreaming about. Your mind compares "rappel down big cliff" with memories of previous cliffs you have descended. Everything looks fine. You are used to this, so your brain registers no threat to survival. Down the cliff you go, happy and undisturbed.

If you are not a mountaineer and don't know how to rappel down cliffs but decide to do it anyway because you really, really want that burger, one look down that cliff will throw your brain into "hold it" mode. Jiminy Lizard jumps up and down, shouting in your ear, telling you a million reasons why you should not get near that cliff. He flips the switch that pumps out a good, healthy dose of fear. You realize that your life is more important than a cheeseburger.

We have the same survival system as the frog, a system that is wholly dedicated to the survival of our bodies. We also have another, more complicated one that operates in our psyche. We all have an identity, an ego, a solid sense of who we are and who we're not: "I'm this kind of person and not that; I believe this and not that; I can do this but not that," and so forth. As far as our human survival system is concerned, this is the equivalent of the setting on the thermostat. Instead of a simple setting like 70 degrees, however, our human survival system compares everything we think of doing with what we have done in the past. When we start thinking of doing something that would stretch us out of our usual, everyday comfort zone, the survival system (Jiminy) starts making noise.

I used to know a guy who was a real-life Rambo. He snuck into a Cambodian village in the middle of the night and silently slit the throat of a Viet Cong leader. This was not particularly scary to him. Years later, however, he found that, like many men, he was terrified of having a deeply intimate relationship with a woman. Does this make any sense? Of course it does, if you understand how our brains work. The Rambo stuff was an everyday, nonthreatening part of his life. It didn't ring his survival bells. But the intimate relationship was new, unknown, and therefore very frightening.

As you can see, the survival system doesn't make a lot of sense. It is a machine, and not a very intelligent one. And guess what? It runs your life. It operates on one simple principle: you survived in the past by doing what you habitually do. Anything that looks different from that predictable past sends up warning signals as a possible threat to survival. This is a perfect system for a cave dweller, whose life stays the same forever and who needs to deal with the same old threats day after day—the lion, the occasional pissed-off cave bear.

It is not a system that is always appropriate for our complex and very different modern lives. Unlike with our ancestors, change is often to our benefit. Stretching out into new territory—out of the comfort zone, going further than is comfortable—is a powerful and positive trait, and a necessary one to employ if you want a career that fits perfectly and provides a level of satisfaction beyond what most people seek or achieve.

YEAH-BUTS

The frog deals with threats to survival by jumping in the pond. You have a much more subtle survival system, the yeah-buts. Every time you make a big stretch, a little voice in your head tells you why you shouldn't do it, why it wouldn't work, why it is dangerous, why you should just keep doing what you were doing before you started getting these wild ideas. Jiminy Lizard will do a perfect imitation of your voice and say something like, "It is so unrealistic to expect to have the perfect career. Why should I expect to have a better life than most people?"

Sometimes, when you recognize some yeah-but running through your head, you can tell that it is silly and absurd, but most yeah-buts sound like the truth. Spend a few minutes looking back to times when you had a major attack of the yeah-buts. Here are some common ones:

I'm too young, too old, not smart enough, too smart.
I'm the wrong sex.
I'm the wrong color.
I'll never get into the right grad school.
The circumstances are like a vise holding me here. I can't do anything about them.
I'm not a risk taker.
I'm not committed enough.
If only I could decide. It's just so difficult to decide what to do.
Work is not supposed to be enjoyable. That's why they call it work.
I'm doomed. Might as well give up.
I'm afraid, and that means I shouldn't move forward.
I didn't/don't/won't have the right opportunities.
I don't have enough willpower.
I have this habit of quitting.
I couldn't do anything I would really want to do.
I'm really trying. It's not my fault. Really!
I don't have enough money.
I don't have enough talent.
I can't do what I want because the fun careers pay less.
I'm sensitive, an artist. I couldn't possibly have a regular job because I see through the banalities of crass materialism.
I want to help people, but this is a cruel, heartless world where only the lawyers win.

It takes putting my shoulder to the grindstone, year after year, and that's not my style.
It's hopeless. I have this fatal flaw.
It's my karma.
I'm an immigrant. My English isn't good enough.
I should have been born in an earlier time.
I don't have the courage to go out and make cold calls and do the other things that I need to do to get the kind of job I want.
I'm over-/undereducated, over-/underqualified, have too much/too little experience, and the experience I have is really a detriment because it's in the wrong field.
I just got out of college. They didn't teach me what Shinola is anyway.
I went to the wrong college/didn't have enough college/didn't go to college.
I picked the wrong major.
My degree is completely useless in today's marketplace.
My skills are antiquated, outdated, underrated.
What makes me think I can decide now, when I have failed so far?

Did you recognize any of these yeah-buts? The further we stretch beyond our usual, comfortable path, the louder they get. This internal survival system is not the enemy. All it wants is for you to be safe. Its notion of "safe," however, is based in the past, within the range of what you're used to.

Some yeah-buts are emotions, not thoughts. The most powerful of them is fear. Whenever I think of doing something really new that would stretch me into new territory, I feel fear in the pit of my stomach, and Jiminy tells me that fear means stop, quit, don't move forward, danger. People today nonchalantly ride roller coasters so steep and scary that they would scare Genghis Khan to death, so it's not the fear per se that's the problem. The voice that goes along with it—the yeah-but that says, "I'm scared. Fear means stop. Don't ask out that girl who seems so far out of my league"—is the problem.

AUTOPILOT

Yeah-buts are just one example of human autopilot. In fact, nearly everything we do is habitual behavior.

In many ways, autopilot is a brilliant solution that allows us to pay attention to what's important right now and leave the driving to habit. It is not just your heart that is operating without your intervention. When you walk, you don't have to say, "Left leg, prepare to lift. Now lift. Left leg, move forward. Body, lean forward. Left foot, prepare for contact. Left leg, lower. Body, shift weight to left leg."

If you had to think about how to open a door each time you did it, how to turn on the lights, brush your teeth, start your car, or do any of a multitude of other things, your life would be way more complicated. Ask someone who has sustained a stroke and has to relearn such basic acts. Our autopilot system frees us to give our attention to other things, to be creative without getting swamped with all the details.

A good question is "Just how much of my life is on autopilot?" An even better question might be "How much of my life is *not* on autopilot?" If you pay very close attention to a one-hour slice of your life, you may discover that most of it is running on autopilot. When you get hungry, you eat. When you itch, you scratch. When the phone rings, you answer. When you are accused, you defend. When you watch the tube, your hand reaches in the bag and puts chips in your mouth with absolutely no thought or conscious action.

TRIBES

Just like our hunter-gatherer ancestors, we are what zoologists call "tribal primates." In ancient times, each of us belonged to one tribe. Now we belong to and are influenced by the wisdom, values, and rules of multiple tribes.

If you grew up in the United States, one tribe you belong to is "American." As an American, you are highly influenced by the values, points of view, customs, beliefs, fears, and behaviors of your tribe. You absorbed them without thinking about it. You didn't choose to speak the language you grew up speaking, for instance. Within the tribe "American" are many subtribes: New Yorkers, African Americans, New Englanders, liberals, Catholics, Jews, evangelicals, teenagers, Goths, creative nerds, Latinos, and many others. People who seem kind of alien to you are probably just members of tribes you don't belong to, so they seem strange or hard to understand. You also belong to sub-subtribes such as the friends you hang around with, the school you go to, the company you work for, and the family you come from.

Each of the tribes you belong to influences what you think and believe and how you behave, no matter how much of an independent thinker you consider yourself to be. When Ronald Reagan was president, nearly all Republicans supported and nearly all Democrats opposed what was called "Star Wars," a shield that would supposedly protect against incoming missiles. The members of both of these huge tribes were sure their opinions were right, and most people believed that they had formed their opinions independently. But that just isn't possible. How could opinions be so neatly divided if people were thinking independently? What was actually happening is what always happens: everyone inherits their opinions from their tribes. We are mesmerized, hypnotized into believing what our tribes believe.

Each tribe has its customs, both ancient and modern. Some of any tribe's customs may not make a lot of sense to someone from another tribe. For example, the ancient Thracians were polygamists. When a man died, his multiple wives competed for the honor of being killed and buried with him. Somehow that doesn't seem like much of an honor to me. But to a Thracian it all made perfect sense, just as what your tribes believe and how they behave make sense to you. The habitual way the American tribe chooses careers doesn't make any more sense than the Thracians' burial customs, but we keep doing it just the same. You know this tribal career-choosing method doesn't work or you wouldn't be reading this book. But remember, these tribal customs have tornado-force winds that will do all they can to suck you back into their grasp.

Each tribe has its own ideas of which careers are acceptable and which aren't. Remember, your family is one of your tribes, as are the people around you, your culture, and your country. All of them have their own fixed beliefs about nearly everything, including which careers are acceptable. In my own family we were taught that sales and entertainment were taboo. There were many other unspoken career taboos, including all the trades, the arts, anything dirty, risky, not professional, and so on. Hundreds of women gave up on dreams because the only careers their family approved for women were nurse, teacher, secretary, or housewife. Fortunately, the big American tribe has expanded what is available for women. But the tribe still rules. What percentage of U.S. senators are women? How many famous female lead guitar players can you think of?

Here in America, millions seek careers at the top of their tribe's list of cool careers. A cool career, however, only fits you if it does. If it doesn't, you spend your life going to work each day at a job that looks good and tastes bitter. Tribal customs intend safety, not harm, but safety usually means sticking to the status quo. And sooner or later "sticking" can start to feel like "stuck."

So there may be a tremendous urge to put this book away and forget what I'm saying, to just go along with the conventional way careers are chosen in your tribe. Jiminy Lizard will do what he can to keep you within the safe bounds of the tribe's career selection rules, and the tribe may apply pressure directly: your friends or family may think you are a little weird to be working so hard on this career design stuff. Please don't cave in on your commitment to live a life you love, to choose the perfect career.

CHAPTER 14

PROBLEM SOLVING 101

The purpose of this chapter is to introduce you to some basic problem-solving principles. If you gain some mastery in applying these principles, you can usually devise solutions to even the thorniest problems. You will notice that some of the most powerful problem-solving principles involve concepts and skills we have talked about earlier. This is no accident.

The reason we have brains bigger than a cat's is that the better a critter can solve problems, the more likely its species is to survive, especially one with weak muscles, no fur, and pathetic little teeth and claws. That's why it's us, instead of the Neanderthals, running all over the place polluting the planet. From day one, we have been learning to solve problems. But we tend to rely on whatever problem-solving method pops into our heads to deal with the obstacle in front of us.

We frequently rely on problem-solving methods we adopted when we were young. We keep on using the same old methods and never really consider how well they work. A tantrum seemed to work well to get you what you wanted when you were five. Plenty of managers still use this technique in spite of its limited effectiveness at age thirty-five. As children, we had a very limited ability to develop powerful, resourceful strategies, at least compared with the capacities we have now as adults.

Kids always pick from the options that are immediately obvious. Mastering the art of problem solving requires seeing beyond the obvious to discover the real source of the problem, and then devising creative solutions. The world is filled with people who think they are on a journey but in fact are just hopping around in circles. They may complain about boredom and seeing the same scenery over and over without noticing that their foot is nailed to the floor. They are blind to what is keeping them stuck.

THE PROBLEM WITH PROBLEMS

One thing that keeps them stuck is the belief that we shouldn't have problems. Most of us have this silly notion that if we solved our problems, we would have fewer of them. Fortunately, life just doesn't work that way. Problems never stop, and you will never have fewer of them until they put you in a box and cover you up with dirt. If you solve one, another pops up.

Here's an example. You have an old beater of a car that has a hole in the muffler and the inside smells like a dead cat. Plus the air-conditioning is broken and you live in Florida. You've got a problem. So you save to buy a shiny new Mercedes. Now you have a new set of problems. Your best friend, who leaves a trail of dirt and cigarette ashes wherever he goes, often rides with you. You didn't mind the grunge in the old beater, but now you don't know how to tell him that he needs to clean up his act or he can't ride in the new car. Your friendship is in jeopardy. You work at the edge of a rough neighborhood. Nobody bothered your car before. Now you have to park twenty blocks from work because you worry somebody might scratch the paint or steal the hood ornament. Still, you sit at work worrying about your baby. Will someone steal it, scratch it? Will a bird crap on it? You don't get rid of problems. If you're living a vital life, you just exchange old problems for new ones. People dealing with the same problems over and over are not really dealing with them. Their foot is nailed to the floor. The scenery gets very boring. It repeats and repeats and repeats.

LOVE YOUR PROBLEMS

The ability to both solve problems and create new ones is one of the main talents that distinguishes us from other animals. Cows have just a few basic problems. Our prehistoric ancestors had more problems than a cow but fewer than we do because their problems were relatively basic, such as getting enough to eat and avoiding becoming somebody else's lunch. You have problems that run on a higher level—problems that arise when you are up to something big, when there is a gap between what exists and what you are committed to. These problems are not thrust upon you like a noisy neighbor or a prowling tiger. You create them because you get what you want when you solve them.

Earlier I said that power is the ability to go through accomplishment cycles quickly. Another way of saying the same thing is that power is the ability to exchange your old problems for bigger and better ones. Since your entire life will consist of a series of problems, I suggest you learn to love and honor the problems you have and seek bigger, more interesting ones.

Inquiry 14-1 **MY RELATIONSHIP WITH PROBLEMS**

This is the shortest inquiry in the book—short but not easy. I ask that you choose and commit to one of the three statements below. Don't pick the one that is the obvious "right answer" because you hope picking it will make your life better or easier. It won't. What works is to be ruthlessly honest. You can always come back later and make a new choice.

- I'm going to keep looking at problems the same way I have been.
- I promise to love problems, to solve them with liveliness and enthusiasm, to seek out more and better ones, to consider them a creative challenge, to honor them as I honor life itself, to notice when I'm not keeping this promise, and to recommit to it as often as it takes, for the rest of my life.
- I'm not sure. I want more time to think about this.

WHAT'S THE SOURCE OF THE PROBLEM—INTERNAL OR EXTERNAL?

Most problems appear to occur outside of us, as something in the external world we have to deal with. But more often than not the solution is found inside. Suppose your parents won't pay for the summer "research" trip you want to take to Thailand. It seems like the outside world is putting an obstacle in your path. But is that really the case? Do you see a tall brick wall looming above you? If you turned your mind around and changed the way you looked at your problem, you could gain new power over your circumstances.

Looking at it as an internal problem, you can see all sorts of possibilities. You could communicate with your parents in a new way, without nagging or demanding or begging or whatever it is you are doing that is not real communication. You could sell something. You could decide to put off the trip until you have saved the money to pay for it. You could come up with a creative plan—find a way to do it on the cheap, hitch a ride in somebody's private jet, find an ultracheap fare and backpack, stay in hostels, write articles about your trip for an adventure magazine, borrow from a rich friend. There are endless possibilities if you are willing to stretch. Every potential solution involves looking at things differently, learning a new skill, stretching out further than usual, communicating better, making requests.

You are dead set on becoming a doctor but have been rejected by every medical school you have applied to. Seems like an external obstacle, doesn't it? But the solutions are mostly internal. The first step might be to decide that you are not going to take no for an answer, that you are willing to do whatever it takes to become a doctor even if it stretches you way beyond anything you have ever done in your life. Even though you would need to do all sorts of things in the external world to reach the goal, this promise to yourself is the nucleus of the solution. I've known people who didn't have the grades or the money yet got into medical school by sheer unstoppable determination combined with a creative approach.

In the years after World War II, Japan was not known for high-quality cars and electronics, as it is now. The stuff the Japanese made was mostly cheap, low-quality junk, things like papier-mâché kaleidoscopes made from old newspapers. Once they created a national commitment to transform their economy, they searched for a way to make it happen. The answer was an American productivity expert named Dr. W. Edwards Deming. He became the wizard who turned Japan around. His principles taught the Japanese to build the amazingly high-quality stuff they now do. One of his central principles concerned figuring out the cause of problems. He said that most of the time, managers look for what he called a "special cause" for their productivity problems, blaming unique, usually external things such as the weather or the competition. He said that the solution to nearly all problems is to look for "common causes"—ordinary, everyday things nearly always internal, that hold the problem in place. For example, companies Deming worked with often discovered that the real problem was how the company is managed rather than some external circumstance. If you've noticed that your friend's Toyota is still running perfectly with 250,000 miles on it while your nearly new Chevy leaves a trail of parts behind it as you motor down the road, you might take a lesson from Dr. Deming—the solutions to nearly all your problems are internal.

WHAT IF THERE IS NO SOLUTION?

There is never no solution! Well, almost never. But there are times when what you want is either impossible or beyond what you are ready, willing, and able to do to achieve the goal.

If it really isn't going to happen, if you aren't going to get what you want, let it go! The worst thing you can do is to hold on to it and drag it along with you like a ball and chain. That's not giving in to a yeah-but. That's nursing a futile hope, which is one way of sticking with the familiar and not stretching beyond your comfort zone.

Ninety-nine percent of the time, we give up too soon after being sucked in by a yeah-but. Persistence, therefore, is usually the wisest course, no matter how difficult the obstacle. How long you've been attempting to solve the problem is a factor to consider in deciding when enough is enough. If you have been trying to make it in acting for several years and your only recent speaking role was an "erk" as you were vaporized by aliens in a crowd scene, you may be right that it's time to hang up the dream. But don't give up until you have done ten times as much as other people would do to fulfill your dream.

A useful viewpoint to look from: the problem is not the difficulty you are facing but figuring out how to deal with it in the most resourceful, powerful way.

PROBLEM SOLVING

Now we're going to look at those principles of problem solving I was referring to at the beginning of the chapter. These are basic principles, skills to learn and practice and use both with your current problems and for the rest of your life.

Wake Up

After reading some of the previous chapters, you've started to notice how much we humans run on autopilot. Autopilot serves useful functions in areas that require no creativity, but it fails to handle the big, important stuff.

We have been running on autopilot in career choice, and we have the results we might predict: 70 percent of people are not happy with their work. (It's almost a miracle the figure isn't higher.) "This is the way we've always done it" is a justification for autopilot. If you shake off the habit of autopilot, however, you very well might think: "Wait, wait, wait. This is crazy! If a garage was only successful in fixing my car 30 percent of the time, would I keep taking it there? So why should I entrust my life to a process with a 30 percent success rate?" As soon as you recognize you are sleepwalking, you're awake. Let's conduct an experiment where you can actually measure whether or not you wander around lost in thought.

Inquiry 14-2 MINDFULNESS

Mindfulness is about paying attention to what's going on moment to moment. With some mindfulness practice, you will start to notice for yourself many of the things I have talked about in this book. You will start to recognize just how much of the time we humans are running on autopilot, lost in thoughts, how often what we do and the decisions we make are no more conscious than a trout jumping for a fly. Remember, there is nothing wrong with autopilot. It is the default operating system for human beings and, for the most part, the only system available to other creatures.

Mindfulness teaches us how to be awake, how to live in the present moment instead of being lost in thought. The technique described in this inquiry has been used worldwide by people from all cultures for thousands of years, and is now recognized by scientists, clergy, and creative business leaders as an extraordinarily powerful technique to wake up and live in the real world. The goal isn't a peaceful feeling. It is to be at one with reality, to pay attention to what is happening, within us and without us.

1. Find a quiet, private spot where you won't be disturbed.
2. Set an alarm for a minimum of twenty minutes. Sit upright in a chair with your spine straight, your head erect and balancing comfortably on your shoulders, and your hands in your lap.
3. Close your eyes and take three big breaths, in and out.
4. Relax your body from head to foot, letting go any tight places.
5. Begin to breathe naturally. Let your body do the breathing without controlling it in any way.
6. Start to pay attention to your breath, either by feeling the air coming in and out of your nostrils or by feeling your chest rise and fall. Keep paying attention to your breath, in and out.
7. Your mind will soon wander. When you realize that your attention has drifted away in thought, return your focus to your breathing. Keep at it.
8. There is no goal to this technique. You are not trying to control your thoughts or force anything. Just pay attention. That's all there is to it.

You will probably notice that your mind has a mind of its own. It just wanders around without your doing anything. It doesn't do this just when you are watching your breath. It does it all the time. It is running on autopilot. People who practice mindfulness daily say the beginner's unfocused mind is like a "drunken monkey." This is the instrument that is making your decisions.

Think for Yourself

> Few people think more than two or three times a year. I have made an international reputation for myself by thinking once or twice a week.
>
> —*George Bernard Shaw*

Every word in this book is intended to teach and coach you to think for yourself and to create your own life with freedom and power. But how to start? Since we all *think* we think for ourselves, actually doing so starts with noticing when you aren't, as in the previous mindfulness inquiry. A good place to start is in the last chapter. How much are your beliefs influenced by the tribes you belong to? Are certain careers attractive because they fit the tribe's standards? Do you think or dress like your fellow tribe members? Once you begin to notice how much of your reality is handed to you already formed, you are ready to build your independent thinking muscles. Then you can find ways to look beyond the conventional.

When you face a specific problem or obstacle, you've actually got two problems—the problem itself and the habitual way we humans look for conventional solutions. Let's use a simple example. Say you want to ask some questions of the top expert in a career field you are considering. The conventional answer would be to write a letter or e-mail or make a phone call. If you don't get a response, most people would give up, or perhaps not try in the first place because they've already decided the expert would never respond. Thinking for yourself always involves finding new ways of looking at the situation by actively creating new possibilities. That's why step one of accomplishment cycles isn't just "What do I want?" but "What do I want *and* what's possible?" One way to come up with new possibilities is to brainstorm.

How to Brainstorm

Brainstorming is a way to come up with lots of new ideas, possibilities, and solutions. Sit down with a piece of paper, frame the question to brainstorm, and write down as many ideas as possible. Push yourself to come up with more ideas. The rules are simple.

1. Frame the question. In this example it might be "How could I get to talk with Ms. X?"
2. Sit down with your computer or pen and paper and think of ideas. The focus is on coming up with lots of new ideas. Write down every potential idea, solution, and answer that you can think of. Let your mind run free in an enthusiastic, uncritical way. Don't listen to the yeah-buts your mind comes up with. Don't edit. Don't get stuck in one train of thought. Write down the ridiculous

ones as well as the seemingly practical ones. You might give yourself new instructions when you run dry, such as: "Now write down some practical answers. Now write down some exciting answers. Now write down some really smart answers. Now write down some answers ___________ [some historical figure you especially respect] might come up with. Now write down some wild answers." Stretch your boundaries. Don't expect to do this all at once. Write down whatever you can think up until you run dry. Then wait a day or two and do it again. There are endless ideas that might work in the present example. Here is a wild one that worked: find out what the person cannot resist and send him or her some. A friend wanted to speak with a high White House official, discovered her quarry had a huge jones for M&Ms, sent that person a big bag, and got her call returned. Another idea is to write an article that involves interviewing the person in question.

3. Individual brainstorming works well. Group brainstorming works even better. If your brainstorm is no more than a slow drizzle or you need a broader perspective, call in a few friends. Not just the ones who think like you. You also want the ones who are least like you. Pick friends with wild imaginations and outrageous or different points of view as well as your most practical, realistic friends. Pose the question to them from different angles. Ask them to come up with lots of possibilities rather than their soundest advice. Encourage them to come up with wild ideas. Make sure they are playing the brainstorm game and understand the one rule: no evaluating, judging, complaining, commenting on, or criticizing anyone's ideas, no matter how ridiculous or impractical they may seem. Push yourself and your friends to keep coming up with as many ideas as they can. Quantity, not quality. The goal is to loosen up and get the creative juices flowing. Become an idea vampire. Only when you have drained every drop of creative juice from yourself and your friends is it time to evaluate the ideas you have collected.
4. Once you have all of the many ideas and solutions collected in one list, sit down alone with your list. It is time to pare them down to the very best. What you are looking for are the ideas that provide the most powerful and effective means to solve your problem. Pick the good ones. Dump the ideas that wouldn't work. Don't throw out any interesting idea, no matter how radical, until you have considered it from an open-minded perspective. You could write down lists of "why this idea would work" and "why this idea wouldn't work." Most people who do this with an open mind discover that some of the "why it wouldn't work" list reveals more about what they are afraid of or think they couldn't do than it reveals about why the idea wouldn't work.

Do some further head scratching, analysis, and research to pare things down further and discern which answer or combination of answers is the one you like best. The best ideas are not necessarily the most obvious or the most practical. Often it is some wild, outrageous idea that turns out to be the best one.

Talk With Lots of People

Thinking for yourself doesn't require you to come up with the solutions yourself. All you need to do is get out of the box of conventional thinking. One way to do that is to include others in the process of devising solutions. Talk with lots of people. Get their feedback, ideas, and inspirations. Ask world-class experts, not just your roommate. This is research, not brainstorming. What you want to do here is not simply adopt the solution of some wiser person but learn enough from experts to form your own independent opinion so you can choose the solution that's best for you and your unique situation. If you talk with just a few people, you will get a perspective that's too narrow to help you form your own viewpoint. If I was thinking of becoming a marine biologist, I would talk with at least a dozen of them to get a wide and deep variety of perspectives. I would formulate my questions ahead of time. Ask each person you speak with to suggest other useful people.

Don't blindly trust the opinion of anyone who is selling whatever you are considering. That applies to anyone who has a personal stake in what you want to find out about. At Rockport Institute, we have heard from hundreds of clients who say they made a huge mistake and decided on a major or a career field after trusting the opinion of a college advisor or professor. If you are thinking about starting a certain type of business, don't trust the advice of someone who has the same sort of business near where you plan to open yours. Ask people in another part of the country who will not be threatened by potential competition.

Get Your Hands on the Wheel—Turn It Into a Project

Remember way back there when I was talking about personal power, saying power is the ability to go through accomplishment cycles quickly? Since everything occurs in cycles, you have more power when you go with the flow instead of fighting it. Loving your problems and turning them into projects is one way to do that and passionately surf the big waves instead of fighting them. No need to do this with the little guys. But it is nearly impossible to succeed with larger, more complicated problems unless you give them the respect they deserve and turn them into formal projects that you take through all the steps of an accomplishment cycle.

The Power of Committent

Nothing has more problem-solving power than giving your word and sticking to it no matter what obstacles arise. When you approach a problem with "I'll try" or "Maybe I can solve it successfully and maybe not," you have already nailed your foot to the floor, because what you are really saying is, "The circumstances will determine what happens. I have no real power." Your wholehearted commitment to the result is the fuel that powers you through the hard parts and stands up against the yeah-buts that seek to keep everything the same.

How Good Can I Stand It?

This is a great question to ask when you are sorting out how far you are willing to stretch into new territory. If you agree with my assertion that your biggest problem is likely to be the powerful force of the yeah-but survival mechanism operating to reduce risk, you know that the further you stretch, the more resistance you are going to get. Most people stretch only when it is a matter of life and death. They won't stand up to the forces that seek to keep them from straying from the equilibrium of their everyday lives. If you want a really extraordinary life, you've got to be willing to stand up to a lot of internal and external resistance. Small stretch, small yeah-buts. Big stretch, massive yeah-buts.

Courage

It takes courage to reject the standard methods and design your own future. It takes courage to stand up to the yeah-buts. When you are struggling through one of the difficult parts of turning your dreams into reality, you may wonder why you always get stuck with having to put up with so much fear and uncertainty. "Why," you wonder, "couldn't I feel more courageous, like those other people do?" You don't feel courageous because courage is not an emotion, not something you feel. Rather, courage consists of doing what you said you would do even when you don't want to. In the face of danger you have a choice to be the delegate of either your commitments or your feelings. It's as simple—and as difficult—as that.

Steer Skillfully

You don't have to become a master of steering your ship. Just a little bit of waking up and steering has a big effect. In fact, some steering when you make the big choices, such as designing your future work, will improve your life immeasurably. Then you can go back to sleep if you want, with the ship heading in a good direction. Couples who cruise around the world on a sailboat, going from port to port, sail twenty-four hours a day on long passages, with one person on watch at a time. During the night, the person on watch sits in the cockpit, dozing off, and awakens every half hour or so to check for danger, such as approaching ships or changes in the weather. That's all you have to do to successfully steer your ship. You don't have to be awake all the time. You don't have to turn into someone else. Who you are now is perfectly capable of steering your ship. You don't have to make radical changes to have a life that heads toward your chosen port. By the way, right now you may be saying, "What chosen port? I don't know where I'm heading." By chosen port I mean heading toward any chosen destination. In this case the port would be successfully completing this project of choosing a career that fits you perfectly.

Mastering the Yeah-buts

Yeah-buts are by far the biggest obstacle to having a career you love. Here's how to deal with them.

Inquiry 14-3 **MY PERSONAL YEAH-BUTS**

Make a list of the yeah-buts that have power over you. Get some hints from the list of common yeah-buts in the previous chapter, but think of some others too. Look back through your memory to times when you had a big decision to make or were considering doing something that was a stretch. What were the objections you thought of? What did you worry about? Read over the list on pages 92–93 for ideas.

Get to know how your own individual survival system works. Which yeah-buts have hooked you like a trout and killed off a dream or plan? Notice which ones pop up most often when you step out of your comfort zone, which ones can be counted on to shut down any attempt to stray out of the safe zone. Remember that emotions can be yeah-buts. Fear is almost always a yeah-but. It arises to keep you from doing something that your system considers dangerous but which may in fact simply be new or unfamiliar.

Some people have hair-trigger yeah-buts that kill off even the thought of sticking a toe out of the comfort zone. Other people's systems let them fantasize about stepping into the unknown and then attack when they start to get serious. Notice what is within your comfort zone and what sets off alarms.

Inquiry 14-4 **MASTERING THE YEAH-BUTS**

1. When you have an attack of yeah-buts, look over your list and notice which ones are making noise right now. See if you can convert each one of them in your mind from "the truth" to a yeah-but.
2. Yeah-buts always point out an objection to your idea or plan. Then the objection gets mixed in with the thought "Therefore I should give up on this." Notice what happens if you separate the two parts. "I would have to get a PhD, so I should give up this silly idea" turns into simply "I would have to get a PhD." Without the extra baggage, you could then consider what it would take to get a PhD or even research how you might do what you want without the PhD.

   How can you tell if it is actually a yeah-but? A yeah-but opposes doing whatever you are considering; it carries a hidden (or not-so-hidden) message that you can't or you shouldn't. A problem, on the other hand, occurs simply as a statement of a circumstance. "To get to Oz I would have to climb over that mountain, so I should go home and watch the game instead" is a yeah-but because it counsels you to quit. "To get to Oz I will have to climb this mountain" is a problem you can solve.

3. Just because it is a yeah-but doesn't mean it lacks useful information. Many yeah-buts contain at least some truth. See if you can convert them into problems to solve in order to reach your objective. When you recognize yeah-buts for what they are, you have a choice: you can drop your goal and run for your life, or you can turn them into a list of problems to solve in order to reach your goal. Let's say you start thinking you might like to climb Mount Everest. Right away, Jiminy Lizard goes wild with objections:

My Yeah-buts

Why I Should Give Up This Crazy Idea

- I climb only little teeny safe mountains.
- I don't have the skills needed.
- I'm not in condition.
- I can't afford to pay to join an expedition.

Notice that all of these yeah-buts have one function: to get you to give up. What if you converted them into a to-do list? They would instantly transform into a list of things to handle:

My To-Do List

Stuff to Handle Before I Climb Everest

- Climb some big mountains to prepare.
- Learn the skills needed.
- Get in condition.
- Raise the money so I can join an expedition.

The words in both lists are similar, but the meaning is completely different: a yeah-but list has been transformed into a to-do list. If you are just considering an idea, you can make the conversion from yeah-but to to-do as a speculative what-if exercise. But if you are totally committed to climbing Everest with no possibility of quitting, your yeah-buts automatically transform into a to-do list. Once there is no turning back, the yeah-buts tend to quiet down. When you are committed, "I don't have the necessary skills" automatically turns into "Learn the needed skills." Once again the power of commitment waves the magic wand that transforms the ordinary to the extraordinary.

The Career Design Toolkit

CHAPTER 15 THE CAREER DESIGN TOOLKIT GUIDE

If you have been merrily turning pages thinking that sooner or later you might actually dig into this career and life design project, you have just reached the end of the ground-school lessons on how to fly. No more sitting in a classroom. Now it is time to step into the cockpit, rev up the engine, and take off. For the rest of the book, we are going to be flying. From this point on, the book changes from something to read to a project to do. If you have not yet read Section 2, I suggest you do so before you start the toolkit. Otherwise you are flying blind.

If you are not quite ready to take off yet and want to learn more about topics such as how to choose the perfect career, yeah-buts, what to do when you get off track, meaning, mission, purpose, personal marketing, and writing a masterpiece of a resume, you might want to read my other book, *The Pathfinder: How to Choose or Change Your Career for a Lifetime of Satisfaction and Success*. It will give you much to munch on. But please take this coaching: Don't wait! Begin now! You are ready!

The three first sections of the Career Design Toolkit are:

Section 4: "Who You Are." This section is about discovering more about who you are (your natural gifts), including your talents and personality.
Section 5: "Why You Work." This section focuses on goals, the subjects that interest you, your values, and what is meaningful to you.
Section 6: "Where You Work." This section is about where you will work.

In each of these sections, you operate in two different roles, Detective and Decider. As Detective, you search for clues and gather them in a notebook. You "work" the strong clues by asking questions and doing research until, as Decider, you turn some clues into definite career design components. These design components are the specifications for your future career.

Once you have enough definite career design components to start identifying some specific careers, it is time to move on to the next part of the toolkit: Section 7, "Making the

Final Choice." In this section you jump into the role of Designer, where you will use the definite components you chose to develop a list of careers to explore and research, then narrow the list of those that fit best until you can make your final choice.

Part 3 of this book is called "The Career Finder." It has several chapters containing lists of careers that fit various combinations of natural gifts. Use it as a resource to assist you in coming up with a really excellent list of careers to explore.

The diagram below illustrates the career design process.

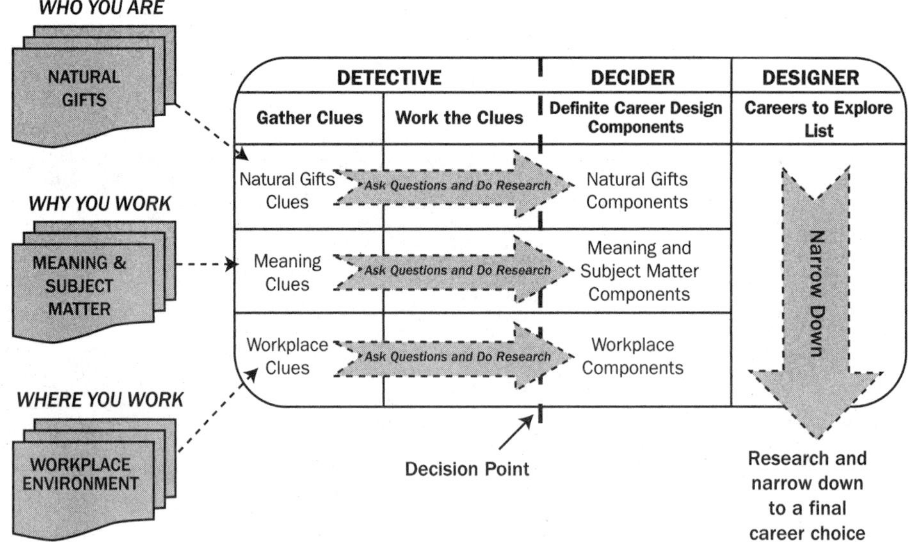

HOW TO USE THE CAREER DESIGN TOOLKIT

Each chapter in the first three sections of the toolkit introduces a topic and then asks you to do inquiries to search for clues from a variety of different angles. Keep these important things in mind as you navigate the Career Design Toolkit:

- **Start at the beginning** with the "Natural Gifts" section. Complete one section before moving on to the next. For example, stick with examining your talents and personality until you "get it" in your bones. Don't shortchange yourself: explore each section fully to get to the heart of it before moving on.
- **Do what's useful.** Skip what's not useful to you. There may be inquiries that are not particularly helpful in your specific situation. You don't have to do everything in the toolkit. If you are impatient with detail, feel some parts are too complicated, have a special situation, or just want a set of steps through the career design process that fits your personality and style, go to the Rockport Institute Web site for specific recommendations on how to use this book in a way that doesn't

drive you up the wall. For most people, however, I recommend that you do all or nearly all the inquiries. Your life may depend on it. Why? Because you probably won't be able to tell which inquiries will bear the juiciest fruit. Often the ones you are least inclined to do will produce the best clues.

- **Don't quit in the middle.** The Rockport Career Design Method works with nearly everyone if you keep at it all the way through to the end. Some of you may be tempted to quit because this method may seem confusing or complicated at first. Remember when learning anything new seemed hard—until you mastered it? If you start at the beginning and go step by step, it will all work out.
- **Use a notebook** to gather and work on your clues. You want all your information in one place. This is especially important for terminally disorganized people.
- **Remember:** Some inquiries will provide strong clues, some won't. Don't worry.

START A NOTEBOOK

As you work through each chapter of the Career Design Toolkit, the instructions will send you to your notebook to record clues and career design components.

In your role as Detective, your curiosity and questioning help you discover clues. In the movies, detectives always have a pocket notebook they flip open at the scene of the crime to make notes. You too need a handy detective's notebook to help you collect your findings. As you go forward, your notebook will fill up with clues and career design components. Use your notebook often.

As I noted earlier, the best way to set up your notebook may be to download notebook components from the Rockport Institute Web site (www.rockportinstitute.com). This will save you the trouble of drawing worksheets yourself.

Create a folder on your computer where you can keep everything related to your career design project. If you are comfortable with a paper-free lifestyle, your computer can be your notebook. If you prefer paper, however, get a three-ring notebook and a three-hole paper punch. Or you can use whatever combination works for you. Do not try to hold this information in your head.

HOW TO SET UP AND USE YOUR NOTEBOOK

Create five major parts in your notebook (separate word-processing documents or actual tabs in a loose-leaf notebook):

- Clues
- Work Strong Clues
- Definite Career Design Components
- Careers to Explore
- Narrow Down to Final Choice

Step 1: Gather Clues

The Clues part of your notebook has three clues lists, to which you'll be adding and subtracting regularly. Each list has its own page:

- Natural Gifts Clues
- Meaning and Subject Matter Clues
- Workplace Environment Clues

As you go through each section of the toolkit, you'll explore each of the above areas. When you discover what you think might be a good clue, write it in your notebook on one of the lists.

What Is a Clue? To recap, a clue is anything *you* consider to be potentially useful information that could lead to being selected as a definite career design component. In the personal realm, a clue can be about who you are, what you do well, how you behave, what you care about, and so on. (Check out the illustrations a little further ahead in this chapter to understand what I mean.) A clue can be about the external world: "I love the idea of building Conestoga wagons, but there are only two small shops that make them now, and employment opportunities look dim." A clue could be an idea to investigate: "Maybe I could make all sorts of wagons and carriages for the movie industry." Some clues feel like hunches, things that you've noticed about yourself throughout life but which you're not sure about. Here's a simple rule: if you've got a hunch, it's probably a good clue. If you're not sure about a clue, you can do some work on it with questions and research to see if it has any lasting value. Don't dismiss clues too quickly in the early stages. Remember, since you are designing a career to fit you, many of the best clues will be about you.

What Is a Strong Clue? As you collect clues, you want to focus on investigating the strongest ones. As every detective knows, working clues takes time and effort, so pick clues that could turn into big and useful definite career design components. You have to judge for yourself what a strong clue is. Avoid getting lost in a gigantic and complex clues list. As you find clues and perform other detective work, be on the lookout for especially strong clues. When you find a strong clue, mark it.

Step 2: Work the Strong Clues

The second part of your notebook is where you investigate the strong clues. Make one page for each strong clue. You can design the pages your own way or use something like the sample below. This form is a compressed example. You want to have lots of room for all the questions, research, and findings you come up with. Then work each of the strong clues. (Read the part in Chapter 10 about how to work clues in case you missed it earlier.)

In working clues, you aim to move them closer to deciding whether or not they lead to a definite career design component.

- **Observation.** If the clue pertains to you—what you do well, how your personality works, what you enjoy, and so on—the best way to work the clue is to observe yourself as if you were a scientist studying some rare and unique creature. Don't go by what you think you already know; observe yourself. If you think you like to solve problems with physical objects, start paying attention when you do it: "How often do I like to do it? How engrossed do I get in solving this sort of problem? Am I having fun? What quality of results do I produce?" Make notes of what you see.
- **Notice connections among clues.** When you consider your strong clues all together, do any themes stand out? Are there any patterns among your clues?

Here's a table to illustrate how to work a clue. In this example, the clue relates to the workplace environment (Chapter 25).

SAMPLE TABLE: WORK STRONG CLUES

Work the Strong Clues—Workplace Environment

Work This Clue	Ask Questions	Research and Things to Do	Answers and Findings
Clue #5: I'm drawn to work in a small, start-up company	What is it about a small company that attracts me? Is there something about big, bureaucratic companies that would impede the use of my talents and personality? Are smaller companies really more dynamic? What makes a company's culture more innovative?	Do some Internet research to learn about the different kinds of corporate culture. Talk with people who work in various kinds of small start-ups to find out more about what it is like to work at one.	I am going to work in a very small organization with fewer than fifty people and a casual culture with progressive, innovative, brilliant scientists and engineers who are passionate about making the world a better place.

How Much Time Should You Spend Working on a Clue? Be patient. You may need several hours, days, or even weeks to work a clue. That's why you want to focus on the strongest ones. Don't waste your time on clues that you think might have limited importance.

Don't shortchange yourself. Solving your career choice mystery requires going deep and wide. Do more research than you feel like doing. Working clues allows important information to come to the surface that you would normally miss. Extra care now may save you from years of agony later. Stay loose and open-minded; some clues will pan out and become big parts of your career, and some will fall by the wayside.

Step 3: Create a Career Design Components List

The third part of your notebook is the Definite Career Design Components List. Organize this list into three sections:

- Definite Natural Gifts Components
- Definite Meaning and Subject Matter Components
- Definite Workplace Environment Components

Dividing up the list makes it a little easier to think about each of these areas separately. Everything on the list is an answer to the big question: "What am I sure will definitely be some of the components of my future career?"

In this third step, you jump from Detective to the second role, Decider. Your job is to choose definite components of your future career. Do any clues stand out as ripe and ready to become definite career design components? Some will be easy to decide. For instance, if you are a very talkative, outgoing person, you might as well commit to that as a part of your career right now; this aspect of you isn't going to change. (Again, if you missed Chapter 10, read the Decider part there.)

Step 4: Careers to Explore List

The fourth part of your notebook is a list of careers to explore. Save room to write notes on what you find out about each career.

As you go through the Career Design Toolkit, write down any career ideas that pop up. This is a rough, preliminary list, so write down any and all careers that seem interesting or seem to fit what you know about yourself. Later on, in Designer mode, you will create a more definitive and specific version of this.

Look for clues. Notice if careers on this list seem to point in any specific direction or have other similarities. As you work your way through your career design project, come back to this list from time to time to look for new clues and keep a fresh perspective.

Step 5: Narrow Down to Your Final Career Choice

In the fifth part of your notebook, you research, compare and contrast, and pare down your Careers to Explore list until you can make a final choice. Don't do anything now except reserve a section for it in your notebook.

SECTION 4

Who You Are

In this section you will investigate your natural gifts: talents and personality traits.

Your natural abilities and personality traits form the centerpiece of what you have to offer the working world. To truly love your work, you want a career that elegantly matches your innate abilities and personality traits. Your natural gifts form the foundation upon which all the other factors rest and depend. Why? Because although we are beings whose cultural evolution is moving as fast as a train with no brakes on a mountain railway, we are also critters, biologically based beings living in the physical universe. The rules of that material world are certain, constant, and unforgiving. You mess with them at your own peril. Every creature other than human beings uses its talents and personality traits fully and constantly in its work. You never see an eagle trying to do a hummingbird's job, hovering over a delicate, trumpet-shaped blossom and trying to get at the nectar with its big beak.

CHAPTER 16 NATURAL TALENTS

Drop a duck into a pond. Even if the duck was raised in the desert and has never seen a pond, that duck will automatically exhibit natural mastery in a matter of minutes, doing what ducks do. Ducks are perfectly designed to make a living in the pond environment. They have an ideal set of talents and the perfect personality for their job.

In the duck world, everyone swims well. No one plays the piano. In the human species, on the other hand, extraordinarily wide variations exist in the realm of natural talents and personality. One person might learn multiple languages with incredible ease, while another person has very little language facility but a gift for building things. Each of us has already been dealt a very specific hand of talent/ability cards by our genetic inheritance that gives us a knack for playing a fairly narrow range of roles in the working world with natural ease and mastery.

When you see someone windsurfing gracefully in a high wind, moving quickly and powerfully across the sea, you are viewing the result of extensive training and a commitment to improve a body that was born with a special gift for balance and agility. People who were born with less coordinated bodies rarely are the ones out there in the stronger winds. It is more difficult for them to master the skills and usually not as much fun as it is for someone with natural talent. This is equally true with regard to the mental and physical talents we use in our work.

These different innate gifts make each of us an incomparable, one-of-a-kind individual, with a special ability to do certain kinds of things easily and happily. A lack of a talent can make other tasks seem like pure torture. Inborn aptitudes are completely different from acquired knowledge, skills, and interests. Your interests can change. You can gain new skills and knowledge. Your natural, inherited talents remain with you, unchanging, for your entire life. Mother Nature dealt you this hand of abilities, and you can't change them. But you can learn to take the hand you were dealt and play it brilliantly, to your best advantage. The better you understand your unique genetic gifts, the more likely you can choose a satisfying and successful career.

People are happiest when they combine their strong abilities in a career that makes full use of all or most of them. The further people stray from using their natural gifts, the greater the chance that they will be dissatisfied with their careers. This dissatisfaction can show up in two ways: boredom and burnout. Boredom frequently signals that your abilities are not being fully expressed. On the other hand, if certain parts of the job remain difficult or unpleasant, no matter how many times you do them, you may not have a natural gift in that department. Therefore, it's possible to be bored and burned out at the same time.

If you want a career that's fulfilling and gives you the best chance for a high level of success, it's critical to understand your innate talents, both as individual abilities and in combination. You could think of individual abilities as musical instruments. Before you can learn how they might combine and what kinds of music would fit the combination, you have to understand the individual instruments. The first step in understanding your abilities is to learn about them as separate pieces of the puzzle.

Your profile of abilities is like a fingerprint. It is different from everyone else's. There are many things in life that are difficult or impossible to change, including the weather and your innate abilities. Rather than compare yourself with others or wish you were different, you can embrace your talents, honor them, and figure out how you can make use of them. Deep personal satisfaction comes from making full use of these natural abilities rather than trying to swim against the current.

PEOPLE ENJOY DOING WORK THEY DO WELL NATURALLY

When people become highly skilled at anything they were not forced to learn, they are probably expressing a natural gift. Someone born with the collection of innate abilities it takes to be a master skier, for example, turns each progressive skill corner much more easily. The same amount of energy and commitment that takes a less gifted person around one corner takes someone naturally gifted around ten. To get your work life flying, choose a career where you have exceptional natural talent and then put in the time and energy to become a real master. Talent and developed skill are an unbeatable combination.

When people are doing something they enjoy, they get more done, and they do it better. Performing at a level of mastery makes use of acquired skills and experience in conjunction with a strong foundation of natural talent. People who are highly successful and also love their work year after year spend most of their time at work engaged in activities that make use of their strongest abilities. They spend very little time performing functions for which they have no special gift. Their lives are concentrated on doing what they do best. The people you envy because they are both successful and happy with their work have found their natural self-expression. Their talents are perfectly aligned with what they do.

SELF-ASSESSING YOUR NATURAL ABILITIES

Our culture accidentally provides the tools to learn about some aspects of our individual abilities. For example, after years of gym classes, you probably know a great deal about your innate athletic talents or the lack thereof. Beyond physical performance abilities, however, few of us have done more than scratch the surface in regard to recognizing and appreciating our unique profile of talents. What we think we know about our talents rests on what we have done before or what people have told us from their perspective. It's useful to take a fresh look outside of the trap of preconceptions, to look at the deepest level.

It is also very important to understand how your innate abilities and your personality interact. Your unique personality and temperament profoundly affect the expression of your innate abilities, complicating any self-assessment. For instance, two people with the same abilities but starkly different personalities would not be suited for the same career. Not even close.

Since your natural talents are the single most important part of you to understand and use in designing your career, it is important to get this part right. This is not easy to do with self-assessment, no matter how well you know yourself. If possible, I strongly recommend going through a natural talent assessment program such as the Rockport Career Testing Program. Since many of you will never get around to doing in-depth natural abilities testing, however, I'll do the best I can to help you assess yourself.

I'll start off coaching you to notice what comes naturally for you and then go deeper as this section continues. Later, I'll help you add your personality into the mix, which will really get things moving.

Uncovering your talents requires some detective work. Your talents constantly provide clues to their nature, but you have to learn to read these clues. This takes observation, paying attention to how you think and act and what you do so easily that you take it for granted. It's easier to recognize what you dislike.

Some parts of what comes naturally to you will be easy to sort out. If you spent your childhood camped out in your bedroom reading books, lost in a fantasy world, your imagination may be one of your natural strengths. If you led a gang of kids on the playground or had a natural affinity for fixing your friends' crashed computers, use that knowledge of yourself as clues.

If you haven't had opportunities to use some of your stronger abilities, then you will need to follow hunches and experiment.

Inquiry 16-1 **WHAT COMES NATURALLY TO ME?**

1. **List activities in the Clues part of your notebook.** Look back over your life for activities, roles, or behaviors that came naturally to you. List anything that you do or did naturally well or that put you in the zone and made you lose track of time. Look back as recently as today or as far back

as childhood. Don't leave out your favorite childhood activities, no matter how childish you now think they are. Here are some places to look:

- Workplace tasks you enjoyed
- Favorite activities in school
- Favorite activities in your free time
- Favorite subject matter(s)
- Problems you enjoyed solving
- Projects you enjoyed
- Hobbies
- Roles you played in favorite events
- Roles or positions you enjoyed on a team (captain, facilitator, expert, supporter)
- Acknowledgment you've gotten from others for a job well done
- Anything else that captured your attention and imagination

2. **Select any strong clues about your natural talents. Work the clues.** Ask questions and do some research. Carefully examine each clue and decide if it could be a strong clue about your natural talents. Is it something you love and do regularly or just like to do once in a while? Do you look forward to it? Is it something you do naturally, without thinking about it? Put a check mark in the Clues part of your notebook next to the activities that really stand out as strong clues. Move the strong clues to the Work Strong Clues part of your notebook and work the clues.
3. **Any definite career components?** If there are any clues you're ready to turn into definite parts of your future career, move those to the Definite Career Design Components part of your notebook.

Inquiry 16-2 NATURAL TALENTS AND ABILITIES SELF-ASSESSMENT

This inquiry provides a way for you to assess your natural abilities. Still in the role of Detective, read through the following descriptions of talents and abilities and rate yourself in each talent area. You can do this right in the pages of this book. Don't rush. Spend some time looking back over your life to see how much evidence you find for each talent/natural ability.

1. **Rate your talents and abilities.** To help with rating yourself in the natural talents listed below, remember situations that came easily and naturally to you as a kid, as a teenager, in college, on the job, hanging out with friends, and so on. After reading about each ability, check one of the circles to rate yourself in that ability: ① for low, ② for midrange, ③ for high. If you're not sure, check the diamond with a question mark. Don't guess. If you aren't sure, check the diamond. Don't worry about how many diamonds (or any other categories) you checked. After you've finished assessing your talents, further instructions will tell you what to do next.

PROBLEM-SOLVING TALENTS

①②③◈ Diagnostic Reasoning

Diagnostic reasoning is the ability to get to the heart of a problem without going through a logical thought process, to diagnose, to critique, to go directly from clues and observations to an accurate answer, to derive a general, unifying principle from some specific clues, to instantly understand what is wrong in a given situation and, perhaps, how to fix it. People who are high in diagnostic reasoning usually pick up flaws instantly. They may be critical of the shortcomings of others, of the world around them, or of themselves. They are rarely oblivious to flaws, and they may not be patient and accepting of them. Of course, habitually finding flaws can come from some sort of personal insecurity, but this behavior often indicates diagnostic reasoning munching away on whatever you are paying attention to.

This ability is useful whenever there is a need to diagnose. Imagine a veterinarian with a little gray kitten on the examination table. The kitten obviously feels very ill, but the vet cannot ask it questions or even pick up much in the way of visual clues, since it is covered with fur from head to tail. The vet has to determine what's wrong from just a few clues. A person with good diagnostic reasoning ability has a gift for problem solving that involves making a leap from some specific clues to a diagnosis, critique, or solution. This happens all at once. It is the "aha" kind of problem solving. Forty years ago, few people believed the highly diagnostic scientists who predicted global warming.

This gift can be a curse: people with an extremely strong diagnostic talent cannot easily turn it off. They constantly critique anything in the field of their attention, often including themselves and others. People with this ability who can employ it in the right career, however, look brilliant. High-diagnostic-ability detectives quickly see connections between (apparently) unrelated clues. The ER doctor quickly diagnoses a patient from available symptoms. Talented comedians surprise an audience with their ability to see unusual connections and creatively critique human foibles.

People who are lower in diagnostic reasoning ability often are more accepting and patient. They usually do not spend every moment looking for flaws. They can more often enjoy the food and the company in a restaurant without turning into a critic. For most kinds of work, low or midrange diagnostic reasoning ability is an advantage.

Career fields that use diagnostic reasoning: **physical, life, and social sciences; emergency medicine and all medicine in general; consulting; litigation and criminal law; investigative journalism; forensic science; critiquing professions (comedy, art critic, food critic, social satire); political pundits, op-ed columnists; innovators (inventors, entrepreneurs, all design fields); troubleshooting technical problems; persuasive fields such as advertising and marketing, product buying; quality improvement; copyediting**

①②③◈ Analytical Reasoning

People high in analytical reasoning ability think systematically and logically. Unlike the diagnostician's ability to make connections from disparate clues, analytical people can easily organize information within a set of *existing* rules and theories. They can quickly make logical connections in a step-by-step fashion, like consummate chess players and puzzle masters. When high, this aptitude compels people to bring order to chaos, to systematize, prioritize, synthesize, categorize, and boil down information to the most important components.

Analytical reasoning is the most used and trusted problem-solving talent in our computer-centered world. Practically every aspect of business, science, and technology requires planning, systematizing, and organizing people, information, and things. Scientists and engineers use mathematical equations to make sense of data, while executives plan and implement new strategies. Writers use the ability to organize ideas and information.

***Career fields that use analytical reasoning:* business management, engineering, science, mathematics, law, social science, research and writing, editing, planning, strategizing, accounting, finance, technical writing, computer programming, journalism**

SPATIAL/TANGIBLE/NONSPATIAL ORIENTATION

We all look at the world in our own way. Some people have a spatial or 3-D orientation. Others have a nonspatial point of view. Others are somewhere in the middle. See if you can identify where you fit on this scale. The range of this ability is best described on a continuum from nonspatial to tangible to spatial, as below:

NONSPATIAL	TANGIBLE	SPATIAL (3-D)

Let's use the field of law to illustrate different parts of this continuum. Spatial people are most at home thinking and working with three-dimensional reality. This fits only one legal specialty, patent law. Patent lawyers look at inventions to see what features could be patentable. They have to understand machinery and physical things and how they operate. At the other end of the spectrum are nonspatial people who most naturally operate in a world of concepts that has little relationship with physical reality. This describes the work of most lawyers, people who spend their days operating in a completely nonspatial world of legal concepts. At the farthest end of the nonspatial world are constitutional lawyers, whom you could consider philosophers of law. In the middle are tangible lawyers, people for whom the real physical world is important in their point of view but not as dominant as with spatial people. This area of law, frequently trial law, depends on a facility with tangible questions and issues, such as suspect identification, physical evidence, how long it takes someone to go from point A to point B, and so forth.

In the field of medicine, surgery is spatial, as are other specialties such as radiology, where it is important to think three-dimensionally. Most medical specialties fit someone who tests in the tangible part of the continuum. For example a dermatologist's day is spent with real, tangible skin, but he or she does not need the degree of spatial ability a surgeon does. At the nonspatial end of the scale is the psychiatrist.

Businesses appropriate for a spatial-oriented person include such things as landscaping and construction management. Even though the manager of a construction company performs many of the same functions as any other businessperson, much of the construction manager's day involves three-dimensional thinking. Most business management is nonspatial and intangible, especially in larger corporations and in service businesses. The great majority of what is taught in an MBA program lies far over on the nonspatial end of the scale. Tangible businesses fall between the extreme ends of the spectrum; for example, managers in retail businesses, restaurants, and printing companies and supervisors in manufacturing businesses often test in the tangible range. Tangible-oriented people can often perform well in fields such as electrical engineering, which is less spatial than most engineering fields.

You may or may not be able to accurately pin down where you are on this scale. Look at what you do well, think about, talk about, your hobbies, and so on. Some people, very often women, who score exceptionally high in spatial orientation may not easily find evidence of this talent as children if they were not encouraged to pursue activities considered "normal" for boys, such as building things. A rough but still helpful way to look into this for women is to remember how you played with dolls. Girls on the spatial side tend to concentrate on the physical world their dolls live in—the Barbie Beach Bungalow with real pink sand and tiny margaritas. The nonspatial girl usually gets into acting out doll relationships: "Ken! Malibu Stacy and I are leaving. We are moving to her place on the beach without you."

①②③◈ Spatial Orientation

High spatial orientation is an aptitude for visualizing in 3-D. The more easily and naturally you visualize in 3-D, the higher your spatial aptitude. About one-half of men and a quarter of women score above the 50th percentile in spatial orientation.

Career fields that use spatial orientation: **most medical specialties (except psychiatry); forensic science; physical therapy; chiropractic; dentistry; speech pathology; architecture; most engineering disciplines; physics; microbiology; organic chemistry; robotics; computer architecture; computer game design; electronics; most design fields; hairstyling; culinary arts; sports (gymnastics, golf, basketball, football, and many others); construction; kitchen and bath design; auto mechanics; carpentry; flying airplanes; navigating; battlefield command; manufacturing; dance and choreography; special effects in film, sculpture, and other fields that require an ability to mentally visualize in 3-D. Careers that fit people with a tangible orientation are sometimes appropriate for spatial people as well.**

①②③◈ Tangible Orientation

A tangible orientation, in the middle of the continuum, suggests work that intimately involves the physical world but without the necessity to actually think in 3-D. People with this quality tend to apply ideas or things to get a real-world result. This is the information technologist's ability to mentally visualize network connectivity, like a picture of a schematic in the mind's eye. FBI agents use this ability to pull together real-world facts and evidence to solve a criminal case.

Career fields that use a tangible orientation: **computer programming, IT and network engineering, database design, electrical engineering, industrial engineering, wildlife biology, zoology, botany, naturalist, family medicine, nursing, practical psychology, graphic arts, cartooning, Web site design, display design, product development and brand management, interior decorating, jewelry design, cosmetology, gardening, cooking, business management in manufacturing and product distribution, car wash owner, retail dry cleaner, retail furniture, car dealer, retail clothing sales, home furnishings, restaurant management, personal coaching.**

①②③? Nonspatial Orientation

Nonspatial-oriented people work naturally with ideas, data, and information and usually have little desire to work with three-dimensional objects. People with an MBA use this ability to run and improve business operations. Constitutional lawyers' nonspatial inclination enhances their work with legal concepts. Sociologists work with ideas about group behavior, and economists construct conceptual models of consumer trends.

Please note that some nonspatial people do have hobbies that involve tinkering with objects, but they tend to do these only occasionally. We've met trained surgeons and engineers who tested nonspatial who said they had to work harder than their peers to perform well.

Career fields that use nonspatial orientation: **all business disciplines: marketing, advertising, public relations, finance, accounting, human resources, sales, management; social sciences: economics, sociology, psychology, political science, demographics, actuarial mathematics, statistics, politics, cultural anthropology, gender studies, social history; humanities: philosophy, religion, language, literature; diplomacy, international relations, public policy; counseling, psychology, organizational behavior; journalism, publishing, editing, poetry**

SPECIALIZED TALENTS

①②③? Abstract ①②③? Mixed ①②③? Concrete

Some people are naturally driven to seek concrete results—obviously an important trait in any get-the-job-done business. Others are perfectly happy to cogitate forever on abstractions, a trait that lends itself to theoretical work. Many economists, for example, remain unperturbed when their predictions about economic trends prove inaccurate. They show little interest in the practical aspects of reality. To them, economics is a theoretical abstraction. Check which part of the spectrum you think you occupy.

Here is a grid that combines natural abstract-concrete talents with the spatial-nonspatial continuum to show sample career paths:

	NONSPATIAL	TANGIBLE	SPATIAL
CONCRETE	Business executive Stockbroker Tax auditor	Tech sales Pharmacist Electrical engineer	Dentist Surgeon Mechanical engineer
MIXED	Advertising director Psychologist Federal judge	Brand manager Documentary filmmaker FBI analyst	Environmental "green" architect Neuroscientist Human-computer interaction designer
ABSTRACT	Poet Economist Constitutional lawyer	Composer: film Science journalist Criminal lawyer	Astrophysicist Thematic sculptor (like Rodin) Patent lawyer

①②③◈ **Rate of Idea Flow**

Idea flow involves the rate at which your mind generates thoughts and ideas. Idea flow is a gauge of the quantity, not the quality, of your ideas. Like water coming out of a faucet, there could be a tremendous flow of polluted water or just a trickle of the tastiest water you've ever had. A fast flow of ideas doesn't mean that you necessarily have brilliant thoughts or ideas; it means they come quickly.

Your position on this scale is a good indicator of how much "flow" you need in your work during the course of each day. People with high idea flow feel more at home with, and are usually better at, work that lets this swift flow of thoughts continue unimpeded most of the time. People with lower idea flow usually enjoy work that involves focus and concentration. As with the other abilities, there is no good or bad score. Whatever your score, it is simply a clue about what sort of work would fit you best.

People with high idea flow are especially good at coming up with spur-of-the-moment ideas. They have minds that move quickly from one thought to another, from one idea to the next. They often have trouble concentrating on one thing for too long, especially if they aren't particularly interested in the task at hand. They have more difficulty than other people in concentrating on repetitive tasks. In school, they often have more trouble than other people at keeping their attention focused on the professor who drones on and on. They respond especially well to teachers who breathe life into their presentation, and to subjects they are personally, passionately interested in. Many high-idea-flow people have a gift for improvisation and enjoy conversations that involve a continual flow from subject to subject. They are often good at thinking on their feet and responding quickly, although introverted people with this trait may not see themselves that way. Introverts sometimes don't notice they possess this ability because it operates inside their heads.

People with a lower rate of idea flow can be just as creative as people with a fast flow. It simply means that the ideas come more slowly. Often the best ideas come from thinking things out carefully. People with lower idea flow can concentrate their energies on a particular task for a longer period of time. You'll find these people in business management, fine engraving, and accounting, all fields needing an ability to focus. For many jobs in the business world, a rapid flow of ideas is a hindrance. Thomas Edison experimented with hundreds of filaments before he came up with one that led to the lightbulb. Someone with high idea flow might have given up and gone on to other projects.

Career fields that use high Idea flow: advertising, marketing, comedy, acting, emergency medicine, teaching, consulting, improvisational music and arts, cartooning, newspaper journalism, TV and radio media, sales

Midrange idea flow: business management, design engineering, architecture, some sales, project management

Low Idea flow: dentistry, surgery, banking, accounting, auditing, insurance, computer programming, house painting, engraving

①②③? **Interpersonal Intelligence**

Interpersonal intelligence, a form of social intelligence, is the natural ability to perceive and understand the moods, motives, and behaviors of others.

Career fields that use interpersonal intelligence: film directing, acting, screenwriting, creative writing, psychology fields, counseling and coaching fields, nursing, physical therapies, child care, teaching K-12, mentoring, diplomacy, training, organizational development, people management, marketing, sales, advertising, humanities, social sciences, public policy, politics

①②③? **Intrapersonal Intelligence**

Intrapersonal intelligence is a form of social intelligence that is focused inward. This is the natural ability to perceive and understand your own moods, motives, and behaviors.

Career fields that use intrapersonal intelligence: poet, playwright, novelist, musician, fine artist, actor, journalist, mediator, counselor, coach, therapist, teacher, professor, social scientist

SENSORY AND PERCEPTUAL ABILITIES

①②③? **Intuition**

Intuition is an imaginative way of perceiving the world around you. While your five senses see factual detail, your intuition sees the nuances or shades of meaning. For intuitives, the world is full of possibilities, and exploring new ideas, people, places, and things is what gives life its zest. They love to seek what's possible in the future; they aim to understand whole systems rather than just the parts. This is the aptitude used by scientists to raise new questions and think outside the box. Poets employ intuition to create metaphors and playfully manipulate the commonsense meaning of words. Actors use it to imagine the inner life and motives of the characters they portray.

Career fields that use intuition: **physical sciences, life sciences, social sciences, humanities, abstract arts, poetry, acting, filmmaking, advertising, marketing, design, psychology, investigative journalism, media studies, entrepreneurs, trend forecasters**

①②③⟨?⟩ **Sensing**

Sensing is a factual way of perceiving the world. Strong sensors trust the literal details perceived by their eyes, ears, and sense of touch more than the vague impressions and hunches that come from intuition. Rather than giving their attention to speculating about possible futures, sensors love to jump in and get the job done. They feel at home with practical ideas and things. As sensors, accountants precisely apply detailed and static rules. Police officers use this ability as rigorous observers of the physical world.

Career fields that use sensing: **engineering, medicine, dentistry, business administration, dance, physical therapy, cooking, cinematography, sales, accounting, landscape architecture, information technology, broadcast journalism, social work**

①②③⟨?⟩ **Visual Dexterity**

Visual dexterity is the ability to quickly and accurately see details, spot errors, and process written information. Fields such as public administration, accounting, law, teaching, proofreading, and editing use this ability constantly. Visual dexterity also comes in handy in careers needing acute attention to minute tangible and spatial details, such as microsurgery, pathology, genetic research, and forensic medicine or CSI-type fieldwork.

Career fields that use visual dexterity: **accounting, auditing, banking, biotechnology, business management, computer programming, finance, forensic science, informatics, language translation, law, legal research, library science, medical research, microbiology, nanotechnology, public administration, publishing, editing**

MEMORY

①②③⟨?⟩ **Associative Memory**

Associative memory is a key ability in learning the vocabulary of foreign languages or computer languages. It even helps with remembering people's names.

Career fields that use associative memory: acting, ad copywriting, computer science, curriculum design, consulting, career coaching, creative writing, education/teaching, humanities, journalism, language, law, medicine, museum docent, physical sciences, life and social sciences, politics, sales, training and development

①②③⟨?⟩ **Number Memory**

Number memory is used to learn and work with numbers and informational details. You probably have it if you can remember all your friends' phone numbers.

Career fields that use number memory: accounting, allied health, anesthesiology, auditing, banking, bioinformatics, business journalism, business management, computer science, engineering, finance and investing, financial planning, information technology, library and information science, mathematics, management information systems, nursing, retail sales (e.g., auto parts, grocery cashier), physical and earth sciences, sports journalism, statistics, tax law

①②③⟨?⟩ **Design Memory**

Design memory is the ability to memorize visual information and tangible forms in the world around you. It also plays a role in navigating. Many people who are high in it quickly learn their way around a new city.

Career fields that use design memory: architecture, adventure guide, antiques appraiser, archivist, botany, chemistry, dance and performance arts, dentistry, earth sciences, engineering, graphic arts, fashion design, filmmaking, forensic science, interior design, industrial design, law enforcement, mechanical engineering, material science, microbiology, patent law, aircraft piloting, physical science, medicine (especially surgery), tour guide, sports coaching (playing field strategy), surveying, taxi and truck driving, visual arts

OTHER SPECIALIZED ABILITIES

①②③⟨?⟩ **Mathematical Ability**

People who display a natural talent for a specific niche of math may have a mix of several natural abilities working together. For example, mathematics used to solve 3-D problems such as geometry and advanced calculus (used in engineering fields) engages a combination of high analytical reasoning, high spatial reasoning, high number memory, and a logical temperament, the perfect "recipe" of strengths for math talent. Adding intuition to this mix of talents can suggest the ability for abstract mathematics such as differential calculus, used in theoretical research fields in the physical and life sciences.

Career fields that use mathematical ability: actuarial science, architecture, computer science, engineering, financial engineering and investing, marketing research, mathematics, physical sciences, earth sciences, economics, operations research, statistics and probability

①②③◈ Language Ability

People who display a natural talent for learning and using language usually have a mix of several natural abilities working together. People with high associative memory and high analytical reasoning tend to learn languages easily. Adding in some musical talent provides the mix of abilities necessary for speaking a second language with perfect inflection.

Career fields that use language ability: acting, screenwriting, print journalism, languages, law, poetry and literary arts, literary agents, editors, social sciences and humanities, politics, publishing, technical writing, scientific writing and research, science journalism

①②③◈ Artistic and Musical Abilities

People who display a natural talent for the arts have a mix of several natural abilities working together. Each artistic expression (music, performance art, dance, and plastic or other visual arts) engages a different set of innate abilities. In all art forms, from the classical and traditional to the contemporary and improvisational, different talent combinations tend to pull the artist in the direction that comes easily and naturally.

Career fields that use artistic and musical abilities: acting, advertising and commercial arts, architecture, computer video game design, dance performance arts, most design fields, filmmaking, film editing and production, film scoring, film special effects, graphic arts, music composition, musical performance arts, photography and photojournalism, literary arts, sound engineering, speech therapy, visual arts, Web site design

①②③◈ Body Kinesthetic Ability

People who excel at gymnastics and other sports, dance and other performance arts, and martial arts have just the right mix of kinesthetic talents for their specific field of performance. Other fields that require regular use of kinesthetic talents include modeling, acting, circus performing, exploring, diving, search and rescue, and law enforcement.

Choosing a sport that fits your talents is more complex than it seems. It involves a number of factors, including muscular-skeletal makeup, heart-lung capacity, mental-sensory perception, and other traits. A world-class cross-country skier needs larger lung capacity than a top-notch tennis player. The skier needs more endurance muscle fiber, whereas the tennis player needs explosive sprint muscle fiber. Both skiers and tennis players benefit if they have a lower center of gravity, which means their legs are somewhat short in proportion to their upper bodies. Someone who excels at swimming butterfly would find the broad chest and shoulders that is such an advantage in that sport a disadvantage in bicycle racing because it would create wind resistance.

Career fields that use body kinesthetic ability: **acting, dance and performance arts, farming, fashion modeling, forest and park management, hunting/fishing/trapping, federal and local law enforcement, firefighting, heavy equipment operation and construction, military, national guard, paramedic/EMT, team sports, Olympic sports, sports coaching, sports medicine, search and rescue, trades**

2. **Search for the best clues.** Transfer your self-assessments to your notebook or the grid below by checking the box that you think best represents your strength in each area. If you're not sure of your strength in a certain area, check the "Not Sure" column to remind yourself to look for more clues about that ability. Think about the abilities you think may represent strong natural talents. Spend a few weeks paying attention to your activities, noticing which talents you use often and what you do well. Also notice what you don't do well naturally.

Natural Talents and Abilities	High	Mid	Low	Not Sure	Definite Career Components
Diagnostic Reasoning					
Analytical Reasoning					
Spatial Orientation					
Tangible Orientation					
Nonspatial Orientation					
Abstract Orientation					
Concrete Orientation					
Rate of Idea Flow					
Interpersonal Intelligence					
Intrapersonal Intelligence					
Intuition					
Sensing					
Visual Dexterity					
Associative Memory					
Number Memory					
Design Memory					
Mathematical Ability					
Language Ability					
Artistic and Musical Abilities					
Body Kinesthetic Ability					

3. **Any definite career design components?** Do any talents stand out as especially strong? Don't worry if you are uncertain or find this a little confusing. It is extremely difficult to accurately assess many of your own natural abilities. Check off any natural talents you are sure will be definite components of your career design. Add these to your Definite Career Design Components list in your notebook.
4. **Round up all the good clues.** You will likely have some good clues that need more investigation. Put them in the Work Strong Clues list in your notebook.

CHAPTER 17

PERSONALITY TRAITS

Designing your career so that it fits your personality can mean the difference between success and failure, satisfaction and career hell. The trick is to live your life so you get rewarded for being who you are; that way you don't have to pretend to be someone else. If you are driven to criticize and find fault with everything that crosses your path, find a way to get paid for it. If you are enthusiastic and expressive, choose a career where these traits are needed and appreciated. Swim with the stream, not against it.

Investigating your personality is a bit like trying to see the back of your own eyeballs. That's why this section of *Now What?* has a number of different ways to look at who you are. If you were buying a new car, you would walk around it, checking it out from all sides. These inquiries help you kick your own tires. You don't have to do all of them now. Don't get overwhelmed. Some people find it best to do an inquiry or two and absorb what they learn before moving on. You want to get to know yourself better, not just rip through the inquiries and jump to some conclusions. Since we don't usually pay attention to the subtle nuances of our personalities, it may be useful to spend some time noticing how you behave in different situations. By using these inquiries to notice how you act and react, you can become acquainted with yourself in new and vital ways. Get to know yourself really well. That way, when you choose definite career design elements based on your personality, you will be quite certain that you are making a solid choice.

In the following inquiries, you will focus on who you are and how you behave, think, and feel naturally, rather than the ways you conform to the expectations of the tribes you belong to. We all may be different individuals, but we also live in a culture that pushes us toward certain ways of behaving. For example, when I first met a Chinese gentleman, he seemed very passive and cautious. It soon became clear, however, that, growing up in the political climate of Communist China, he had *learned* to be this way. After just a few years in America, his natural self-reliance and assertiveness emerged, and he now pursues a career path of his own design. Do your best to notice your natural tendencies, not how you have been trained to behave by your boss, school, or family.

Inquiry 17-1 **WHAT AM I LIKE?**

1. **Look for clues.** The chart below lists a variety of personality traits. For each, check the appropriate box, from Not at All to Always, to rate how often you exhibit each trait.

Rating Scale

- *Not at All*—I am never ever this way.
- *Rarely*—I may be this way on occasion, but rarely.
- *Sometimes*—I am this way now and then, or when it's necessary.
- *Usually*—I am this way much of the time; it's comfortable.
- *Always*—I am this way all the time; I can't imagine not being this way.

These traits are listed in pairs. You might fit on both sides of a pair of opposites. You could be usually talkative and sometimes quiet. The goal here is to sort out your strongest, most definite personality traits. So just be honest with yourself in making selections.

PERSONALITY TRAITS	**WEAK <<**			**>> STRONG**	
	Not at All	**Rarely**	**Sometimes**	**Usually**	**Always**
Outgoing, talkative					
Ingoing, quiet					
Warm, friendly					
Reserved, aloof					
Emotional					
Rational					
Calm					
Excited					
Logical, objective					
Personal, subjective					
Leading, taking charge					
Rather operate than lead					
Cheerful, upbeat					
Serious					
Persistent					
Easily distracted					
Adventurous					
Cautious					
Bold					
Shy					

(continued on next page)

PERSONALITY TRAITS	WEAK <<			>> STRONG
	Not at All	Rarely	Sometimes	Usually	Always
Tough					
Tender					
Independent					
Depend on others					
Suspicious					
Trusting					
Skeptical					
Accepting					
Imaginative, dreamer					
Practical, get results					
Liberal					
Moderate					
Conservative					
Clever					
Straightforward					
Tactful, considerate					
Direct, blunt					
Playful					
Serious					
Experimental					
Traditional					
Do my own thing					
Follow the group					
Inventive					
Follow the rules					
Self-controlled, restrained					
Rowdy, wild					
Energetic, eager					
Laid-back, subdued					
Tense					
Relaxed					
Driven, motivated					
Unconcerned, carefree					

2. **Work the clues.** Examine all the check marks that fall in the "Usually" and "Always" categories.

   Do some research. Ask friends and family what they see as natural tendencies in your personality ("Do you think I'm more emotional or rational?").

   You may find it useful to write down a short description of yourself by combining your strongest traits ("I'm a rowdy, cheerful, talkative, trusting, playful, adventurous, emotional, persistent person.").
3. **Any definite career design components?** Are there any personality traits you choose to be definitely part of your future career? Add them to the Definite Career Design Components list in your notebook. You might phrase it like this: "My career needs to fit my logical, direct, driven personality." Or "My career needs to fit and express my rowdy, cheerful, talkative, trusting, playful, adventurous, emotional, persistent personality."
4. **Strong clues.** Take the clues that are not definite components but which you think might deserve more scrutiny and transfer them to the Work Strong Clues list in your notebook. Then work those clues.

TRIBAL AND MAESTRO

As I've noted, we are all members of a species scientists call "tribal primates" because we live together in a society and interact with each other. But some of us have a personal orientation that is more tribal than others. This distinction says a lot about how we best fit in the working world.

Tribals

The way we use the word *tribal* here communicates what the majority of people (about 75 percent) have in common: they are usually most successful and satisfied working with and through other people as members of an organization, group, or "tribe." They have a broad, generalist frame of reference for life, usually getting bored with work that is highly specialized and too narrow in scope. They are usually at their best contributing to the goals of an organization. They are on the same wavelength as the group. Like a member of a flock of birds or a herd of gazelles, they move with the flow of the group. Because they are so attuned to the tribe, they derive many of their values, goals, and points of view from their tribe. Most of the "in crowd" in high school are outgoing Tribals. They like to be in the part of the beehive where the other bees are buzzing and dancing. For more introverted Tribals, this orientation may not be quite as obvious; they are happiest in a quieter corner of the human beehive, but still working with and through others. Tribals generally understand human nature without specialized training more easily than most Maestros. For example, exceptional managers and salespeople are usually Tribals who have an inborn understanding of human psychology, demonstrated by their ability to motivate people. Their success often depends on their interpersonal abilities or their gift for fitting easily into the culture of an organization. They like the shared risks and rewards of being a part of a group. Tribals often choose careers in general business, management, personnel, high school teaching, supervision, sales, advertising, administration, banking, or human resources.

Maestros

Maestros are in the minority in our society. Maestros usually fit best where they can do a whole and complete job in a particular area, usually an area where they've developed in-depth knowledge or mastery. They're usually paid for their knowledge or special talent in that particular area, such as a doctor, lawyer, scientist, actor, artist, or CPA. That specialization is the heart and soul of what they do.

Maestros comprise about 25 percent of the total population. You could say that they are on their own wavelength. They are individual workers, preferring to be most valued for and paid for their mastery of a particular discipline. Their success usually depends directly on special training or a talent for a chosen field. At work, they like having people seek them out for their mastery, expertise, or knowledge. They most enjoy being appreciated and valued for the unique contribution they make. Maestros usually gravitate to careers that put them on a raised platform of expertise, such as a college professor. They tend to understand the world through a unique, personal, and subjective way of thinking.

The following inquiry will help you identify your spot along the Tribal/Maestro continuum.

Inquiry 17-2 TRIBAL/MAESTRO ORIENTATION

1. **Rate yourself.** Read each pair of opposites (left to right), and put a check mark next to the one in each pair that describes you best. Pick statements that describe how you really are rather than how you would like to be. Do this quickly; don't think about it or quibble with the wording. Just mark the one that rings most true for you. If you can't decide which side describes you better, go on to the next item.

I'm on the same wavelength as most folks. ❑	❑ I am on my own wavelength.
I prefer to be a part of a team. ❑	❑ I prefer to do my own thing.
I am definitely one of the gang. ❑	❑ I float between different groups as needed.
I listen to the same music as my peers. ❑	❑ I have my own unique taste in music.
I read popular books. ❑	❑ I read in-depth subject matter.
I consider myself to be like other people. ❑	❑ I am a unique individual, different from others.

Tribal			Maestro
I know just enough in my interest areas.	❑	❑	I know and learn a lot about my interest areas.
I'm attracted to team sports or activities.	❑	❑	I'm attracted to solo sports or activities.
I like the idea of clubs.	❑	❑	I'm not a club kind of person.
I prefer to collaborate on ideas with others.	❑	❑	I prefer my own, individual ideas.
I see myself as a general businessperson.	❑	❑	I see myself as an expert in a specialized field.
I'm into the popular TV shows.	❑	❑	I have my own unusual taste in TV shows.
I dress like most people I know.	❑	❑	I dress uniquely.
I fit in naturally.	❑	❑	I can fit in if I work at it.
I am good at organizing people.	❑	❑	I'd rather not organize people.
I'm comfortable with all kinds of people.	❑	❑	I'm comfortable with people who are like me.
Life is about friends and family.	❑	❑	Life is about being really good at something.
I keep in touch with my family a lot.	❑	❑	My family has to remind me to keep in touch.
I prefer to follow someone else's lead.	❑	❑	I prefer to come up with my own ideas.
I can take or give orders easily.	❑	❑	I don't like to be told what to do.
I'm pretty much like most people.	❑	❑	I'm different from most people.
I cooperate and do the right thing.	❑	❑	I challenge the typical way of doing things.
Sometimes I wish I stood out a bit more.	❑	❑	Sometimes I wish I were a bit more "normal."
My dreams of the future are similar to my friends'.	❑	❑	I dream of a different and highly personal lifestyle.
Total check marks for Tribal	___	___	**Total check marks for Maestro**

2. **Any definite career design components?** If you are sure you fit on one side or the other you may want to add this information to your Definite Career Design Components list. Here are a couple of examples: "I'm going to have a career that engages my Maestro personality, where I can specialize in an area and be sought out for my mastery of a technical body of knowledge." Or "I am going to have a career that engages my Tribal personality, where I will be a part of a team that collaborates daily."
3. **Strong clues.** If you aren't sure and need to think this over, make an entry in your Work Strong Clues list in your notebook. Then work the clues.

PERSONALITY TYPE

Your personality stays fairly constant throughout life. Yes, you will grow and change, but your personality type will, most likely, remain the same.

This inquiry allows you to sort out your own personality type right after this bit of explanation. This way of measuring personality traits is the most widely used personality testing in the world. The people who originally came up with this kind of test described some of these traits with words that are more technical than useful. I will translate where necessary.

Inquiry 17-3 **ROCKPORT PERSONALITY TYPE INDICATOR**

On the following pages you will find four sets of statements that describe opposite aspects of personality. Each set of statements describes different aspects of daily life. This is a tool to help you make choices for your future, so be true to yourself as you respond to each question.

1. **Rate your personality.** Read each pair of opposites (left to right), and put a check mark next to the one in each pair that describes you best. Choose the statement that describes who you really are, not who you would like to be. Go through this quickly, without too much pondering. Pick the one that jumps out at you, the one that rings most true. If you can't decide which side describes you better, don't check either. Just go on to the next pair.

Set 1

I am mostly outgoing. ❑	❑ I am usually quiet except with close friends.
The more friends the better; I am very sociable. ❑	❑ I prefer a few deep relationships.
I am talkative and prefer to participate rather than observe. ❑	❑ I am reflective and prefer to observe rather than participate.
I prefer to be out there; I like to be seen and heard. ❑	❑ I prefer to be more private; I like to keep to myself.
I like to mingle with many different people at parties. ❑	❑ I prefer one-on-one conversations with a few close friends at parties.
I prefer to study with people. ❑	❑ I prefer to study in private.
I feel lonely when left alone. ❑	❑ I seek time alone and enjoy it.
If I have a problem, I tend to discuss it with many friends. ❑	❑ If I have a problem, I tend to discuss it with only one or two very close friends, at most.
I'd rather be with people. ❑	❑ I'd rather read a book.
I am action-oriented. ❑	❑ I am contemplative.
I tend to work out ideas with others, think out loud. ❑	❑ I tend to work out ideas internally, live in my head.
I tend to talk first, think afterward. ❑	❑ I tend to think first, talk afterward.
Don't just think about it, do something! ❑	❑ Don't just do something, think about it!
My attention is usually focused on the immediate surrounding environment. ❑	❑ My attention is usually focused on my thoughts.
I am easy to get to know. ❑	❑ I am not easy to get to know well.
I love to be the center of attention. ❑	❑ I love to listen.
You might say the phone is my lifeline to the world. ❑	❑ You might say e-mail is my lifeline to the world.

After school, I am eager to hang out with a group of friends.	❑	❑	After school, I stay by myself or hang out with a close friend.
Total check marks Type element E	___	___	**Total check marks Type element I**

When complete, add up the check marks in each column and enter your total at the bottom. Circle the type (E or I) with more check marks. If the scores are nearly the same, circle both.

Continue doing the same process with the following checklists.

Set 2

I imagine things that could be.	❑	❑	I pay more attention to what is real.
I tend to explore new possibilities.	❑	❑	I tend to stick with what is familiar.
I prefer to make up something totally new.	❑	❑	I prefer to improve something that already exists.
I often think about the future.	❑	❑	I prefer to deal with the present moment.
I tend to be conceptual, abstract.	❑	❑	I tend to be realistic, practical.
Other people might say I am insightful, deep.	❑	❑	Other people might say I am sensible.
I think of myself as figurative, poetic.	❑	❑	I think of myself as literal, black and white.
I am good at understanding metaphors, analogies.	❑	❑	I am good at solving practical problems.
I tend to dream up ideas for the fun of it.	❑	❑	I like ideas that can be applied.
I like to imagine future events.	❑	❑	I deal with events when they happen.
I seek to be inspired.	❑	❑	I seek to be useful.
Good friends might say that my head is in the clouds, that I am a daydreamer.	❑	❑	Good friends might say that my feet are on the ground.
I like to pay attention to the big picture; the details are less interesting to me.	❑	❑	I like to pay attention to details; I don't easily see the big picture.
I'd say I have a strong imagination.	❑	❑	I'd say I am practical.
I tend to imagine things I'd like to have someday.	❑	❑	I tend to shop and buy things I'd like to have now; why wait?
Often restless, I yearn a lot.	❑	❑	Usually content, I don't yearn much.
I tend to come up with original ideas that others have not thought of.	❑	❑	I prefer to work with existing ideas.
I don't mind sacrificing present pleasure to work on reaching future goals.	❑	❑	I dislike sacrificing present pleasure to work on reaching future goals.
Total check marks Type element N	___	___	**Total check marks Type element S**

Set 3

When making decisions, I rely more on hard facts. ❑	❑ When making decisions, I rely more on my gut instincts.
I approach life using logic and observable facts. ❑	❑ I approach life using my sense of style, passion, and taste.
I am more natural with numbers. ❑	❑ I am more natural at understanding people.
My personality is logical, cool-headed. ❑	❑ My personality is compassionate, warmhearted.
I like to dissect arguments and point out the flaws. ❑	❑ I like to seek harmony and point out the best in people.
I am exacting; I like to ask specific questions to get the true facts. ❑	❑ It's okay for me to get the gist of something; I don't need all the facts.
I am analytical and levelheaded; my judgment is not easily blinded by my feelings. ❑	❑ I am caring and passionate; at times my feelings can cloud my judgment.
In competition, it is important for me to win, be the best. ❑	❑ In competition, it is important to me that everyone is happy; winning is less important.
Laws are to be strictly followed. ❑	❑ Laws should be adapted to fit the situation.
Principles are most important. ❑	❑ People are most important.
I am impatient with people's emotions; I don't pay much attention to their feelings. ❑	❑ I easily understand people's emotions and automatically notice how other people feel.
I want people around me to do their best without having to be told. ❑	❑ I like to coach others on how to improve their performance.
I am mainly interested in information or things. ❑	❑ I am mainly interested in human behavior.
It's best to be frank and direct, tell it like it is. ❑	❑ It's best to be tactful, smooth the tension.
I prefer to be brief, concise. ❑	❑ I prefer to be warm, friendly.
I seek justice, truth. ❑	❑ I seek harmony, mercy.
Competition is in my bones. ❑	❑ Helping people is in my bones.
My friends might say I am reasonable, logical. ❑	❑ My friends might say I am forgiving, emotional.
Total check marks Type element T ___	___ **Total check marks Type element F**

Set 4

I like to decide and move on. ❑	❑ I like to leave my options open.
Once my mind is made up, I don't budge. ❑	❑ I am flexible; I'll change my mind and adapt.
Work now, play later. ❑	❑ Blur the line between work and play.
I like to be planned, structured, orderly. ❑	❑ I like to be spontaneous, open-ended, random.

My friends might say I play it too safe. ❑	❑ My friends might say I take too many risks.
Life is about seeing results. ❑	❑ Life is about trying new things.
Take the tried-and-true path. ❑	❑ Follow the road less traveled.
I am sometimes too rigid, inflexible. ❑	❑ I am sometimes too indecisive, up in the air.
Do what you should. ❑	❑ There are many roads to the same end.
I prefer to be definite, clear-cut, final. ❑	❑ I prefer to experiment, leave things open.
Do the right thing. ❑	❑ Experience as much as possible.
My personality is usually more cautious, hesitant, serious. ❑	❑ My personality is usually more trustful, adventurous, playful.
Conform to the rules. ❑	❑ Change the rules to fit the situation.
Plan to avoid unexpected experiences. ❑	❑ Let things unfold as they may.
It is most important to make a steady effort, get the job done. ❑	❑ It's okay to make a sporadic effort, leave room for change.
I like to have precise steps and detailed instructions. ❑	❑ I like to start from scratch, make it up as I go.
Some would say that "exacting" is my middle name. ❑	❑ Some would say "adjustable" is my middle name.
Total check marks Type element J ___	___ **Total check marks Type element P**

2. **Tabulate your personality type.** Look back at your scores to see which side of the pairings received the most check marks and record them in the chart below. As in the sample directly below, the first designation will be either an E or I; the second either an N or S; and so forth. If you have a tie between two types, enter a question mark in that box as a placeholder until you can do more investigation. Anytime you have both numbers almost the same, consider it to be a tie. For example, if you have seven check marks for E and six for I, consider that a tie. The final four letters with the highest scores make up your personality type.

Sample Scorecard

# check marks	# check marks	Sample Personality Type
1. **E** 16	**I** 2	**E**
2. **N** 1	**S** 17	**S**
3. **F** 4	**T** 4	**? (tie)**
4. **P** 4	**J** 14	**J**

Your Scorecard

# check marks	# check marks	My Personality Type
1. **E** ________	**I** ________	
2. **N** ________	**S** ________	
3. **F** ________	**T** ________	
4. **P** ________	**J** ________	

How to break a tie or an almost equal score: Go back to the set of opposites where your scores came out with an equal or nearly equal number. Cover one column and read the other column from top to bottom. Try to get an overall sense of what that column describes. Then read the opposite column from top to bottom. Which column best describes you? If one is more like you than the other, go to the scorecard and replace the question mark with the letter that is more descriptive of you. If both are still about equal, don't worry. Just consider yourself to be a mix of two personality types.

3. **Look for clues.** Locate your type among the descriptions that follow. If you are a mix of two, read the personality description for both. Get a highlighter, go through the description of your personality type, and mark the parts of the description that stand out as clues about who you are and how you behave. You don't need to mark every word that seems to describe you. The whole point of this inquiry is to find some strong clues. Go through the list of careers for your type in Chapter 28. Highlight any that jump out as exciting or worth looking into further.
4. **Work the clues.** Ask questions, do some research, verify your findings. Show your closest friends and family your type description and ask if they think it describes you well. Do they say "Absolutely!" to any particular parts of the description? (That's a strong clue.) Do they say "Not really" to any other parts? There are several good books about personality type. The best one about personality type and career is called *Do What You Are,* by Paul and Barbara Tieger.
5. **Any definite career design components?** Add any definite elements to your Definite Career Design Components list. This could include any word or phrases from the description of your type that you highlighted and that you know will play a part in your career.
6. **Add to your Careers to Explore list.** Do any of the careers listed for your type in Chapter 28 stand out as interesting enough to consider further? Remember, just because a career fits your personality does not necessarily mean it's the right career for you. Personality type is only one slice of a bigger pie.

Go to your Careers to Explore list in your notebook and write down any career titles you would like to add to your career choice research effort.

ROCKPORT INSTITUTE TYPE INDICATOR: PERSONALITY TYPE DESCRIPTIONS

The preceding inquiry measured four pairs of opposite traits that make up important parts of your personality. Combining the letters that best describe you produces a four-letter personality type. There are sixteen different types.

Extroversion (E) and Introversion (I)

You are either more outgoing and social (E) or more private and ingoing (I). Generally, spending a lot of time with people charges the batteries of Es and drains Is.

Intuition (N) and Sensing (S)

A better way to think of intuition (N) is as being possibility-oriented and sensing (S) as being oriented to present reality. If you tend to look into the future and imagine what could be possible, you are an N. If you like to deal with the real world around you as it is now, you are an S.

Feeling (F) and Thinking (T)

People who lean toward the feeling (F) side trust their feelings and emotions in making decisions. People on the thinking side (T) trust logic more. Let's say you were a judge deciding the case of a scruffy fellow who stole a loaf of bread to feed his starving mother. If you were an F, you might say the circumstances mitigate the crime, so you would go easy on him. As a T, you would be more likely to say that, for the sake of the rule of law, you couldn't go easy on him.

Perceiving (P) and Judging (J)

The traditional terms for this pair, *perceiving* and *judging*, are not particularly helpful. More descriptive terms are *open-ended* or *flexible* (P) and *decisive* (J). People who are perceiving (P) don't want everything planned and decided; they like to stay open to the moment. Js, on the other hand, like things planned out; they get nervous if they don't have things worked out and decided. Based on your results in Inquiry 17-3 above, find your four-letter type below and see how well the type description fits who you are. Most people fit into a single type, while others are a combination of two types. If you tested as partly one type and partly another, read both descriptions.

ENFP

Enthusiastic, expressive, emotional, warm, evocative, imaginative, original, artistic, improvising, perceptive, affirming, supportive, cooperative, positive, open, responsive, sensitive, playful, fun-loving, multifaceted, gregarious, zestful, spontaneous, idealistic. Initiators of new projects and possibilities, change agents. Their focus is on self-expression and possibilities, what could be rather than what is. Life is a celebration and a creative adventure. Enthusiastic initiators of new projects, relationships, and paradigms. Masters of the start-up phase. Lose interest when the project or relationship gets routine or when the primary goal is well on the way to accomplishment. Often eloquent in expressing their vision of a world where ideals are actualized. They might say the glass is full rather than half full or half empty. They are quick to see the potential in people and situations. Frequently have a positive attitude in situations others would consider to be negative. May enjoy a rainy day as much as a sunny one. Management style focuses on the people rather than the tasks. Encourage and serve as mentors rather than command. Work in bursts of enthusiasm mixed with times when little gets done. Need careers that are personally meaningful, creative, allow for full self-expression and contribute to other people in some way. Extremely versatile. They may have friends from many walks of life, a wide range of interests and hobbies, and gain a professional level of mastery without formal training.

INFP

Idealistic, warm, caring, creative, imaginative, original, artistic, perceptive, supportive, empathetic, cooperative, facilitative, compassionate, responsive, sensitive, gentle, tenderhearted, devoted, loyal, virtuous, self-critical, perfectionist, self-sacrificing, deep, multifaceted, persistent, determined, hardworking, daydreamers, improvisers, initiators of new projects and possibilities, change agents. Drawn to possibilities, what could be rather than what is. Values-oriented with high level of personal integrity. Their focus is on understanding themselves, personal growth, and contributing to society in a meaningful way. Under surface appearances they are complex and driven to seek perfection and improvement in themselves, their relationships, and their self-expression. If their career does not express their idealism and drive for improvement, they usually become bored and restless. Dislike conflict, dealing with trivialities, and engaging in meaningless social chatter. Thrive on acknowledgment and recognition so long as they are not the center of attention. Need a private work space, autonomy, and a minimum of bureaucratic rules.

ENFJ

Enthusiastic, caring, concerned, cooperative, congenial, diplomatic, interactive, diligent, emotional, sincere, interpersonally sensitive, warm, supportive, tolerant, creative, imaginative, articulate, verbal, extraordinary social skills, smooth, active, lively, humorous, entertaining, witty, facilitators, persuasive motivators, teacher/preachers, natural leaders. Values-oriented. Uncannily perceptive about others' needs and what motivates them. Often rise to leadership positions. Concerned with the betterment of humanity and effecting positive change. They have such a gift for persuasively using language that others may consider them to be glib and insincere when actually they are forthright and openhearted. Do not deal well with resistance and conflict. Easily hurt and offended if their well-meaning crusades meet with criticism and rejection. Take everything personally. Put people before rules. Strong desire to give and receive affirmation. Manage by encouragement.

INFJ

Gentle, introspective, insightful, idealistic, intellectual, inquisitive, sincere, steady, dependable, conscientious, orderly, deliberate, diligent, compassionate, caring, concerned, peace-loving, accepting, intense, sometimes stubborn, dreamers, catalysts, with quiet strength and many interests, seek and promote harmony. Many feel at home in academia, studying complex concepts, enjoying theoretical courses. They are quietly aware of the dynamics between people. Because they are gentle and quiet, their gifts and rich inner life may go untapped. Their caring, nurturing nature can remain unnoticed since they may not find it comfortable to express these feelings openly. Consequently, they may feel isolated. Need a great deal of solitude and private personal space. Dislike tension and conflict. Give a great deal of focused energy and commitment to their projects, both at work and at home. Although usually compliant, they can become extremely stubborn in pursuit of important goals. Seek careers that further their humanistic ideals and engage their values.

ENTP

Enthusiastic, objective, inventive, independent, competitive, questioning, gregarious, witty, involved, strategic, versatile, clever, adaptable, energetic, rebellious, conceptual thinkers, creative problem solvers, entrepreneurial risk takers, improvisers, rule breakers, puzzle masters, action-oriented change agents. Improve systems, processes, and organizations. Relentlessly test and challenge the status quo with new, well-thought-out ideas and argue vehemently in favor of possibilities and opportunities others have not noticed. Can wear out their colleagues with their drive and challenging nature. See the big picture and how the details fit together. The most naturally entrepreneurial of all types. Usually not motivated by security. Their lives are often punctuated with extreme ups and downs as they energetically pursue new ideas. They have only one direction: ahead at full speed, leaving a trail of incomplete projects, tools, and plans in their wake. Their idea of fun and creative self-expression involves devising new conceptual modeling and dreaming up imaginative and exciting ventures. Need lots of room to maneuver. When forced to dwell on details and routine operating procedures, they become bored and restless. Respect competence, not authority. Seek work that allows them to solve complex problems and develop real-world solutions. Often surrounded with the latest technology.

INTP

Logical, original, speculative, ingenious, inventive, cerebral, deep, ruminative, critical, skeptical, precise, reserved, detached, questioning, quick thinkers, reflective problem solvers, flaw finders, architects and builders of systems, lifelong learners, absentminded professors. Seekers of logical purity. They love to analyze, critique, and develop new ideas rather than get involved in the implementation phase. Continually engage in mental challenges that involve building complex conceptual models leading to logically flawless solutions. Because they are open-ended and possibility-oriented, an endless stream of new data pours in, making it difficult for them to finish developing whatever idea they are working on. Everything is open to revision. Consequently, they are at their best as architects of new ideas where there are endless hypothetical possibilities to be explored, and no need for one final concrete answer. Their holy grail is conceptual perfection. May consider the project complete and lose interest when they have it figured out. To them reality consists of thought processes, not the physical universe. Often seem lost in the complex tunnels of their own inner process. Seek work that allows them to develop intellectual mastery, provides a continual flow of new challenges, privacy, a quiet environment, independence. Thrive in organizations where their self-reliance is valued and colleagues meet their high standards for competency.

ENTJ

Born to lead, outgoing, involved, fully engaged, ambitious, take-charge, impersonal, hearty, robust, type A, impatient, bossy, controlling, confrontational, argumentative, critical, sharp-tongued, intimidating, arrogant, direct, demanding, strategic, tough-minded, organized, orderly, efficient, long-range planners, objective problem solvers. Self-determined and independent. Skilled verbal communicators. Firmly believe that their way is best. Hold on to their point of view without alteration or compromise until some brave soul is able to convince them, through extensive argument and definitive proof, that another way is better. They consider all aspects of life to be the playing field for their favorite game: getting to the top. Their energy is focused on winning, getting to the top, beating the competition, reaching the goal. See life and evaluate other people as part of this game. Assess others hierarchically, above them or below them on the mountain. Tend to look down on people who will not engage them in competition. Often generate hostility and rebellion from their employees and children. Show affection for others by helping them improve. Seek power. Learn by fully engaged discussion (also known as arguing). At their best planning and organizing challenging projects, providing the leadership, straight-ahead energy, and drive to keep up the momentum, and efficiently managing people and forces to reach the objective.

INTJ

Innovative, independent, individualist, self-sufficient, serious, determined, diligent, resourceful, impersonal, reserved, quick-minded, insightful, demanding, critical, strategic, tough-minded, organized, orderly, efficient, argumentative debaters, may seem aloof to others, global, long-range visionaries, planners, objective problem solvers. Self-determined and independent. Use resources efficiently. Do not waste time on trivialities. True to their own vision. Can become stubborn when told to do things in a way that differs from their own opinion of the best methodology. Oriented toward new ideas, possibilities, and improving systems. Their motto is "everything could use improvement." This includes processes, systems, information, technology, organizations, other people, and themselves. Many earn advanced degrees and use education as a path to success. Usually early adopters of the latest computers, software, and other technology. Show affection for others by helping them improve. Learn by in-depth study of the subject and by discussing and arguing. May not realize that other, more thin-skinned people do not interpret arguing in the positive way that INTJs do. Attain personal growth by confronting anything within themselves that could be ameliorated. Constantly stretch themselves in new directions. Highly competent. Read and understand both conceptual and practical materials. See both the forest and the trees. Excellent at planning, execution, and follow-through. They see the big picture and ably organize the details into a coherent plan. Often rise to the top in organizations. At their best where they can conceptualize a new project, push it through to completion, then do it all over again with a new project.

ESFP

"Live for today, face the consequences tomorrow." Warm, positive, friendly, popular, vivacious, animated, open, tactful, helpful, generous, inclusive, tolerant, enthusiastic, gregarious, fashionable, action-oriented, robust, zestful, spontaneous, flexible, energetic, alert, fun-loving, playful, optimistic, impulsive, thrill seeking. Realistic, practical, instructive, useful. A great deal of common sense. Focus on people. Attentive, entertaining, chatty, informal, relaxed. Sunny disposition, accepting, live-and-let-live attitude, go with the flow, love life. Laugh easily, even at themselves. Adventurous, fearless, willing to try anything that involves sensation and risk. Tuned in to and relish the world around them. Smell the roses without stopping. Plunge in headfirst. Live in the present, spurred into action to meet today's needs. Seek immediate gratification, harmony, positive experiences, avoid or repress unpleasant or negative experiences. Do not naturally plan ahead. Dislike routines, procedures, limits, conflict, and slow-moving, long-range projects. Learn by interactive, hands-on participation. Do best in careers that allow them to generate immediate, tangible results while having fun and harmoniously relating with other people in the center of the action.

ISFP

Gentle, sensitive, sensual, quiet, modest, self-effacing, gentle, giving, warm, genuine, service-oriented, helpful, generous, inclusive, tolerant, people-pleasing, considerate, respectful, loyal, trusting, devoted, compassionate, caring, supportive, nurturing, encouraging, serene, easygoing, fun-loving, open, flexible, realistic, practical, independent. Extremely observant and in touch with the sensual world, both externally and within themselves. Consider form and function equally important, strive to make a practical, beautiful world. Savor the sweetness of life, tactile, super-attuned to sights, sounds, smells, flavors, textures. A great deal of common sense. Accepting, live-and-let-live attitude, go with the flow. No need to lead, compete, influence, or control. Seek harmony. Do not impose their values on others. Find their own practical and creative way to do things. Often seek self-expression through crafts or hands-on arts. At their best in work that expresses their personal values and helps or provides a service to others. May forgo college for a practical education in the trades, crafts, or service professions.

ESFJ

Gracious, amiable, affirming, gentle, giving, warm, genuine, cordial, kindly, caring, concerned, dutiful, reliable, punctual, polite, tactful, socially appropriate, thoughtful, self-sacrificing, nurturing, people-pleasing, goal-oriented, helpful, cooperative, consistent, extremely loyal, traditional, rule-bound, uncomplicated. Confident with people, perfectly in tune with others' needs and sensitive to nuances, they are the world's natural hosts and hostesses, efficient managers, event planners. Their presence contributes graciousness, harmony, fraternity, and fellowship to whatever they are engaged in. Both female and male ESFJs relate with people in a way that combines warmhearted "mothering" and caring, considerate "innkeeping." So eager are they to please that they put others' needs before their own, ignoring their personal well-being as they care for the people most important to them. They seek harmony, avoid conflict, follow the rules, keep their commitments, and ignore problems by pretending they do not exist. Sensitive to criticism. Need appreciation and praise. Particularly concerned with etiquette, shoulds and shouldn'ts. Family and home are often their central passion; can be happily consumed by the details of homemaking and raising kids. Value stability, harmony, relationships, and practical, hands-on experience. The day-to-day events in their lives are carefully planned and meticulously managed. At their best in professions that provide helpful, caring, practical service to others and do not require them to learn theories. Pay little attention to information outside their immediate reality, rarely read the newspaper. They are particularly good at planning events, organizing people, and managing the day-to-day aspects of projects that deal with producing tangible results. When they learn an effective new method, it becomes standard operating procedure. Their extraordinary effectiveness comes from picking the perfect, tried-and-true procedure from their internal database at exactly the right time.

ISFJ

Warmhearted, conscientious, loyal, considerate, helpful, calm, quiet, devoted, gentle, open, nurturing, practical, patient, responsible, dependable, very observant, sensitive, holistic, inclusive, spontaneous, pragmatic, tactile, respectful, giving, noncompetitive, sympathetic, painstaking and thorough, efficient, traditional. The most service-oriented of all the types, caretakers. Very much in touch with their inner process as well as the world around them. Seek harmony for themselves and all others, the managers everyone loves. Drawn to the healing professions. Serene, appreciative, in tune. Do not impose themselves or their opinions on others. Do not need to control, unassuming, shy, prefer lots of solitude. Find their own creative way to get the job done. Learn by doing. Uninterested in abstractions and theories, would rather execute than plan, comfortable with routine. Guardians of natural resources, conservation-oriented. Use standard operating procedures only when they are the best method for reaching the goal. Often creative and highly skilled but so averse to imposing that they are easily overlooked and their contributions go unnoticed.

ESTP

Outgoing, realistic, action-oriented, robust, zestful, fun, spontaneous, energetic, alert, direct, fearless, resourceful, expedient, competitive, spontaneous, flexible, gregarious, objective, expressive, pragmatic problem solvers, take-charge, convincing, smooth talkers, negotiators. Adventurous, willing to try anything that involves sensation and risk, entrepreneurial, witty. Plunge in headfirst, then analyze. "Live for today, face the consequences tomorrow." No tolerance for theories and abstractions, no-nonsense. Useful, constructive, handy. Short attention span. Usually have a laid-back attitude, value individual rights and personal freedom. Do not naturally plan ahead. Prefer to deal with what life throws at them, troubleshoot. Adapt to the present situation. React to emergencies instantly and appropriately. A passion for tackling tough jobs and winning in impossible situations. Football-hero mentality. Break the rules more often than any other type. Often find themselves in trouble in strict bureaucracies. Dislike being tied down. Learn by doing; rarely read the manual. Want a big return for their investment of time, energy, money. Lively, entertaining center of attention. The ultimate party-hearty soul. Always willing to put off mundane tasks for the thrill of something new and exciting. Often attracted to motorcycles, fast cars, power boats, skydiving, and similar quick thrills, the new and the unexplored, tactile pleasures, high-risk sports. May enjoy working with their hands.

ISTP

Independent, reserved, cool, curious, expedient, flexible, logical, analytical, realistic, spontaneous, action-oriented. Function over form, workability over beauty. Adventurous, willing to try anything that involves sensation and risk. Usually have a relaxed, laid-back attitude, value individual rights and personal freedom. No-nonsense, straight talker. Enthusiastic about and absorbed in their immediate interests. Constantly scanning and observing the world around them, attentive. Do not naturally plan ahead. Prefer to deal with what life throws at them, alert. Adapt to the present situation. Follow the path of least resistance. React to emergencies instantly and appropriately. Live-and-let-live philosophy, laissez-faire approach to life. Dislike rules, being tied down, or imposing themselves on others. Often attracted to motorcycles, fast cars, power boats, skydiving, and similar quick thrills, the new and the unexplored, tactile pleasures, high-risk sports. Usually enjoy working with their hands; have natural mastery of tools. Things or objective information are the focus rather than people.

ESTJ

Systematic, serious, thorough, down-to-earth, efficient, decisive, hard-working, dutiful, loyal, sincere, conservative, aggressive, in charge. Focused, controlled and controlling. A strong sense of responsibility, generous with their time, civic-minded. Gregarious, active, socially gifted, partygoers. Make their point of view known. Macho. Often rise to positions of responsibility, such as senior-level management. Want their work to be practical, pragmatic, immediate and objective, have clear and unambiguous objectives, require follow-through and perseverance, involve facts and produce tangible, measurable results. Natural managers, supervisors, administrators. Type A personalities. Keep their commitments at any cost. Think in terms of shoulds and shouldn'ts. Have difficulty appreciating and learning from other points of view. Work first, play later. Drawn to work in established, stable, structured, hierarchical organizations using standard operating procedures. Follow the rules. Seekers of security and stability. They safeguard and maintain traditions and traditional values, toe the line, do their fair share. Protectors, guardians of rules. A tendency to trample other people (usually unknowingly) as they plow straight ahead to accomplish their goals. A high percentage of military sergeants have this personality type.

ISTJ

Systematic, serious, thorough, detailed, objective, analytical, down-to-earth, efficient, decisive, hardworking, dutiful, loyal, reserved, sincere, conservative, legalistic. A strong sense of responsibility. Very dependable, trustworthy. Very private but learn extroverted social behaviors for the sake of practicality. Want their work to be practical, pragmatic, immediate and objective, have clear and unambiguous objectives, require follow-through and perseverance, involve facts and produce tangible, measurable results. Often have type A personalities. Keep their commitments at any cost. Think from the point of view of shoulds and shouldn'ts. Work first, play later. Simple tastes, no frills, classical, traditional. Drawn to work in stable, structured, hierarchical organizations using standard operating procedures. Seekers of security. They safeguard and maintain traditions and traditional values. A high percentage of military people, engineers, surgeons, and financial analysts have this personality type.

CHAPTER 18

CORE PERSONALITY

Here is another way to learn more about yourself and what careers might fit you. To make this chapter useful to you, you must have done two previous inquiries—Inquiry 17-2, where you sorted out whether you are a Tribal or a Maestro, and Inquiry 17-3, where you figured out your personality type. Here we combine what you discovered in these two inquiries. If you came out in the middle in the extrovert/introvert scale or in the middle in the Tribal/Maestro scale you are very likely a combination of two core types. Read about both types.

FOUR CORE TYPES

If you are definitely on one side or the other as either an extrovert or an introvert and either a Maestro or a Tribal, then one way to understand yourself is to think of yourself as one of these four core types: introverted Tribal, extroverted Tribal, introverted Maestro, or extroverted Maestro. This is a quick and powerful way of sizing up your basic personality.

The following diagram illustrates the four quadrants. Recall your extrovert/introvert and Tribal/Maestro self-ratings from earlier inquiries. Which of the four quadrants do you fit into? Read through the descriptions for each of the four types below and see which of the types describes you best.

Extroverted Tribal	Extroverted Maestro
Introverted Tribal	Introverted Maestro

Tribal Personality

Introverted Tribal. What do you get if you mix introversion with a Tribal personality? People with this combination like working as a part of the human beehive, often as a part of an organization, but they are happiest in a quieter part of the hive where they can mainly work internally rather than spending most of the day interacting with other people. They are team players, but they participate in their own way. Because they are more introverted, they do their best work either alone or with a small group of people they know well. Since their Tribal side gives them the inclination to cooperate with teammates, the best way to satisfy this need is to work among like-minded colleagues. Many modern office-cubicle settings are well suited to introverted Tribals: they excel at project-based work that allows them to contribute to the whole by working in a semiprivate space. They can sense the hum and hustle of other Tribals rubbing their wings together. Even though they may not interact with others as much as their extroverted Tribal officemates, they know that at any moment they can grab a cup of coffee and collaborate with a buddy around the corner. They are the true unsung heroes. Quietly working through and with people, introverted Tribals serve as the backbone of an organization. Professionally, they fit into thousands of different jobs in organizations, wherever they can contribute to the goals of the organization in a way that allows them to spend a considerable portion of their day working internally.

Extroverted Tribal. If you have friends who seem to have a cell phone permanently attached to their ears, they are probably extroverted Tribals. They are happiest spending most of their day working with and through others, interacting, talking, and socializing. Extroverted Tribals need a double dose of people. Their Tribal side drives them to be a member of a community; their extroverted side has them interacting all day within that community. They are nonstop, people-oriented, the shiny happy party people in all those beer and cola ads.

Getting things done with and through other people most of the day is how they work and play. They may ask themselves, "Why write an e-mail when I can talk to someone?" Professionally, they excel as sales representatives, hosts, greeters, people managers, executives, spokespersons, promoters, supervisors, day care providers, recreation therapists, nurses, advertising account managers, marketing presenters, K-12 teachers, and personal trainers.

Maestro Personality

Introverted Maestro. We think of introverted Maestros as professionals. They mainly work internally in their area of specialty or expertise, thinking and solving problems internally in their area of specialty. Introverted Maestros prefer to do a whole project or job, mainly working internally. They live mainly in a private inner world. Some may feel like outsiders, with little desire to join a tribe. They are inclined to be scholarly, scientific, or professional, and occasionally eccentric. They perceive and do things their own way. Many introverted Maestro physicians work with patients all day but direct much of their attention internally, figuring out what is broken and how to fix it. Even though we call their extroverted Maestro cousins "performers," in fact many fine performers, including some of the greatest actors and singer-songwriters, are introverted Maestros.

Professionally they excel as artists, master craftsmen, musicians, poets, novelists, scientists, pioneers, specialist physicians, attorneys, inventors, and consultants, to name a few. This group is responsible for most of the greatest breakthroughs throughout the history of humankind.

Extroverted Maestro. I like to think of extroverted Maestros as performers. They may not necessarily perform in front of a large audience or on a stage, but even with an audience of one, they communicate their expertise to others. They're experts or masters in a particular area and are at their best performing their mastery out in front of others—for example, the college professor who loves the classroom, seminar leader, spokesperson for a technical subject, politician, actor, comedian, performance artist, consultant, trainer. Some are charismatic leaders or entrepreneurs who speak for a new idea or product that has complexity and depth. They are geared to take a lead role: As an expert, they direct, advise, and guide others in their field of mastery. Not only do they see the world in a highly personal way, but they are compelled to share their talent, knowledge, and wisdom.

Inquiry 18-1 **MY CORE PERSONALITY GROUP**

1. **Look for and work the clues.** Are you clear which of the four types above describes you best? You may be a combination of types. For example, you could be a Tribal who is 40 percent extrovert and 60 percent introvert. If that is the case, you want your career to fit your unique combination.
2. **Any definite career design components?** Add any definite elements to your Definite Career Design Components list. An example: "I will work as a Tribal in an organization, with my work split fairly evenly between extroverted work with other people and working quietly on my own."
3. **Any good clues?** If you need to think about this more, make an entry in your Work Strong Clues list.

CHAPTER

19

NATURAL ROLES

All the world's a stage, and all the men and women merely players; they have their exits and their entrances, and one man in his time plays many parts.

—*William Shakespeare*

Each of us plays natural roles throughout our lives. As the man said, the world is a stage, and we are the players, acting out basic roles and tendencies. Even as children, we exhibited some of our main character roles. Think of kids you knew who were natural leaders, comedians, rebels, risk takers, or artists. These roles, also called archetypes, stay with us for our entire lives. Each of us has several roles that come to us most naturally. They are almost like different characters who take turns having a lead role in a chapter of our lives. These roles don't necessarily have any consistency or relationship among them. For example, a Mafia hit man may be an absolutely ruthless criminal at work and a loving and devoted parent at home.

Throughout your life, different roles take the lead at different times. Most of these roles have a genetic component: they choose you, not the other way around. For example, one of the roles described below is Risk Taker. Scientists have linked risk-taking behavior in mice to a single gene. Some mice with a particular genetic structure are willing to walk along an unprotected walkway high above the ground, while most seek a safer, more secure path. Like the men willing to walk unprotected on narrow steel beams to build the great skyscrapers, or extreme-sport athletes joyfully performing dangerous feats, some people are born risk takers.

Recognizing these natural inclinations can provide more clues for deciding what to do with your life. Someone whose dominant roles are Builder/Designer and Risk Taker leans toward a very different career than someone with the combination of Healer and Leader.

Your challenge in this chapter is to get into Detective mode and sort out your own unique collection of roles, how you function in the more dominant roles, and how roles combine. Because we tend to go through life more conscious of *what* we do than *why* we do it, you may not have given much thought to the roles you play. We all take ourselves for granted, so it's going to take looking at yourself with new eyes.

There is no simple formula for turning roles into careers that fit you. This inquiry simply provides another kind of access to who you are.

Inquiry 19-1 **MY NATURAL ROLES**

There are two different ways of doing this inquiry. The short and simple way is to do it yourself, just you and this book, without involving anyone else. However, I recommend that you also involve some people who know you intimately, perhaps your best friends, your parents, even your evil little brother. Doing it this way often reveals things about you that you might not notice if you didn't include other people's assessments. One woman gave herself a zero for the role of Hero, but after everyone else gave her high marks, she saw she had a very limited view of herself.

IDENTIFY YOUR NATURAL ROLES IN DIALOGUE WITH OTHERS

1. Make some copies of this chapter and staple them together in sets.
2. Pass them out to other people who are big players in your life. Ask them to check roles that they see as part of your personality. Really strong roles get the ③ checked. Roles midrange in importance get a ②. Minor ones get a ① or perhaps a ⓪.
3. Go through the chapter yourself. Identify roles you actually play rather than ones you like.
4. After you have gone through this inquiry, check out how other people's perceptions of you match your own.

HOW TO IDENTIFY YOUR NATURAL ROLES

1. **Look for clues.** As in all the inquiries in this book, you are a Detective looking for clues about your personality and behaviors that will be useful in choosing your career.

   Select a total of up to ten natural roles. Read through the following pages of natural roles and put a check mark on the line in front of the role that you think describes an important aspect of who you are. Be thoughtful; carefully consider your choices. We suggest that you pick no more than ten roles. You'll have a chance later to sort out which are the lead actors in your life. Don't worry if you don't recognize many roles as fitting you. Sometimes it takes paying attention to yourself in new ways or puzzling over the list before you notice some of your roles. Your connection with a particular role may not hit you like a bolt of lightning.

   The roles are divided into groups. Four of these groups are based on the middle letters of your personality type. Pay particular attention to roles listed under the letters that fit you. For example, if you determined in Chapter 17 that you are an ENFP, the middle letters of your personality type would be NF so you should pay special attention to roles listed in the category called "Roles Common with Intuitive-Feelers (NF)."

   Zero in on the real you. You are looking for roles you actually play as a regular and significant part of your life. The younger you are, the less likely it is that you will have had much actual experience playing a particular role in the outside world. In that case, what to look for is the connection, the recognition, the sense of familiarity.

   Note: Instructions will resume after the list of roles.

BASIC UNIVERSAL ROLES

___ ⓪①②③ **Child.** This is a role we all inhabit. To some degree we all carry our childhood with us, for better or worse, throughout our lives. The positive side of this role is the eternal child, the person who remains eternally young at heart. They are lighthearted and fun to be around, preserving a charming innocence, a spirit of playfulness, and a vital, energetic youthfulness.

On the negative side, some people never fully grow up, remaining irresponsible as a childish adult. Afraid to face the unknowns and unpredictable aspects of life, the Child yearns to be protected and taken care of by others. They may care only about filling their own needs. They may be bratty, need to always be the center of attention, or be unable to form mature relationships. When it comes to career choices, the Child wants someone else to decide for them or just hopes it all works out rather than treating career choice as one of life's most important decisions. When times get tough, nearly everyone has bouts of the Child role; the hope of being rescued from tough choices and dangers is woven deeply into human nature.

___ ⓪①②③ **Mother.**The nurturer, the vital giver of life. The Mother is protective, devoted, caring, and unselfish. Although most women can biologically function as a mother, this role describes people of either sex who embody these characteristics in their everyday life. They may have their own children or passionately look forward to having a family, or this role may show up in many other ways—for example, in a devotion to protecting the environment or the well-being of anything else they care about.

___ ⓪①②③ **Father.** Even beyond the immediate family, some people embody the bold and courageous male patriarch. The Father role initiates, takes charge, and leads through the tough decisions in life. People who embody the spirit of the Father role will find ways to apply this talent in the workplace as the wise manager, on the playing field as the nurturing sports coach, and as a parent to their own children as the ultimate "cool" dad. On the dark side, the Father may also abuse his authority by being overly controlling, dictatorial, or a know-it-all.

___ ⓪①②③ **Warrior.** The Warrior takes a stand and fights for something. The adversary can be anything—other Warriors, an injustice, a disease, a shortcoming of society, a personal weakness, a belief system, an unfulfilled goal. The Warrior is willing to do what it takes to reach the goal, no matter what obstacles arise, no matter how uncomfortable he or she feels. The more evolved Warrior seeks to win without a fight, the objective being the goal rather than the need to go to battle. Men and women drawn to defend their country on the battlefield embody the physical Warrior, willing to put life on the line for a cause. Others manifest the Warrior in fighting for social injustices or on the proverbial battlefield of the competitive business world. On the dark side is the Warrior who can't stop, who loves the battle more than the goal.

___ ⓪①②③ **Hero.** The Hero arises in many forms. The true Hero begins as an ordinary person, called to a mission beyond his or her present capacities. Out of dedication to the goal, the Hero undergoes difficulties and emerges transformed by the experience. Many tales handed down to us from ancient days follow this theme. The character Frodo in *The Lord of the Rings* is the perfect embodiment of this role in modern literature. The Hero's journey can involve an adventure in the external world or an inner quest for wisdom or personal transformation. The Hero's quest always involves overcoming those very weaknesses or inner demons holding the Hero back. Many of you reading this book with a strong desire to find a career you love are on a Hero's journey: you are working against a prevailing belief that not enjoying work is normal ("If it were fun, they wouldn't call it work").

___ ⓪①②③ **Comedian.** The consummate class clown, prankster, fool, and jokester. The Comedian thrives on making people laugh, cry, or think about things differently. They see the humor and absurdity in everyday life. They make us laugh at ourselves and our foolish ways. Some are court jesters, a role that gives them special permission to reveal the truth that most of us, caught up in trying to be politically (or otherwise) correct, aren't seeing.

___ ⓪①②③ **Leader/King/Queen.** Without much effort, some people carry an air of authority, confidence, clarity, vision, or majesty; they are recognized by others as natural leaders. As if born with royal blood, they have natural authority. While Managers administer projects and work the details, Leaders see the whole forest while maintaining a practical eye on the trees. They are at their best when they know the difference between power and force. A truly powerful Leader is benevolent, using wisdom, persuasion, and the example of their actions. People follow them because they want to. They direct their kingdom, company, organization, family, or team without needing to use force and domination.

___ ⓪①②③ **Prince/Princess.** Deserving, entitled, the Prince/Princess needs to be taken care of. They think of themselves as special, born to be honored and adored. They are vulnerable, seek attention, and usually find others to worship them, dote on them, and generally treat them as royalty. Rarely independent or self-sufficient, they often trap themselves in relationships and situations where they are completely reliant on others and never fully develop their own powers to live independently in the real world.

___ ⓪①②③ **Money Person.**Since the dawn of civilization, some people have had a strong affinity for money—acquiring it, saving it, investing it, understanding the complexities of it, working with it. Just because you want a lot of it doesn't mean this role is one of yours. Look instead for a real affinity. This may be one of your natural roles if you spend a lot of time looking for the good deal or reading about investing and enjoy the financial intricacies of business, balancing your checkbook, or doing financial spreadsheets.

PUBLIC OR "SOCIAL FACE" ROLES

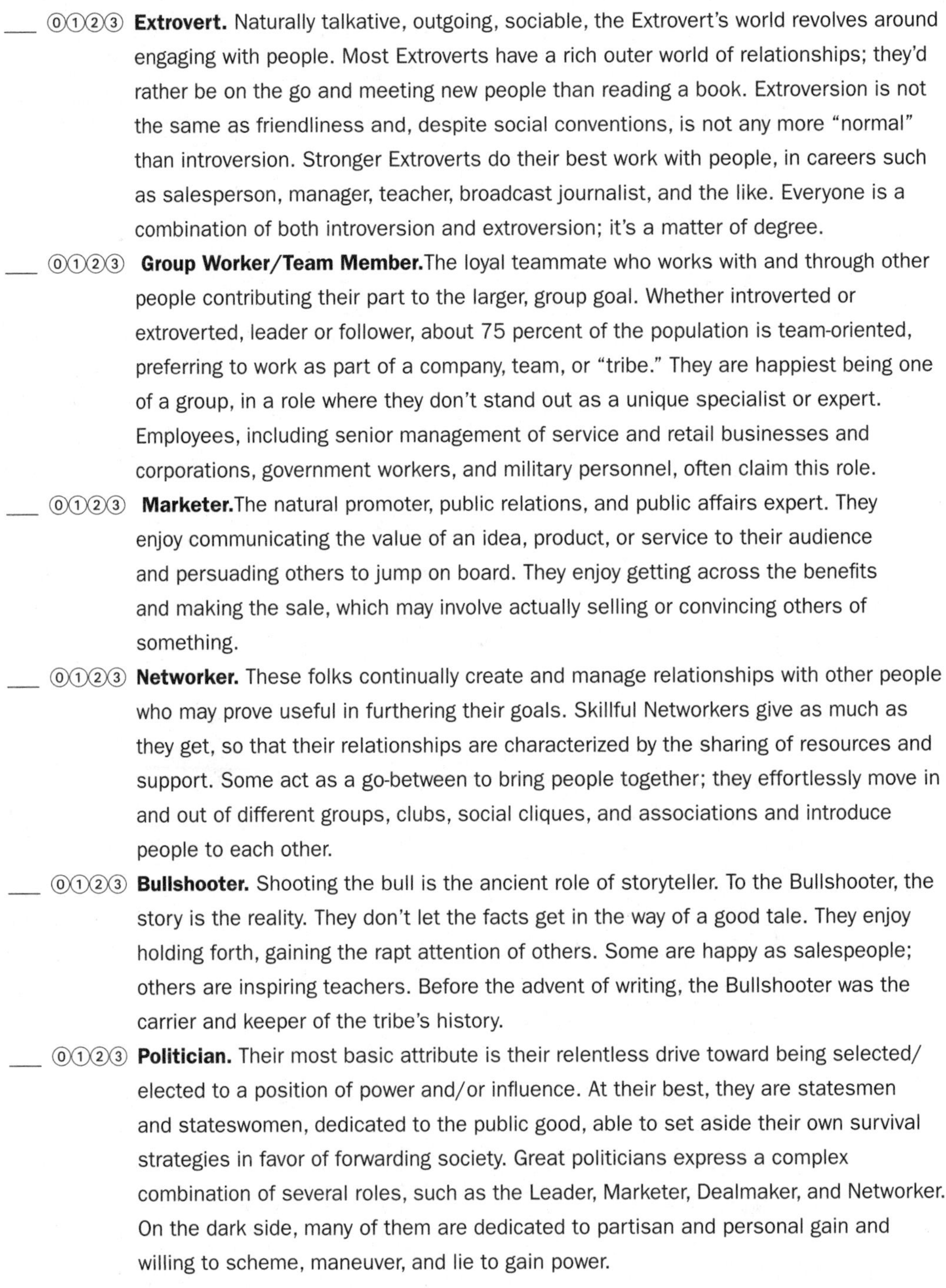

___ ⓪①②③ **Extrovert.** Naturally talkative, outgoing, sociable, the Extrovert's world revolves around engaging with people. Most Extroverts have a rich outer world of relationships; they'd rather be on the go and meeting new people than reading a book. Extroversion is not the same as friendliness and, despite social conventions, is not any more "normal" than introversion. Stronger Extroverts do their best work with people, in careers such as salesperson, manager, teacher, broadcast journalist, and the like. Everyone is a combination of both introversion and extroversion; it's a matter of degree.

___ ⓪①②③ **Group Worker/Team Member.**The loyal teammate who works with and through other people contributing their part to the larger, group goal. Whether introverted or extroverted, leader or follower, about 75 percent of the population is team-oriented, preferring to work as part of a company, team, or "tribe." They are happiest being one of a group, in a role where they don't stand out as a unique specialist or expert. Employees, including senior management of service and retail businesses and corporations, government workers, and military personnel, often claim this role.

___ ⓪①②③ **Marketer.**The natural promoter, public relations, and public affairs expert. They enjoy communicating the value of an idea, product, or service to their audience and persuading others to jump on board. They enjoy getting across the benefits and making the sale, which may involve actually selling or convincing others of something.

___ ⓪①②③ **Networker.** These folks continually create and manage relationships with other people who may prove useful in furthering their goals. Skillful Networkers give as much as they get, so that their relationships are characterized by the sharing of resources and support. Some act as a go-between to bring people together; they effortlessly move in and out of different groups, clubs, social cliques, and associations and introduce people to each other.

___ ⓪①②③ **Bullshooter.** Shooting the bull is the ancient role of storyteller. To the Bullshooter, the story is the reality. They don't let the facts get in the way of a good tale. They enjoy holding forth, gaining the rapt attention of others. Some are happy as salespeople; others are inspiring teachers. Before the advent of writing, the Bullshooter was the carrier and keeper of the tribe's history.

___ ⓪①②③ **Politician.** Their most basic attribute is their relentless drive toward being selected/elected to a position of power and/or influence. At their best, they are statesmen and stateswomen, dedicated to the public good, able to set aside their own survival strategies in favor of forwarding society. Great politicians express a complex combination of several roles, such as the Leader, Marketer, Dealmaker, and Networker. On the dark side, many of them are dedicated to partisan and personal gain and willing to scheme, maneuver, and lie to gain power.

___ ⓪①②③ **Dealmaker.** Part Networker, Politician, and Marketer, they can get the deal done and the contract signed. Some are gifted at making friends, building relationships, and proposing the win-win deal. Others have a talent for getting others to agree to deals that favor only the Dealmaker. They understand what makes people tick and know what it takes to motivate others to make up their minds and sign on the dotted line. They often become salespeople and also excel as marketing executives, politicians, and diplomats.

___ ⓪①②③ **Introvert.** Naturally quiet, ingoing, reserved, talks little but thinks constantly. Introverts have a rich inner life and do their best work in their heads or with their hands, such as writers, craftspeople, accountants, lawyers, researchers, scientists, artists, and so on. Introversion is not shyness or a lack of confidence. Introverts have an inward focus, which is just as normal as extroversion. Everyone is a combination of both introversion and extroversion; it's a matter of degree. Some may try to hide their natural tendency and force themselves into more extroverted careers. Introversion is not a weakness; it's a natural trait that, if not taken into account, can lead to exhaustion on the job.

___ ⓪①②③ **Hermit.** A small percentage of people are happy to live in solitude. Most introverts are not Hermits. The difference is that introverts have a social life. Hermits don't. Rather, they prefer to live and work alone and consider contact with other people a bother.

ADVENTURER ROLES

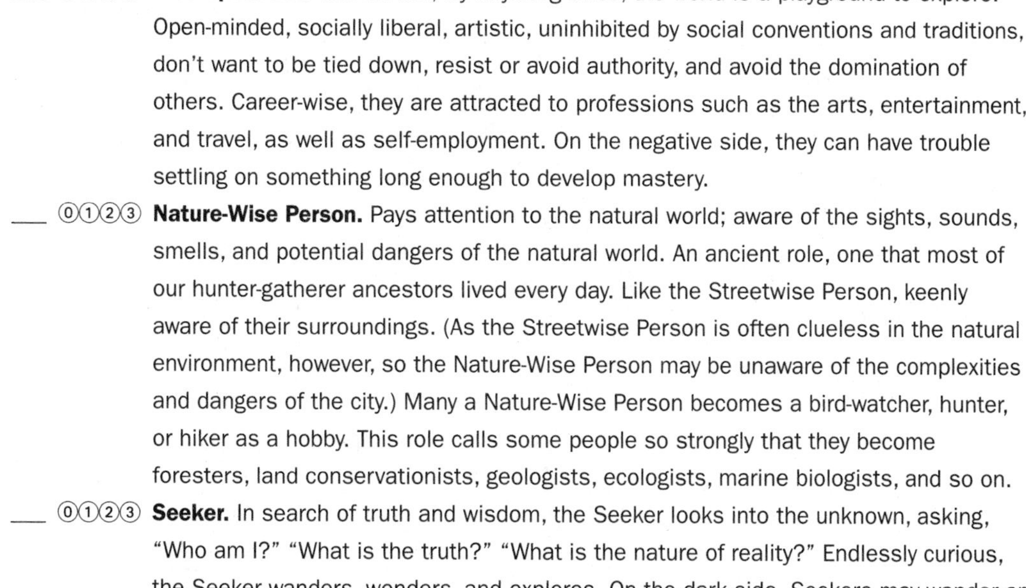

___ ⓪①②③ **Free Spirit.** Live and let live, try anything twice, the world is a playground to explore. Open-minded, socially liberal, artistic, uninhibited by social conventions and traditions, don't want to be tied down, resist or avoid authority, and avoid the domination of others. Career-wise, they are attracted to professions such as the arts, entertainment, and travel, as well as self-employment. On the negative side, they can have trouble settling on something long enough to develop mastery.

___ ⓪①②③ **Nature-Wise Person.** Pays attention to the natural world; aware of the sights, sounds, smells, and potential dangers of the natural world. An ancient role, one that most of our hunter-gatherer ancestors lived every day. Like the Streetwise Person, keenly aware of their surroundings. (As the Streetwise Person is often clueless in the natural environment, however, so the Nature-Wise Person may be unaware of the complexities and dangers of the city.) Many a Nature-Wise Person becomes a bird-watcher, hunter, or hiker as a hobby. This role calls some people so strongly that they become foresters, land conservationists, geologists, ecologists, marine biologists, and so on.

___ ⓪①②③ **Seeker.** In search of truth and wisdom, the Seeker looks into the unknown, asking, "Who am I?" "What is the truth?" "What is the nature of reality?" Endlessly curious, the Seeker wanders, wonders, and explores. On the dark side, Seekers may wander on an endless, aimless journey to nowhere and avoid finding something for fear that it will end their search. Evolved seekers become finders.

___ ⓪①②③ **Rule Breaker/Rebel.** The outsider and maverick who questions conventions and deviates from the norm. Rebel energy often helps society break out of habits that no longer work. Social activists and critics, scientists, comedians, artists and poets, visionary leaders, and change agents who move the world to see things anew or challenge the status quo have the Rule Breaker in their makeup. Matt Groening, creator of *The Simpsons,* is an example of the artistic, comedic Rule Breaker. On the dark side, some Rebels are on a path of destruction, bringing harm to themselves or society as professional criminals, con artists, tricksters, and scammers. This group's white-collar representatives often show up in the news: Politicians and Criminals with MBAs and law degrees, manipulating the public for their own ends.

___ ⓪①②③ **Risk Taker.** The daredevil, willing to do things that most people would consider dangerous, chancy, speculative, or foolhardy. The Risk Taker may take physical risks, like the mountain climber or stunt person, or thrive on beating the odds, like the day trader or the entrepreneur. Much of human history was made by successful Risk Takers. Many of the advances and advantages we most cherish exist only because someone took a big risk and won. On the dark side, some get their kicks by trying to beat the system. At the far end of that spectrum lies the Criminal role.

ANTISOCIAL ROLES

Some of what is commonly considered antisocial may be just pushing the boundaries of what is known or accepted, and that is the engine that moves humanity forward. The roles in this category are different, however. When playing these roles, people have no intention of making a contribution to society. Their impulse is narrow, in service to the ignoble in humanity or to cause intentional harm.

___ ⓪①②③ **Sell-out.** At one time or another, each of us plays this role. Whether or not it is a dominant role for you depends on how much time you devote to playing it. Sell-outs make choices they know are based on expediency, what's easy rather than right, cashing in their values and dreams for money, power, comfort, security, or status. Common expressions of this role occur when you choose a career you don't enjoy, or marry someone you don't love for security or status. Selling out damages not only you but also the fabric of life around you.

___ ⓪①②③ **Criminal.** This role is somewhat different from the everyday use of the word. Most people in prison fit the common definition: someone who commits acts against the law. But not all fit the role described here. The Criminal role includes people without much moral or ethical concern about the damage they inflict on other people as they pursue their own advancement, power, or wealth. They may have antisocial or psychopathic tendencies or simply not care how their actions affect others. The bad guy in the movies, the Mafia hit man, and the soldier of fortune fill this role wonderfully, but so do some perfectly respectable citizens who happily rob you with a fountain pen. Computer virus creators fall into this category. Wherever you find hired guns, you also will find people playing the Criminal role: some lawyers, lobbyists, politicians, financial finaglers, and so forth.

___ ⓪①②③ **Bully.** The bully dominates others through force—either physical force or just a dominating personality focused on getting its way no matter what.

ROLES GROUPED BY PERSONALITY TYPE

From this point on, the roles listed are grouped by the personality types that are often linked with them. Any of these roles could be one of yours, no matter what your personality type. The reason I put them in groups is because these roles are especially common in people of certain personality types. So look especially carefully at the group listed under your personality type, but check them all out to see if they describe one of your dominant roles.

Roles Common with Sensor-Thinkers. The next group of natural roles could fit you no matter what your personality type but is especially common in people with a sensor-thinker (ST) personality (ESTJ, ISTJ, ESTP, and ISTP). If yours is one of these personality types, you should read this group of roles with special care.

___ ⓪①②③ **Manager.**The natural organizer and administrator of people and projects. Although often in a leadership position, a Manager is not necessarily a natural authority or visionary leader. Supervisor, captain of a team, gets the job done. Whether in the workplace, at home, planning a vacation or dinner party, the Manager brings order to chaos, sets the agenda, plans the project, orchestrates the activities, and manages the resources to make it all happen.

___ ⓪①②③ **Builder/Designer.** The natural engineer is born to build, tinker, and find practical solutions to tangible problems. Builders often show signs of their gift early in life, engineering things out of Lego blocks that often astound their parents. All engineering specialties, the trades, architecture, and the hardware and software sides of information technology are playgrounds for Builders. They are the tool makers and tool users who build and improve the efficiency of our everyday lives, following in the footsteps of Henry Ford and Alexander Graham Bell. Crafting and shaping the physical world of objects and things to serve human purposes is their joy.

___ ⓪①②③ **Athlete.** The embodiment of strength, character, commitment, and determination to push the human body and mind to its limits. The Athlete's spirit is expressed in the relentless pursuit of physical and mental mastery, and in someone less competitive is sometimes expressed as simply loving a sport or other athletic activity for the sheer joy of it. Olympic and professional athletes, classical musicians, circus performers, dancers, stunt people, soldiers, fighter pilots, explorers, rescue personnel, and outdoor adventurers.

___ ⓪①②③ **Streetwise Person.** Walks the urban landscape keenly aware of what's going on, the intentions of people they encounter, and potential threats. Their movements and actions are consistent with survival—they know when to cross to the other side of the street. This is one of the most ancient roles. Imagine you and your tribe are walking down the trail twenty thousand years ago and suddenly come upon a strange group of people. You would want to have someone in your group who could pick up the vibes of the other people and know instinctively if they meant you harm. People with this trait are often attracted to police work, undercover intelligence, firefighting, and emergency medic/paramedic fields, including animal rescue and disaster relief.

___ ⓪①②③ **Protector.** Keeper of traditions, guardian of the rules, laws, customs, and socially accepted morals. The Protector sees the world through a lens of shoulds and shouldn'ts, judging rights and wrongs, holding life as black and white. Plays by the rules. Defending homeland and honor, Protectors are usually loyal to whatever they identify as their tribe: country, organization, belief system. Usually socially conservative, they strive to maintain important values and ways of life. Protectors are attracted to professions that enforce and make more rules, as law enforcement personnel, federal agency regulators, and armed forces.

___ ⓪①②③ **Right-Hand Person (Helper/Sidekick/Companion/Server).** The ultimate "right hand" who gets the job done. Their strength, dedication, loyalty, and supportive nature are often the real backbone of an organization. Vice presidents, chief operating officers, general managers, executive assistants, and secretaries often say they are not interested in being the main person out front, but thrive as the one who makes it all work behind the scenes. Some are Companions or Sidekicks with a giving nature who find joy in serving, hosting, and pleasing others. Some become waiters or work in other hospitality industry careers; others work as cooks, manage a bed-and-breakfast, drive a taxi, or run a hotel. Helpers are often grossly underappreciated.

Roles Common with Sensor-Feelers. The next group of natural roles could fit you no matter what your personality type. They are especially common in people with a sensor-feeler (SF) personality (ESFJ, ISFJ, ESFP, and ISFP). If yours is one of these personality types, you should read this group of roles with special care.

___ ⓪①②③ **Teacher/Mentor.**Drawn to educate, instruct, and pass on knowledge or wisdom to students and apprentices. Teachers instruct groups of students, where Mentors take an individual apprentice under their wing to pass on their mastery.

___ ⓪①②③ **Healer.** The modern-day descendant of our hunter-gatherer ancestors' shaman. The Healer is called to heal the sick and restore well-being to those suffering. Strangely enough, many modern physicians do not identify with this as a dominant role. They practice medicine in another role.

___ ⓪①②③ **Caregiver.** An innate desire to take care of other people or animals is the main characteristic of this role. The Caregiver's nonjudgmental, responsive, and nurturing spirit calms people who come in contact with them. With their power of empathy, they nurse others back to health, help them through a crisis, and care for the elderly. They make the perfect nurse, hospice counselor, or physical therapist.

___ ⓪①②③ **Animal Lover.** Able to bond with the animal kingdom. They enjoy spending time with animals and often have a special ability to communicate with them. People with this temperament will go out of their way to train, care for, or rescue animals in distress. Naturalists, zookeepers, ecologists, racehorse trainers, jockeys, search-and-rescue dog trainers, ASPCA officers, veterinarians, and avid pet owners usually inhabit the Animal Lover role.

___ ⓪①②③ **Artisan.** The crafter of artistic and functional objects, the Artisan is the craftsperson who makes beautiful and functional objects by hand. Many have a designer's aesthetic; their finely tuned senses are sensitive to subtleties of design, color, form, taste, touch. Chefs, fashion designers, interior designers, landscape designers, home remodelers, stonemasons, historic preservationists, antique appraisers, furniture makers, instrument makers, vintners, musicians, makeup artists, massage therapists, and hairstylists often embody the Artisan role.

___ ⓪①②③ **Hedonist.** The pleasure seeker whose philosophy is "Why put off what you can enjoy now?" and who lives for the moment. They are the ultimate shoppers, the impulse buyers. The dark side of hedonism is when it interferes with living sensibly, attaining long-range goals, and forming lasting relationships.

___ ⓪①②③ **Sensualist.** Considers life a grand feast for the senses, finds delight in the sensual world. They may love music, art, food, touch, nature, physical pleasures, scent, or beauty. This is a different role from the Hedonist in that it lacks the compulsive "pleasure, now, now, now" quality of the Hedonist.

Roles Common with Intuitive Thinkers. The next group of natural roles could fit you no matter what your personality type. They are especially common in people with an intuitive-thinker (NT) personality (ENTJ, INTJ, ENTP, INTP). If yours is one of these personality types, you should read this group of roles with special care.

___ ⓪①②③ **Scientist.** Seeking understanding and drawn to experiment, Scientists inquire into the mysteries of life to understand and explain the laws of nature or the universe. Some are interested in the physical universe, others in social or psychological science.

___ ⓪①②③ **Investigator.** Some detectives solve homicides; others seek a cure for cancer. What all Investigators have in common is a nose for a good clue and a mind that can't help looking under the surface to figure out the truth. They constantly pay attention to their environment with a critiquing ability that allows them to discover clues that might not be obvious to others. Detectives, scientists, inventors, mystery writers, counselors, lawyers, and crime scene investigators embody this gift.

___ ⓪①②③ **Entrepreneur.** Innovative by nature, the Entrepreneur builds businesses from the ground up. They make use of a wide range of natural talents, calling on multiple abilities to create something that didn't exist before. They take pride in being able to do it on their own, counting on their own resources, talents, and know-how.

___ ⓪①②③ **Innovator/Pioneer.** Goes where no man or woman has gone before, exploring the unknown territories of inner or outer worlds. Innovators bring new ideas, tools and toys, systems, theories, technologies, and discoveries into being. The ultimate "paradigm shifters," Innovators are drawn to operate on the edge of the unknown. Pioneers are similar, with one difference: their focus is less on creating something new than on exploring unknown territory or making use of a new technology as an early adopter. Both can operate without the agreement of society. They are often subject to the criticism of people who mindlessly defend the status quo.

___ ⓪①②③ **Amateur.** They delight in some specialty without the drive (or sometimes talent) to become a professional. The inspired amateur may love sports, the arts, cooking, cars, or any other area. They are often passionately engaged in their interest, but happy to let others do it for a living. Sometimes their passion takes so much of their attention that they fail to develop the same level of interest in their career. It is especially useful to claim this role if it fits you so you don't get overwhelmed by your hobbies or feel you have failed because your hobby is not your profession.

___ ⓪①②③ **Critic.** Critics have the eye of a hawk, the nose of a dog, the sonar of a bat. Nothing gets by them. Critics are born to find flaws or get to the truth under the surface appearances. They look for "what's wrong with this picture," sleuth out the hidden agenda, the design flaws, let us know why we shouldn't bother to see that movie. They have a built-in lie detector and tend to critique everything that crosses their radar screen.

___ ⓪①②③ **Geek.** Geeks have their attention narrowly focused on scientific or technical pursuits, often to the exclusion of other interests. At one time, *geek* was an insult by nongeeks confusing geekdom with social ineptitude. These days, the fact that many billionaires are geeks has changed public perception of the role.

___ ⓪①②③ **Lifelong Learner.** The perennial student, always curious to learn more. You should hope that your doctor is one of these people.

Roles Common with Intuitive Feelers. The next group of natural roles could fit you no matter what your personality type. They are especially common in people with an intuitive-feeler (NF) personality (ENFJ, INFJ, ENFP, INFP). If yours is one of these personality types, you should read this group of roles with special care.

___ ⓪①②③ **Guide/Coach/Counselor/Therapist.** These four roles are similar in some ways. They all involve working with a person or group to help them reach a goal or learn something new.

The Guide is the highest, most evolved form of teacher. Guides communicate wisdom, based on their personal mastery of a subject that comes from many years of experience. Guides transmit principles, the heart of the matter, and are often the most creative contributors to their field.

The Coach role assists a talented, committed person in reaching a goal. Many years ago, when I made up the term "career coach," I thought the term "career counselor" was insufficient, implying the provision mostly of information and advice. A Coach, on the other hand, figures out what it will take for you to reach your goal, elicits your strengths, assigns appropriate tasks, and makes sure you get to your goal. You do the work, whether that means practicing your sport every day or moving toward some important personal goal. A relationship with a Coach is a partnership between you and your Coach. Today there are personal, life, romance, business, career, and spiritual coaches in addition to the original—the athletic coach.

The Counselor provides advice and information, such as a lawyer, psychologist, the more capable physicians, and some of the best professors. They rely on a deep well of knowledge and years of experience to give you the best advice.

The Therapist works with people needing some form of help, who are suffering from some problem, and who take on the role of patient. What distinguishes this role is that the Therapist helps resolve or cure something that is perceived as a problem or shortcoming.

___ ⓪①②③ **Charming Enchanter.** The person who enchants others with a tale, a tune, an idea, a look. Enchanters are often quick-witted, articulate persuaders who easily influence others with their charisma, charm, or wit. Some, like John F. Kennedy and Ronald Reagan, combine the Enchanter role with the Leader role into a powerful political personality. Others use this role to convince people to buy what they're selling, from CEO to salesperson or museum director who uses charm to raise funds. On the dark side, the Enchanter manipulates or seduces others into their web with selfish designs.

___ ⓪①②③ **Romantic.** The passionate lover of life, people, culture, art, music, food, sex, science, technology, the unknown, the mysterious, or whatever their fancy may be. Floating in a starry sky, the Romantic is rarely realistic, always hopeful, forever seeking passion and connection. They may find reality tiresome.

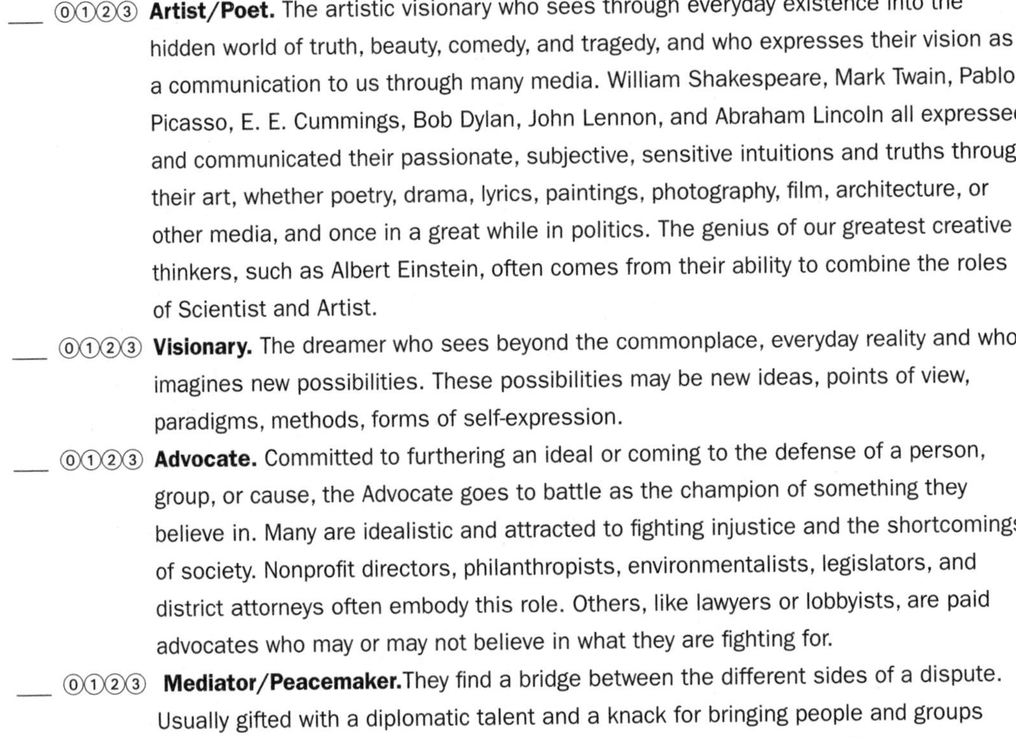

___ ⓪①②③ **Artist/Poet.** The artistic visionary who sees through everyday existence into the hidden world of truth, beauty, comedy, and tragedy, and who expresses their vision as a communication to us through many media. William Shakespeare, Mark Twain, Pablo Picasso, E. E. Cummings, Bob Dylan, John Lennon, and Abraham Lincoln all expressed and communicated their passionate, subjective, sensitive intuitions and truths through their art, whether poetry, drama, lyrics, paintings, photography, film, architecture, or other media, and once in a great while in politics. The genius of our greatest creative thinkers, such as Albert Einstein, often comes from their ability to combine the roles of Scientist and Artist.

___ ⓪①②③ **Visionary.** The dreamer who sees beyond the commonplace, everyday reality and who imagines new possibilities. These possibilities may be new ideas, points of view, paradigms, methods, forms of self-expression.

___ ⓪①②③ **Advocate.** Committed to furthering an ideal or coming to the defense of a person, group, or cause, the Advocate goes to battle as the champion of something they believe in. Many are idealistic and attracted to fighting injustice and the shortcomings of society. Nonprofit directors, philanthropists, environmentalists, legislators, and district attorneys often embody this role. Others, like lawyers or lobbyists, are paid advocates who may or may not believe in what they are fighting for.

___ ⓪①②③ **Mediator/Peacemaker.**They find a bridge between the different sides of a dispute. Usually gifted with a diplomatic talent and a knack for bringing people and groups together, they are facilitators who move people toward resolving conflicts.

Now that you have identified your roles, continue with the instructions that follow.

2. **Work the clues.**

- *Rate your roles.* After you've selected up to ten key natural roles, go back and review the ones you marked and rate the strength of each. Mark the numbered circles with a highlighter or pencil to indicate how strong this role is for you. Three ③ is the strongest rating ("runs my life"), two ② is moderately strong ("a significant part of me"), one ① is a small role ("rings true but is a smaller part of me"), and zero ⓪ ("I never play the role"). If you gave a role a zero, look to see why you picked it as one of your ten. If you truly never play the role, go pick another one.
- *Prioritize.* Now dig in deeper and look for the biggest, strongest, most compelling roles. Prioritize your top roles, with number one being the strongest. See if you can separate out roles that you might want to play somewhere in your life other than your career. For example, one of my roles is Nature-Wise Person. I grew up playing in the woods, had many wild animal pets, and am a sucker for a good nature show on TV. Now I live in a forest, where I see and interact with wild animals every day, which satisfies that role, but I wouldn't want a nature-centered career.

- *Designate your main role or roles.* Of your top natural roles, which one do you think is the big number one that expresses you best or takes the lead most often? If you're not sure, ask friends or family members for their opinion, and give it some time to become clearer. There may not be one that takes the lead. Instead, there may be two or more dominant roles that work together. For example, Abraham Lincoln might select Leader, Hero, Father, Politician, and Dealmaker, among others. No single one of these describes him. Only when you consider all of these roles together do you get more than a glimpse of his life. That may be the case with you too. But you and I aren't Abe—and you are best served by getting it down to one or two dominant roles.
- *How are your main roles expressed in your life?* For instance, you probably have one or more roles that influence the major choices in life. Are some of your biggest goals or common concerns and behaviors shaped by your main roles? For example, someone whose dominant role is Mother may not put much thought into a career choice; anything will do, as long as it leads to motherhood and family. Another person with Mother as a lead role may feel a passion for work caring for other people. The Nature-Wise Person may dislike working indoors. The Critic may find fault with almost everything.
- *Did your parents expect you to play any roles?* Did they encourage you to take on roles that you don't think come naturally? What roles do you think shaped your parents' life choices? Are you following in their footsteps or living authentically, in touch with your own natural roles?
- *Are there dark sides to any of your natural roles that play out now and then?* For example, the dark side of the Child role is acting helpless, throwing tantrums, or being unwilling to grow up. The dark side of the Comedian role is in play when the jokester hurts others to get a laugh. We all know the movie version of the dark side of the Warrior role. It shows up in other ways too—for example, when students forge blindly ahead into the wrong field of study because they want to prove they can do it.

3. **Any definite career design components?** Add them to your Definite Career Design Components list.
4. **Strong clues.** Put anything worth further investigation in your Work Strong Clues list.
5. **Careers to explore.** Go to your Careers to Explore list and write down any career titles you want to add to your career choice research effort.

   - What careers might make use of your dominant roles? You might want to spend some time brainstorming this question and asking some people you know with a lot of knowledge of the working world. (See Chapter 14 for how to brainstorm.)
   - Do careers that attract you have a connection with your natural roles? What connection do you see?

CHAPTER 20

JOB FUNCTIONS

Whether you have a job or work on your own, you are paid for just one thing: performing functions. Nearly everyone who loves their work spends their days performing functions that express their talents and training fully. They do what comes naturally. This is one of the most basic elements of career success and satisfaction. Some functions fit you better than others because they make better use of your natural talents. We have discussed the concept of "natural fit" previously. Now we are going to take another look at this subject from a different perspective.

At the most basic level you want to be good at what you do, but good isn't enough. I used to be talented at shoveling horse manure. I could fling it far and wide. But was it satisfying? It was kind of interesting for the first ten minutes of the first day, but after that it was a drag, even though the farmer said I "had the gift." This chapter is about sorting out the main functions you will use in your work, looking for functions you perform with natural mastery *and also love to do*. Competence alone is the booby prize when it comes to workplace functions. Deciding what job functions you can look forward to performing every day will be one of the most critical choices you'll make in this book, since functions make some of the best career selection clues.

THREE KINDS OF JOB FUNCTIONS

Even though there are more than ten thousand different job titles, a common theme of activity underlies the hustle and bustle of the working world. Human beings perform activities in three general areas, working mainly with *people, information,* or *things*.

Some work mainly in one category. For example, a house painter spends the bulk of the day working with things, like a paintbrush, ladder, house, and paints. Many careers, however, involve combining job functions across categories. A software salesperson works in two categories, people and information. The salesperson's primary job function is selling to people, but a secondary function is understanding and communicating technical information. Surgeons engage in activities in all three categories: they diagnose and work on the human anatomy, a thing, in the same way a mechanic works on a car engine, as their primary job function. Before the surgery they consult with patients as people and educate or present them with information to improve their health. Your task in this chapter is to explore your own perfect combination of future job functions.

Most careers make use of functions in one of these three categories more often than the other two. For example, customer service representatives, supervisors, and therapists mainly perform people-centered functions. Computer programmers, songwriters, and editors mainly perform information-centered functions. Structural engineers, sculptors, and landscape architects work mainly with things, objects, the physical world.

FUNCTIONS ARE AT THE CENTER OF ALL JOBS

One trick to choosing a career that perfectly fits you is to check out what the career actually involves on a functional level. You want to choose the perfect combination of job functions for *you*—not just a career title. A nice title like "garbological operative" may actually involve picking up people's smelly trash. Career titles often don't really tell you enough about what functions you will perform.

If you've got a few career paths in mind, zero in on the primary tasks and activities you are expected to do throughout the day. Remember, *employers hire and pay you to do specific tasks*. Whether you're selling tomatoes or pharmaceuticals, sales is the same function regardless of the field. The functions of technical writing and abstract research are common activities performed in most academic fields, whether the field is biology, physics, or psychology. Careers in the same ballpark usually employ similar job functions.

For instance, jewelry designers, gourmet chefs, hairstylists, and cosmetic surgeons all have very similar job functions. Regardless of the specialized product they create, the daily job functions are very similar—creating works of 3-D art, critiquing physical objects, precisely using tools, an eye for design, and fine hand dexterity. The same holds true for other major career disciplines. Most physical scientists (physics, chemistry, climatology) perform similar functions regardless of their specialty.

Need lots of variety on the job? The more complex the career, the greater the variety of job functions. For instance, a surgeon who works at a teaching hospital will perform a couple of primary functions and a few secondary functions. In a typical workweek the surgeon primarily practices clinical medicine and diagnoses spatial problems for patients, physically repairs the anatomy through surgery, and teaches a group of medical students. Secondary functions might include advising students, and some administrative management activities associated with being part of a big hospital setting.

HOW DO I KNOW WHAT FUNCTIONS SUIT ME?

Getting a handle on your job functions should be pretty straightforward. As you look back over your life, you'll find that some activities come more naturally to you than others. As you consider what job functions to perform, stay grounded in bedrock: do what comes naturally. People always talk about skills as if they are most important. A skill is something you learn to do, whether it comes naturally or not. Your skills may be what matters most to a boss, but before you get to the point of having a boss, figure out what job functions will put a smile on your face so you can have your life rock to a sweet, strong tune year after year.

Ideally, you should know what functions come naturally to you even before you go to college—to help you pick the right major to study. Unfortunately, this usually isn't so. Many young people interested in the business world select accounting to study because it's "business." Sheila, a young accountant working at a bank, quickly realized that she despised the primary job functions that accountants perform all day—analyzing, organizing, and recording data. As an extroverted Tribal, her gifts for networking and bringing people together were useless on the job.

Like most young people, she made a serious blunder by ignoring her natural abilities when choosing her college major and falling for what she thought was a sexy title. Hoping to improve her analytical skills, she chose a field that engaged her weakest abilities. This common mistake never pans out. Without suitable natural talent, all the practice in the world will not make your job functions any more natural or fun. If you're not a natural at analyzing and crunching numbers, accounting or finance will torture you. Obviously, the only way to know what functions will suit you is to have a full understanding and appreciation for your natural talents (see chapter 16).

Inquiry 20-1 **JOB FUNCTIONS**

This inquiry allows you to sort out which job functions you intend to use as major components in your future career. After reading the instructions, you select from a list of functions that you do well naturally. Then you narrow your selections down to several major ones—the functions you want to use a lot, every day.

Your lack of experience may interfere with your selections—you probably haven't done many of the functions listed. So, at least to some extent, you have to guess. Use your self-knowledge, intuition, and gut instinct to make some selections. Obviously, you don't want to rely only on a bunch of guesses, so going through this inquiry may be just the beginning of exploring which job functions, when combined, will give you the perfect career.

The goal here is to separate what comes naturally from learned skills that may not come so naturally. If you were a wind-up toy robot and each morning the kid who owned you wound you up and then watched you perform the tricks you were programmed to do, what would those tricks be? What are the functions you can't help doing? For example, I once had some very logical engineer types working for me. All I had to do to get them to leap at a logical problem was to wiggle it in front of them like a nice juicy worm in front of a fish. That is the sort of thing you want to look for in yourself. These functions don't show up only in a work environment. Even if you've never had a job, look through your entire life to see what worms make the fish in you jump.

1. Start at the beginning of the job functions list. Place a check mark in front of the job functions that come naturally to you or express what you do best. Be selective and just mark the most important stuff. Do your best to limit your selections to just a few—say no more than fifteen. Some entries have several versions of a function on one line. If one or more really stands out, circle it.
2. It may be helpful to ask close friends or parents to go through this inquiry as well—especially if you are a guy, since we guys are often a little dim at noticing this sort of thing. Others may notice things about you that aren't obvious to you.
3. After you've gone through the whole list and made your selections, go back to examine all the ones you marked and rate your natural ability for each by checking or shading the numbered circles: 1 is the lowest rating, 5 is the highest. Don't worry if this takes a while. Once you've rated all your selections, go to the end of the list of job functions, where you can get the next instructions.

People-Oriented Functions and Activities: Primarily One-on-One

Problem Solving, Providing Expert Advice

___ ①②③④⑤ Mentoring, one-on-one teaching, instructing, training, tutoring
___ ①②③④⑤ Counseling, coaching, guiding, empowering
___ ①②③④⑤ Healing, treating the diseases or problems of, rehabilitating
___ ①②③④⑤ Advising, consulting with
___ ①②③④⑤ Assessing, evaluating
___ ①②③④⑤ Diagnosing, analyzing or understanding an individual's needs, mood, motives, responses, behavior, etc.
___ ①②③④⑤ Using intuition or nonverbal clues to understand individuals
___ ①②③④⑤ Observing, studying behaviors
___ ①②③④⑤ Other ______________________________

Supporting, Enabling, Hosting, Entertaining

___ ①②③④⑤ Encouraging, supporting
___ ①②③④⑤ Providing emotional support
___ ①②③④⑤ Promoting, being an agent for others
___ ①②③④⑤ Listening
___ ①②③④⑤ Being understanding and patient with others
___ ①②③④⑤ Enabling, assisting other people to locate information
___ ①②③④⑤ Helping, serving, providing needs of individuals

___ ①②③④⑤ Assisting, caretaking
___ ①②③④⑤ Hosting
___ ①②③④⑤ Entertaining, amusing, conversing with
___ ①②③④⑤ Giving pleasure
___ ①②③④⑤ Using your personal charisma
___ ①②③④⑤ Other ______________________________

Managing, Informing, General Administrative Activities

___ ①②③④⑤ Cultivating and maintaining relationships
___ ①②③④⑤ Selecting, screening, hiring
___ ①②③④⑤ Managing, supervising
___ ①②③④⑤ Giving instructions, providing information
___ ①②③④⑤ Persuading, selling, motivating, influencing, enrolling, recruiting
___ ①②③④⑤ Interviewing
___ ①②③④⑤ Communicating verbally with
___ ①②③④⑤ Bringing together, introducing
___ ①②③④⑤ Networking, building alliances and relationships
___ ①②③④⑤ Negotiating between individuals, arbitrating
___ ①②③④⑤ Other ______________________________

People-Oriented Functions and Activities: Primarily with Groups, Organizations, the Public, or Humanity

Problem Solving, Providing Expert Advice to a Group

___ ①②③④⑤ Empowering, enabling a group
___ ①②③④⑤ Instructing, teaching, training a group
___ ①②③④⑤ Guiding a group through a healing process
___ ①②③④⑤ Diagnosing, analyzing, or understanding a group's existing or potential needs, mood, motives, responses, behavior
___ ①②③④⑤ Using intuition or nonverbal clues to understand a group or individuals in a group setting
___ ①②③④⑤ Consulting to affect a group or organization's productivity, behavior
___ ①②③④⑤ Advising a group, providing expertise
___ ①②③④⑤ Designing events or educational experiences
___ ①②③④⑤ Creating activities, games
___ ①②③④⑤ Other ______________________________

Managing, Leading, Interacting with a Group

___ ①②③④⑤ Managing, leading a group, organization, company
___ ①②③④⑤ Initiating, creating, founding a group of people or a company

___ ①②③④⑤ Supervising, captaining a group or team
___ ①②③④⑤ Supporting a team, work group, orchestra as a member
___ ①②③④⑤ Leading group in recreation, games, exercise, travel, rehabilitation
___ ①②③④⑤ Negotiating between groups, resolving conflicts or disputes, bringing conflicting groups together
___ ①②③④⑤ Inspiring a group
___ ①②③④⑤ Facilitating, guiding a group
___ ①②③④⑤ Other ______________________________

Influencing and Persuading a Group

___ ①②③④⑤ Persuading, motivating, convincing, or selling to a group
___ ①②③④⑤ Using personal charisma
___ ①②③④⑤ Networking with groups
___ ①②③④⑤ Communicating verbally with groups, public speaking, or communicating verbally through the media
___ ①②③④⑤ Communicating with people via art, music, writing, film, or other art forms
___ ①②③④⑤ Other ______________________________

Entertaining and Hosting Group Functions

___ ①②③④⑤ Hosting, entertaining socially
___ ①②③④⑤ Amusing, providing entertainment or pleasure
___ ①②③④⑤ Performing, acting
___ ①②③④⑤ Presenting to people via TV, films, seminars, speeches
___ ①②③④⑤ Selecting, screening prospective members or employees
___ ①②③④⑤ Assisting, serving, helping
___ ①②③④⑤ Other ______________________________

Information-Oriented Functions and Activities: Primarily with Ideas, Data, Media, Knowledge, Wisdom, or Art

Creating, Designing, and Using Imagination

___ ①②③④⑤ Idea generating, creating, inventing, imagining
___ ①②③④⑤ Asking new questions, pioneering new ideas
___ ①②③④⑤ Brainstorming
___ ①②③④⑤ Drawing, painting, filming, photographing
___ ①②③④⑤ Creating original works of art, including music
___ ①②③④⑤ Creating visual or written presentation or presentations using other media
___ ①②③④⑤ Creating marketing materials, advertisements, promotional campaigns
___ ①②③④⑤ Creating activities, games, or other experiential learning activities
___ ①②③④⑤ Designing events or educational experiences

___ ①②③④⑤ Writing fiction, creative writing—poetry, essays, novels, scripts
___ ①②③④⑤ Performing, acting
___ ①②③④⑤ Presenting to people via TV, films, seminars, speeches
___ ①②③④⑤ Information engineering, database design, computer programming
___ ①②③④⑤ Designing information architecture, such as in Web site design
___ ①②③④⑤ Creating software or similar works
___ ①②③④⑤ Designing research experiments to make new discoveries
___ ①②③④⑤ Other ____________________

Problem Solving, Researching, Investigating

___ ①②③④⑤ Diagnosing by seeing the relationship between clues
___ ①②③④⑤ Analyzing by perceiving patterns in data, events, or processes or accurately evaluating information
___ ①②③④⑤ Seeing through masses of information to the central principles or most important facts
___ ①②③④⑤ Breaking masses of data down into components, analyzing
___ ①②③④⑤ Synthesizing: combining parts to form a whole
___ ①②③④⑤ Systematizing, prioritizing, categorizing, or organizing information
___ ①②③④⑤ Deciding what data or information to collect
___ ①②③④⑤ Conducting research to develop new ideas, theories
___ ①②③④⑤ Researching by observing behavior or phenomena
___ ①②③④⑤ Researching by gathering or compiling information
___ ①②③④⑤ Making decisions about the meaning of data or information
___ ①②③④⑤ Other ____________________

Reading, Learning, Mastering a Body of Knowledge

___ ①②③④⑤ Reading, learning, gathering information
___ ①②③④⑤ Interpreting other people's concepts, ideas
___ ①②③④⑤ Adapting information to suit another purpose
___ ①②③④⑤ Combining existing ideas or concepts into new ones
___ ①②③④⑤ Mastering a specialized body of knowledge, expertise, wisdom, lore
___ ①②③④⑤ Other ____________________

Critiquing, Evaluating, Making Recommendations

___ ①②③④⑤ Critiquing other people's ideas
___ ①②③④⑤ Critiquing works of art, such as in script reading, book reviews, film reviews
___ ①②③④⑤ Critical writing, such as nonfiction, journalism, and science writing
___ ①②③④⑤ Technical writing, such as in business, law, technology, medicine, public policy
___ ①②③④⑤ Judging, evaluating, or appraising information

___ ①②③④⑤ Using physical senses to evaluate information
___ ①②③④⑤ Process improvement, making systems more efficient
___ ①②③④⑤ Risk and opportunity cost analysis
___ ①②③④⑤ Making recommendations, providing solutions
___ ①②③④⑤ Troubleshooting, debugging, and maintaining software
___ ①②③④⑤ Editing to improve content
___ ①②③④⑤ Using mathematics, numbers, statistics, working with formulas to evaluate
___ ①②③④⑤ Other ______________________________

Organizing, Planning, Improving, Other General Administrative Activities

___ ①②③④⑤ Organizing information, projects, or events
___ ①②③④⑤ Managing projects, setting goals and milestones, budgeting, status reporting
___ ①②③④⑤ Planning, strategizing, forecasting
___ ①②③④⑤ Translating, interpreting information to another language, medium, or style
___ ①②③④⑤ Copyediting to improve grammar, syntax
___ ①②③④⑤ Retrieving or finding information, researching, compiling information
___ ①②③④⑤ Entering data into a computer, data entry, word processing
___ ①②③④⑤ Comparing, proofing
___ ①②③④⑤ Accounting, bookkeeping, business mathematics
___ ①②③④⑤ Record keeping, storing, filing
___ ①②③④⑤ Other ______________________________

Thing-Oriented Functions and Activities: Primarily with Objects, Tools, the Human Body, or the Physical World

Problem Solving and Understanding Complex Physical Systems

___ ①②③④⑤ Understanding complex physical systems such as in the physical sciences, medicine, engineering, and technology
___ ①②③④⑤ Diagnosing and analyzing complex mechanical systems, such as a mechanic, engineer, physician, or veterinarian does
___ ①②③④⑤ Repairing or improving complex mechanical systems
___ ①②③④⑤ Other ______________________________

Creating, Designing, Inventing Physical Objects, Including Art

___ ①②③④⑤ Designing complex physical systems
___ ①②③④⑤ Creating new theories, understanding or interpreting physical systems
___ ①②③④⑤ Inventing, creating, designing original devices or objects
___ ①②③④⑤ Directing films or plays, choreographing scenes, storyboarding
___ ①②③④⑤ Creating works of three-dimensional art
___ ①②③④⑤ Other ______________________________

Evaluating, Critiquing, Fixing, and Repairing Objects and Things

___ ①②③④⑤ Evaluating and critiquing physical objects, including food, arts, design, or the human body

___ ①②③④⑤ Appraising and judging physical objects, including food, arts, design, or the human body

___ ①②③④⑤ Repairing or restoring things, maintaining physical structures

___ ①②③④⑤ Assembling

___ ①②③④⑤ Other ________________________________

Crafting, Beautifying, Using Tools to Produce Objects

___ ①②③④⑤ Sculpting, shaping, tooling

___ ①②③④⑤ Crafting (combining artistic and motor skills to fashion things)

___ ①②③④⑤ Employing fine hand dexterity (as used by surgeon, dentist, craftsman, artist, musician, etc.)

___ ①②③④⑤ Precision use of tools

___ ①②③④⑤ Manufacturing or mass-producing objects

___ ①②③④⑤ Cooking, preparing, or displaying food

___ ①②③④⑤ Choosing, arranging objects artistically

___ ①②③④⑤ Utilizing eye for design, color, texture, or proportion

___ ①②③④⑤ Using sensual acuity of sight, sound, smell, taste, or feel

___ ①②③④⑤ Other ________________________________

Athletics, Performing Expertly with the Body, Manipulating the Human Anatomy

___ ①②③④⑤ Dancing or choreographing dance routines

___ ①②③④⑤ Using physical agility, fine sensory-motor skills, strength, and dexterity in athletics and other fields such as law enforcement, firefighting, emergency medicine

___ ①②③④⑤ Using spatial visualization for gymnastics, figure skating, diving, and other sports that require visualizing body movements

___ ①②③④⑤ Performing stunts or other extreme physical feats

___ ①②③④⑤ Massaging, adjusting, touching, hands-on healing

___ ①②③④⑤ Other ________________________________

Operating Machines and Equipment

___ ①②③④⑤ Operating an airplane, ship or boat, truck or car, motorcycle or bicycle

___ ①②③④⑤ Using large tools such as bulldozers and other construction machinery, tanks

___ ①②③④⑤ Constructing buildings or other large objects, such as bridges and roads

___ ①②③④⑤ Operating, controlling, or guiding machines

___ ①②③④⑤ Tending machines

___ ①②③④⑤ Fighting, using firearms or other weapons

___ ①②③④⑤ Installing
___ ①②③④⑤ Cleaning, preparing, washing, dusting
___ ①②③④⑤ Moving, storing, warehousing, carrying, lifting, handling
___ ①②③④⑤ Other ______________________________

Interacting with the Physical World, Including Nature

___ ①②③④⑤ Navigating, orienteering, pathfinding, exploring
___ ①②③④⑤ Farming, gardening, growing or tending plants or animals
___ ①②③④⑤ Exploring aspects of physical environment, nature
___ ①②③④⑤ Hunting, trapping, fishing
___ ①②③④⑤ Other ______________________________

4. Look over your selections. Are there any themes or clusters of similar functions? Do most of your highest-rated functions involve people, or information, or things? Are there any clusters of functions in a specific subcategory, such as "Problem Solving Providing Expert Advice" or "Managing, Leading, Interacting with a Group"? (If one section dominates, that's a pretty good clue that your work should concentrate in that area.)
5. Do your selections align well with your profile of talents discovered in prior chapters? For instance, people with a strong spatial orientation, talent for practical hands-on problem solving, and sensory acuity often find their most natural functions in the "Crafting, Beautifying, and Using Tools" subcategory of working with things.
6. Narrow down your strongest functions to just a few, no more than five. Some of you may have a tough time reducing the number to five because you don't want to give up anything you like to do. You don't have to toss anything out—just do your best to focus on those functions you think will be the dominant, most used functions in your future career.

When people describe someone who is good at lots of different things, they may say that person is "Leonardo-like," referring to Leonardo da Vinci. Actually, Leonardo got paid for painting, sculpture, and designing buildings, three similar functions. His other activities, inventing things and studying the physical world, were more like hobbies.

One way to begin narrowing things down is to look for clusters of functions that work together. If you selected a group of activities that can operate as a series of steps in a process, you can group them into a single function. For example, a cluster of functions such as using intuition or nonverbal clues to understand individuals, observing behaviors, listening, assessing, diagnosing moods and motives, and making recommendations can be grouped under a single combined function such as advising or counseling.

Another way to reduce the number of your selections is to imagine performing them for several hours each day forever. Do any of them lose their appeal when put to the volume test? Push yourself to get past the romance of functions that may sound good for only a few hours a week or less. Remember, you don't have to throw anything away for good. Some functions you can perform only occasionally at work or as a hobby.

7. Make commitments. If you are sure any of these functions will definitely be an important part of your careers, put them in your Definite Career Design Components list.
8. If you've come up with some strong clues, put them—you guessed it—in your Work Strong Clues list.

Inquiry 20-2 ADVANCED JOB FUNCTIONS INQUIRY FOR PEOPLE WHO ARE CHOOSING THEIR FINAL CAREER NOW

This is an extension of the previous inquiry for those who need to narrow it down all the way and make a final career or job choice now. This may be too much to handle for those who are still exploring and learning. You may not have the experience to do this part yet. But whatever your age or experience, if you've got to pick that career or job now, this part is for you.

1. **Primary job function.** Most careers/jobs have one primary function and some secondary ones. A surgeon's primary function is all about blades and blood, a musician's is playing an instrument, a mutual fund manager's is picking stocks. Their primary function is what they do most of the time and the main thing they get paid for, even if they may do other things. It is possible to have more than one or two primary functions, but that is most common for entrepreneurs and farmers; it's less common for people who work for an organization. See if you can pick one or two of your final five as your primary function or functions. If you can't, don't worry. Do the next step in this inquiry.
2. **Secondary job functions.** Are any of your final five functions obviously secondary or supporting functions? For example, someone who sells high-end audio gear may have selling as a primary function and teaching, advising, and learning about new gear as secondary.
3. **Having difficulty sorting out what's primary and what's not?** Try this. List your final five in a vertical list. Then try the playful technique we used in Part 1. Imagine that you died and woke up in heaven with an angel wringing his hands and saying he had made a terrible mistake. The person who was supposed to get run over by the bus was right behind you and wearing the same clothes. You get to go back, and you can pick four of your top five functions to use in your job. So you have to drop one of the five. Which one would it be? Now imagine it is 2050, you are the same age you are now, and you were just blown to smithereens by a space alien. Medical science can rebuild you, but they can rebuild only three main functions. Which one would get dropped from what's now your final four? Keep it light. Play around with different scenarios to discover what are likely to be your primary and secondary functions. Want a more serious approach? Try the next method.
4. **Simulate your workday.** Create some experimental pie charts to visually imagine how much of

your day might make use of your top functions. Each slice represents the percentage of the day you would perform each function. The following example illustrates a workday breakout of an actual career, someone who runs her own arts-and-crafts business. There is one primary function and three secondary functions. Notice that the primary function, crafting beautiful objects, comprises about half of the workday, and the secondary tasks and activities are support functions that are performed less often but are just as important to the job. Create some experimental pie charts, simulating several possible workday scenarios by varying the percentage of time for each function. Explore different combinations until one clicks for you.

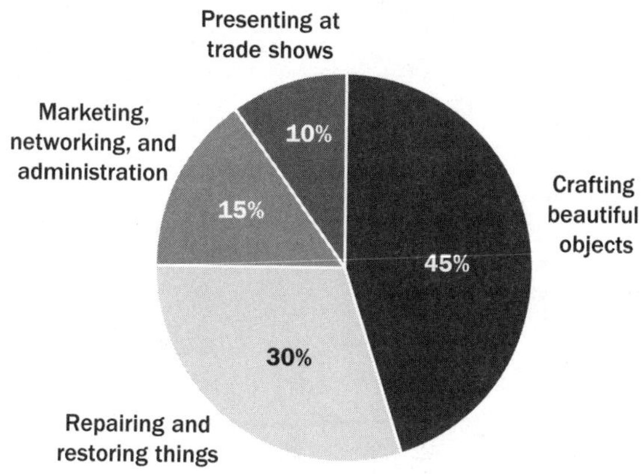

5. **Date your job functions before you marry them.** If you feel a little hesitant to designate some of your job functions as primary or secondary, don't worry. You may need some experience before you can make confident choices here. Flag any of your top functions that need a test drive. Find a way to experiment in the real world in some sort of job, internship, hobby, or volunteer activity. For example, I had one young woman client who measured extremely high in 3-D spatial orientation, but she had never had a chance to use it in her life. She was an advertising copywriter, mainly working with ideas all day. Her spatial talent to design and build things was latent and untested. To test out whether she might enjoy performing the spatial design function, she set up a project to design and build a deck for the back of her house. She bought books, taught herself how to do it all, and completed the design in less than a week. She loved this project so much that she is now studying to be an architect. A test drive is worth a million words; there's no better way to know if you're going to love what you do.
6. **Commitments and strong clues?** If this final part of the functions inquiry yields more commitments and/or clues, you know which lists to put them on.

CAN YOU BE HAPPY WORKING IN A SUBJECT AREA YOU LOVE, NO MATTER WHAT FUNCTIONS YOU PERFORM?

The short answer is no, subject matter alone is not enough. For example, an administrative assistant at an environmental nonprofit was confused: she loved the subject matter and mission of her organization, and the nonprofit was doing great things in the world, but she couldn't figure out why she was bored most of the day and felt guilty about it. She wondered if she was expecting too much from a job. The root of the problem lay not in her expectations but in the job functions she performed. Answering telephones, scheduling meetings, and shuffling papers proved a bad match for her natural talents. Although she loved the subject matter at work, her strongest talents sat idle all day. She went back to school, became a social scientist, and now loves her career.

SECTION 5

Why You Work

The man who sinks his pickaxe into the ground wants that stroke to mean something. The convict's stroke is not the same as the prospector's, for the obvious reason that the prospector's stroke has meaning and the convict's stroke has none. . . . Prison is not a mere physical horror. It is using a pickaxe to no purpose. . . .

—*Antoine de Saint-Exupéry,* Wind, Sand and Stars

So far your work as a Detective has been directed at uncovering and understanding your innate talents, personality traits, and job functions. Although choosing the perfect career demands a good fit between your natural gifts and your work, it takes more to put all the pieces in place. Even if you do something well, if you have no purpose, meaning, or mission in doing it, you'll be like a talented hamster on a wheel. This brings up another major career choice question—why work?

Most people work because they have to, not because they want to. Many talented midcareer professionals say they are either bored stiff or deeply uninterested in their daily job. Although they use some of their natural talents, they say they have no goals and no passion for the job. Giving their best isn't enough.

Having meaningful work and a sense of direction is a huge piece of what makes us happy. What makes a doctor bound around the hospital like a teenager, wearing out interns a third of his age? Why do orchestra conductors live so long? Perhaps it's because they cannot bear to quit what they're doing. It's hard to find a *retired* orchestra conductor. Never underestimate the benefits of passion and enthusiasm in a career.

Each of the chapters in this section will help you explore what careers might light your fire. People can find meaning in interesting subject matter, in the delight of using their best functions in the right environment, or in fulfilling important goals. You might as well go for all three.

Don't overlook the desire to contribute as a major motivation. Research at the National Institutes of Health has shown that generosity and contribution make all the bells go off in a primitive part of the brain—not in the brains of those on the receiving end, but those on the *giving* end. If advertisers have shaped your ideas about what constitutes the good life (emphasis on *getting*), you might have missed this point and cut yourself off from one of the greatest sources of pleasure.

> The only ones among you who will be happy are those who will have sought and found how to serve.
>
> —*Albert Schweitzer*

CHAPTER

21 GOALS

In the long run you only hit what you aim at. Therefore, though you should fail immediately, you had better aim at something high.

—*Henry David Thoreau*

My friend John Goddard sat down at his kitchen table at the age of fifteen, wrote down 127 life goals, and then decided to fulfill all of them. The list included such things as exploring the major rivers of the world from source to mouth, climbing the major peaks, piloting the fastest aircraft, studying primitive cultures around the world, and much, much more. Now in his seventies, he has fulfilled nearly all of the goals on his list and hundreds more he created later. Some of them turned into major adventures. He was the first known person in history to explore the entire length of the Nile River, which he did by kayak. The *Los Angeles Times* called this "the most amazing adventure of this generation." He studied 260 primitive tribes and traveled more than a million miles on his adventures. People call him "the real Indiana Jones." This just scratches the surface of his amazing life.

You might not want as much adventure as my friend John, but you probably don't want "Lived a mechanical life" engraved on your tombstone. You may remember from earlier parts of the book how easily we can let life become automatic. If you want yours to have passion, flavor, and zest, set some life goals that will pull you forward into the future.

The value of setting long-term goals goes far beyond reasonable expectations. Whatever you want, you vastly increase your chances of living a life you love if you write down and commit to long-term goals. What do you want to include in your life? What sort of future are you willing to create for yourself? Before we take on that challenge, let's use a short inquiry to check out the present situation. It may seem obvious, but when you want to get somewhere, it is always useful to know where you are starting from.

Inquiry 21-1 **LIFELINE**

1. Open your notebook to a new blank page. Write "Lifeline" in big letters at the top of the page.
2. Now draw the longest line you can along the length of the piece of paper. This represents your life from beginning to end, your lifeline. Write "The Beginning" at one end of the line and "The End" at the other.

3. Draw short perpendicular lines across the lifeline to represent each decade of your life, past, present, and future up to one hundred (age ten, age twenty, and so forth). Make a mark and write "Now" at the place that represents your present age.
4. Start at the beginning of your life. Write in significant events from your birth to the present time. Focus on events where you experienced significant growth, major life events, tragedies, and times you attempted or accomplished an important goal.
5. Now take a look at your future. Write in the big specific goals you have created for your future.
6. How did you do? If you were able to write in more than a very few goals in the future, you are among a tiny minority. Most people find they can't write much, if anything, in the future part of their lifeline. Few people write anything more specific than "graduate, go to grad school, get a good job, have a family, retire."
7. Okay, enough for now. If you have a clear and compelling set of life goals that stretch way out into the distant future, go on to another chapter. If you don't, please read on.

CREATING YOUR FUTURE

> All men dream, but not equally. Those who dream by night in the dusty recesses of their minds wake in the day to find that it was vanity: but the dreamers of the day are dangerous men, for they may act their dream with open eyes, to make it possible.
>
> —*T. E. Lawrence*

Many studies about wealth creation have looked at how people became wealthy. Oddly enough, most who became rich didn't walk through life with dollar signs in their eyes. In fact, most reported that they hardly noticed that they had become rich. They must have had something else on their minds. That something else was a passion for life. Going for what could be called "inner wealth," they were fulfilling values more important to them than money, and were passionately absorbed in their work. Their primary motivations were things such as solving problems, the adventure of succeeding, making a contribution, exploring possibilities, creativity, and having fun.

Let's stop right here for a minute. I have a question for you. Please think about this question and write down whatever comes to mind before you read any further. Get a piece of paper and a pen. Ready? Here's the question: *How would you know that you did a really good job at something?* Please don't read on after this line until you have thought about this question and come up with an answer.

Okay, let's check out your answers. There are two different kinds of answers people give to this question, external and internal. With external answers, you know you did a good job because the boss gave you a pat on the back or a raise or a gold statue, your picture was in the paper, your record went platinum, or you could afford the mansion on the hill. Internal answers are completely different: you know you did a good job because you were happy with the result, you felt satisfied, you enjoyed using your talents fully, it was fun, you kept a promise to yourself, you fulfilled an important goal, you made a contribution that mattered to you, you built some sort of "inner wealth."

Most people who build major financial wealth give internal answers to this question. They aren't out to please other people or meet some cultural standard. Their main goal is rarely to make a lot of money. Instead, they are motivated by goals that continually add to their inner wealth. We'll call this kind of goal a "meta-goal," which basically translates to "the goal of the goal."

THREE LEVELS OF GOALS

Meta-goals

The highest level of goals are the meta-goals. The prefix *meta-* means "higher" or "more comprehensive." These goals express big, broad, general desires, ideas, and concepts that inspire and motivate you from within, like:

- Pleasure
- Security
- Avoid helplessness
- Self-sufficiency
- Explore possibilities
- Procreate
- Have fun
- Love
- Health/well-being
- Be right
- Avoid pain
- Survive
- Self-expression
- Relate
- Self-control
- Succeeding
- Ecstasy
- Self-esteem
- Dominate
- Contribute
- Create
- Adventure
- Belong
- Longevity
- Develop competence
- Peace
- Desirability
- Avoid domination

Specific Goals

At the second level are specific goals that state more precisely how you will achieve your meta-goals. Someone with a meta-goal such as adventure might have several specific goals, including paddling down the Yangtze, eating fresh red snapper by moonlight, photographing a snow leopard, and trekking Annapurna.

Action Steps

At the third level are the nitty-gritty tasks and action steps you carry out to achieve your goals and plans. Action steps are really a to-do list, much like using a daily planner.

GOAL SETTING 101

Set Meta-goals First

When people set long-term goals, they often look in all the wrong places, focusing on specific goals and action steps. The most productive long-term goal setting begins with meta-goals—your deepest desires, passions, and dreams. Meta-goals are the "real" goals or underlying motives behind your conscious specific goals; they are the reasons why you pursue your more tangible actions and plans. To be absolutely clear about what a meta-goal is, go back to Chapter 7 and review the section "How to Figure Out What You Really Want."

Some meta-goals are hardwired, rooted in basic human instincts such as feeling good, feeling safe, and avoiding pain. You are programmed to fulfill these goals. The nervous, twitchy bunny in the backyard is programmed the same way, to fulfill the most basic meta-goal of all—survival. You don't have to do anything to keep these meta-goals online: they run automatically, no choice. (We'll look at those in the next inquiry.) Unlike the bunny, you can create your own goals.

Make Your Goals Correspond with What You Really Want. When we get what we don't really want, it could be the result of a random accident or the fickle finger of fate, but often it is because we aren't aware of the meta-goal behind our choices. Remember Leo the lawyer, back in chapter 7: he concentrated on his specific goals without looking to see if they truly supported his meta-goals. By the time he finished, he had almost the opposite of what he really wanted. But because he'd achieved his specific goals, he had no idea why he was miserable.

Set lower-level goals consistent with your meta-goals. Don't set goals you aren't fully committed to achieving. Just writing down some words won't make anything happen. You've got to sort out what you most want, what you are willing to stretch for even if huge obstacles arise.

Create Goals for Every Important Category of Your Life. Each part of your life overlaps other parts. In addition to your career goals, create goals for the other major areas of your life, including family, friends, relationships, self-expression, health, fitness, fun and adventure, emotional well-being, self-development, spirituality, and education and learning.

State Your Goals Clearly. Well-founded goals contain specific ingredients that boost their effectiveness. Make them highly specific—sharpen up your goals, avoid fuzziness, and say exactly what you mean. Make them measurable—settle on a definite completion date if possible. For example, "Within three years, I'll have a career that will engage my strongest natural talents solving interesting problems most of the day." "I'll circumnavigate the globe in a sailboat over a four-year period starting in 2020." Setting clear goals is like having a compass to navigate with; you know where you're heading.

Write Them Down. Get your goals down on paper. Your head is about as useful for keeping goals as a crocheted bathtub is for holding water.

Create Both Short-Term and Long-Term Goals. I recommend creating a comprehensive life plan along a timeline to map out your goals. For each major area of your life (career, family, health, and so forth), create goals to achieve within one month, six months, one year, two years, five years, ten years. This exercise will bear sweet fruit if you go back to your goals regularly, perhaps every month or so, to remind yourself and recommit.

Turn Your Important Life Goals Into Projects. Otherwise they'll never happen.

Set Goals That Take You as Far as You Are Willing to Stretch. Most folks set reasonable goals that don't require much of a stretch. In terms of career choices, mainstream wisdom persuades us all to be sensible about career goals. If you want an okay life, set reasonable goals. If you want an extraordinary life, forget about reasonable. Reasonable people adapt to the world around them. Unreasonable people shape the world to fit them. Commit to achieving your goals and turn them into a lifelong adventure.

> Nothing is ever accomplished by a reasonable man.
>
> —*George Bernard Shaw*

What follows are two inquiries that go about goal setting in somewhat different ways. You may find both to be useful. Do the first; afterward, if you feel you've done an excellent and complete job of setting goals, don't bother with the second.

Inquiry 21-2 GOAL SETTING, METHOD 1

Use this inquiry as an opportunity to map out goals for important areas of your life.

1. The aim of this first step is for you to identify your meta-goals, the bottom-line goals that form the underlying basis of your specific goals, and action steps. Look back at the list of meta-goals a little earlier in this chapter. Circle the ones that are most important for you by asking yourself,

"Which of these matter the most to me and my life?" From the circled ones, choose those that are most compelling. Leave wishful thinking out of it. Don't just choose the goals you think are positive and attractive. If one of your meta-goals, for instance, is to dominate, be straight about it. Meta-goals have a way of punishing you for ignoring them.

2. Write your meta-goals on a page in the Clues section of your notebook, leaving several lines between each.
3. Then ask yourself, "What specific goals will help me achieve these meta-goals?" Write down whatever comes to mind, without editing. Do the same for each meta-goal. Example:

   Meta-goal: Self-expression

   Specific goals: Use my talents fully, research as a major job component, master's degree in computer graphics, get good enough at sailing my Lightning to win some local races, take some salsa lessons, get an American Stratocaster and a good amp and learn to play Robert Johnson's "Stones in My Passway" and "Walking Blues."

4. Go through the goals you wrote out for each meta-goal and select ones you are willing to commit to doing. Be as specific as possible, adding beginning and completion dates. Then you can work out the action steps for each specific goal—turning it into a project, in other words. In just a few steps you arrive at a range of goals that both get to the heart of the matter and provide clear action steps.
5. When you are finished, go over your entries. If you have created goals that are important to you, you almost certainly have some things to enter in your Definite Career Design Components list.

Inquiry 21-3 GOAL SETTING, METHOD 2

This is a more detailed approach that takes time and works brilliantly for people willing to use it regularly. It is an in-depth approach to goals for people who want a detailed and ordered method of setting and managing goals. It is useful for setting big goals. It also works extremely well for managing your projects and daily tasks. It requires more dedication and desire for order than I can muster, but it might work very well for you. This is not a to-do list. This is a results-management tool that focuses your attention on what actions will produce the greatest results.

Choose categories that describe the most important areas of your life for which you want to create goals, areas such as career, family, and sports. You can choose as many as you want, although it's easier to work with just a few.

Identify your meta-goals that apply to each of the categories. For example, for the category "work," you might have meta-goals such as independence, competence, security, and contribution.

Set up a goal and project planner like the sample on the next page. This goes in the Clues section of your notebook because your goals are often some of the strongest clues about what careers will fit you best.

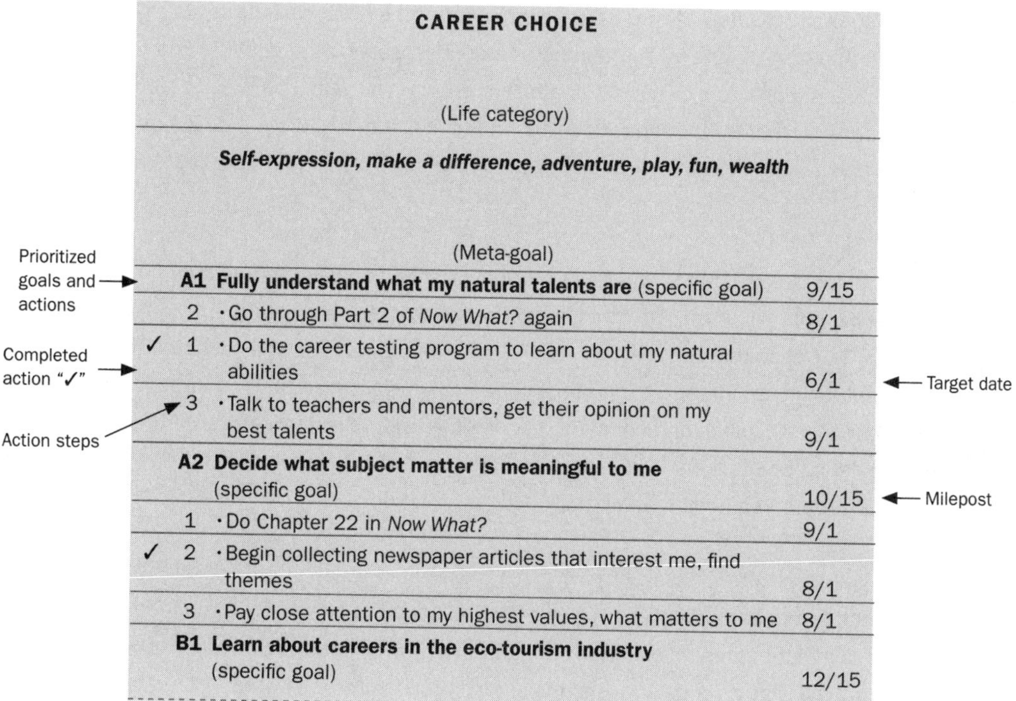

CAREER CHOICE

(Life category)

Self-expression, make a difference, adventure, play, fun, wealth

(Meta-goal)

	A1	**Fully understand what my natural talents are** (specific goal)	9/15
	2	• Go through Part 2 of *Now What?* again	8/1
✓	1	• Do the career testing program to learn about my natural abilities	6/1
	3	• Talk to teachers and mentors, get their opinion on my best talents	9/1
	A2	**Decide what subject matter is meaningful to me** (specific goal)	10/15
	1	• Do Chapter 22 in *Now What?*	9/1
✓	2	• Begin collecting newspaper articles that interest me, find themes	8/1
	3	• Pay close attention to my highest values, what matters to me	8/1
	B1	**Learn about careers in the eco-tourism industry** (specific goal)	12/15

Begin setting specific goals that you think will help you reach your meta-goal. Remember, the whole reason you set specific goals is to achieve your big, top-level meta-goals. In the diagram above, the goal "Fully understand what my natural talents are" is a specific goal. Sharpen your goals so they say exactly what you mean.

Categorize your specific goals using the following three levels to help you prioritize. In goal-setting workshops, participants are shocked to discover how much time they spend on C-level goals and how little is given to the A-level goals that move important goals forward. This is different from the way we talked about goals earlier in this chapter. In this results management method you divide goals into three types based on their potential for moving your life forward.

- **A-level goals** have the highest level of desire and impact. A-level goals have a powerful, long-term impact on the quality of your life. They move you forward in big ways.
- **B-level goals** have an intermediate impact on your life. They may be important and desirable, but they don't transform your life or generate much momentum in terms of fulfillment.
- **C-level goals** are the everyday, mundane things that have no long-term impact, things such as bathing the cat and deciding what to do for the weekend.

If you focus on your A-level goals, you will find a way to handle necessary C-level goals without their taking over your life.

Prioritize your specific goals. Add a priority number after the letter as follows: A1, A2, A3, B1, B2, C1, C2, C3 (as shown in diagram). The numbered priorities serve as a guide to the relative importance or timeliness of each goal. Since A1 is a higher priority, you would be wise to work on completing it before moving on to the other specific goals A2 and B1. When you are sitting around wondering what to do next, you just have to look at your goal and project planner to see what would have the most impact.

5. Plan your action steps. This is where you turn your specific goals into actions. In the diagram, under specific goal A1, there are three action steps that are also prioritized in order of importance (1, 2, 3). Notice that the example has "2" first on the list: you can change the order of your action steps any time. These action steps form your to-do list of tasks and activities to begin fulfilling your specific goals, and ultimately your meta-goals. This goal-setting method asks you to keep considering which goals and actions will produce the biggest impact at any given time. All extraordinary feats begin with small, daily actions. How do you eat an elephant? One bite at a time.
6. Visit your goals list often. Some of your goals may require daily attention; others may be on a weekly, monthly, or yearly timeline. Highly effective people manage their goals daily, constantly working to complete tasks, check them off, and move on to the next priority. You can make adjustments to your list on a daily basis, move goals forward or backward in time or importance, change or abandon others, and so forth. A powerful way to manage your goals is to pick a date every year to reevaluate your goals and accomplishments, set new goals for the coming year, and establish monthly milestones, weekly goals, and daily action steps.
7. When you are finished, go over your entries. If you have created goals that are important to you, you almost certainly have some things to enter in your Definite Career Design Components list.

CHAPTER 22

SUBJECT MATTER

Your imagination is your preview of life's coming attractions.

—*Albert Einstein*

When you were a kid imagining yourself working as an adult, I bet that, whatever your fantasy, the subject was interesting to you. For many people, part of the answer to the question "Why work?" is interesting subject matter. For others, the subject may not matter so much. In sales, for instance, some people don't care if they sell things they personally care about. They just enjoy using their natural sales talents, fulfilling goals, and getting an emotional charge from making the sale. For many of us, however, the subject matter forms a major piece of the career design puzzle.

You may not know what subject matter to choose. Perhaps you have one or more of the following dilemmas:

- I'm just interested in having fun with my friends. I am not thinking about subject matter.
- I'm interested in many subjects; it's hard to narrow things down.
- I can't tell which subject matter interests are strong enough to turn into a career.
- I'm afraid I'll lose interest in the subject matter once I've mastered it.
- I don't seem to have a special passion for any subject.
- My interests change regularly.

Don't worry, if you have one abiding, passionate interest, you already know it. And if you have enough talent in your area of interest to turn it into a career, you probably know that too. Steven Spielberg didn't need a book like this to know he was a filmmaker. You may not be able to pick a specific interest area, however. Most people can't, even most people in midcareer with many years of working experience. As you go through this chapter you will likely find some strong clues about areas of interest.

Most of your interests throughout your life come and go. At the age of ten, you may have been completely captivated by frogs. If you're still interested at twenty-three, that says something important about you. At a recent party, my friend Lonnie, age fifty, was watching the sky, hoping for rain after a dry spring, worrying about all of the nearly dried-up ponds full of tadpoles he studies. He has been wildly passionate about nature since the age of ten. Interests, as well as activities that you don't tire of, are very likely engaging underlying natural talents and personality traits. This is especially true of subject matter that continues to fascinate you as the years roll by. Our studies show that if you lose interest in the subject matter of your career, 90 percent of the time it's because the subject is not tapping your core talents.

For example, many people with innate strengths in intuitive imagination and a high spatial talent have a long-term interest in the physical sciences or spatial arts such as sculpture. People with strong sensor-thinker temperaments, combined with analytical and nonspatial thinking, frequently find quantitative business subjects and sports statistics intriguing.

Because Maestros are usually paid for a deep level of expertise or mastery in a specific area, it is especially important that they choose a career with subject matter that continues to be of interest. I know one doctor, a brilliant cardiologist, who lives and breathes hearts. His friends never mention that word at parties for fear of his launching into passionate, detailed explanations of the latest cardiology research. He didn't grow up doodling hearts in his notebook when bored in high school. He got interested in hearts because they engaged his spatial talent and powerful problem-solving abilities. I know another physician, an ear, nose, and throat specialist, who, if he had the courage, would never hear those three words again.

For some Tribals, the exact subject matter may be somewhat less important. But you have to judge for yourself. If you have one abiding long-term interest, it may be a very strong clue. One fellow spent his entire childhood interested in only one subject, fish. He went fishing several times a week, raised trout, knew everything about fish, got a degree in marine biology, and later discovered that his real love was physical work that involved the sea and boats. Even with a college degree, he chose to become a fisherman, and today fishes and scallops contentedly off the coast of Cape Cod.

Keep in mind that your subject matter interests do not constitute proof that you have the natural talents to make a career out of them. You may love playing basketball and stand just five feet tall. You may love music and have no talent. The best litmus test in evaluating your interests and activities for clues to your career direction is to ask, "How well and how much?" Is this a highly developed interest? Are you headed in the direction of mastery on your own? Can you imagine yourself engaged in the interest or activity several hours every day, year after year? If not, it's probably not a very good career clue.

If you are someone who doesn't seem to have many interests, don't beat yourself up over it. Some people aren't wired to have a lot of interests. For example, people with certain personality types often say they don't have a sense of "passion" for anything specific. This is because their brains are wired to be more levelheaded and utilitarian; it takes a lot to arouse their feelings about something specific.

Inquiry 22-1 SUBJECT MATTER INTERESTS

Choosing a career that brings long-term fulfillment requires exploring what you would be intrigued by and engaged in for substantial periods of time each day over many years.

In the following inquiry, look at each real-life scenario and imagine doing each of the activities or working with the various subject matter topics for most of the day over an extended period of time. Get into Detective mode and remind yourself that you are looking for clues that will shape your career direction.

1. Read each of the scenarios below and imagine yourself in each.
2. Under each scenario there are eight different activities or subject matter topics. Put a check mark in the circle to the left of the top five activities you can imagine doing.
3. In the corresponding white box to the right of each of your checkmark selections, pencil in the rank, 5, 4, 3, 2, or 1, using the following scale to gauge your level of interest:

   5 = *High level of passion*
   4 = *Very interested*
   3 = *Interested*
   2 = *Somewhat interested*
   1 = *Very mild interest*

You will find more instructions at the back end of this inquiry.

SUBJECT MATTER INTERESTS AND ACTIVITIES	**INTEREST RANKING**							
Scenario 1. Imagine being stranded on a small island for two years in the South Pacific with a few others. What activities would you be naturally inclined to do to help the group survive and get along?	Rank your selections (5, 4, 3, 2, 1) in the white boxes below to prioritize your level of interest. Use each ranking only once.							
Select exactly five from the activities below (put a check mark in circles at left)	A	B	C	D	E	F	G	H
○ Invent a fishing net and a spear thrower for hunting								
○ Be the wise sage and draft a constitution for the island								
○ Perform a stand-up comedy act and try to make people laugh								
○ Monitor the food supply and enforce fairness and adherence to laws								
○ Hunt, fish, chop wood, gather berries, carry water								
○ Fashion coconuts into bowls for eating and drinking, make clothes								
○ Construct huts to live in and build a makeshift life raft								
○ Nurse sick people back to health								

(*continued on next page*)

SUBJECT MATTER INTERESTS AND ACTIVITIES	INTEREST RANKING							
Scenario 2. If you were a rock star or part of a team of people putting on a concert, what activities would you look forward to doing every day?	Rank your selections (5, 4, 3, 2, 1) in the white boxes below to prioritize your level of interest. Use each ranking only once.							
Select exactly five from the activities below (put a check mark in circles at left)	A	B	C	D	E	F	G	H
○ I'd invent unique electronic effects pedals for instruments								
○ I'd write poetic and philosophical lyrics								
○ I'd be the drummer or lead guitarist								
○ I'd be the band manager								
○ I'd be the roadie, drive the truck, and haul the equipment								
○ I'd operate the visual light and laser show								
○ I'd set up and troubleshoot the amplifiers and sound system								
○ I'd be in charge of the fan club and social engagements								
Scenario 3. You're on a three-month sailing excursion through the Caribbean islands, as part of a small crew on a 35-foot sailboat. How would you likely spend your time?	Rank your selections (5, 4, 3, 2, 1) in the white boxes below to prioritize your level of interest. Use each ranking only once.							
Select exactly five from the activities below (put a check mark in circles at left)	A	B	C	D	E	F	G	H
○ Play Jacques Cousteau and do marine biology research								
○ Spend long hours reading and pondering the meaning of life								
○ Write a journal, document the trip or the crew's life stories								
○ Be the captain of the ship and coordinate the shipmates' tasks								
○ Do the athletic work of hands-on sailing and getting a good tan								
○ Cook and coordinate meals								
○ Be first mate in charge of navigating and reading ocean maps								
○ Plan events and excursions to nearby islands and go shopping								
Scenario 4. As part of a group of people making a movie about a global-warming disaster, which activities would interest you?	Rank your selections (5, 4, 3, 2, 1) in the white boxes below to prioritize your level of interest. Use each ranking only once.							
Select exactly five from the activities below (put a check mark in circles at left)	A	B	C	D	E	F	G	H
○ Advise on the atmospheric and geological theories for the film								
○ Write a screenplay about the social implications of a global disaster								
○ Direct the film, coach the actors, and shape the overall plot line								
○ Be the film producer in charge of funding and promoting the project								
○ Be a stuntman or stuntwoman								
○ Do the cinematography								
○ Be a carpenter or electrician and build the film sets								
○ Gossip with the actors, organize lunch, schedule the day's activities								

Scenario 5. You and a group of friends have a summer to run a tiki bar and restaurant right on the beach in Key West, Florida. What roles would you play in this endeavor?	Rank your selections (5, 4, 3, 2, 1) in the white boxes below to prioritize your level of interest. Use each ranking only once.							
Select exactly five from the activities below (put a check mark in circles at left)	A	B	C	D	E	F	G	H
○ Be an evolutionary biologist researching the evolution of crustaceans								
○ Find a quiet spot at the bar and observe people playing the mating game								
○ Play guitar and perform Jimmy Buffett and Bob Marley tunes								
○ Operate the bar, track inventory to make sure there's enough tequila								
○ Play volleyball on the beach, dance, take part in wet T-shirt events								
○ Be the bartender								
○ Be the utility person and fix anything that breaks								
○ Be the host/hostess and make sure people have a good time								

Scenario 6. If you were a part of the White House administration, what would you do best?	Rank your selections (5, 4, 3, 2, 1) in the white boxes below to prioritize your level of interest. Use each ranking only once.							
Select exactly five from the activities below (put a check mark in circles at left)	A	B	C	D	E	F	G	H
○ Science adviser on renewable energy								
○ Political speechwriter for the president								
○ Press secretary for the White House								
○ Be the president and call all the shots								
○ Be a fitness trainer to the White House staff or a Secret Service agent								
○ Design handmade decorations for all holiday galas and dinners								
○ IT network specialist for a secure communications system								
○ Secretary of education, interested in improving children's education								

Scenario 7. The president of the United States makes a daring request of the nation—to invent a totally new kind of automobile in the next decade. How would you see yourself participating in this effort?	Rank your selections (5, 4, 3, 2, 1) in the white boxes below to prioritize your level of interest. Use each ranking only once.							
Select exactly five from the subjects below (put a check mark in circles at left)	A	B	C	D	E	F	G	H
○ Get a PhD in physics to understand complex 3-dimensional systems								
○ Study sociology to learn the impacts of new technology on society								
○ Write content for a Web site to promote the program								
○ Study finance and economics to balance the federal budget								
○ Run in a marathon to raise money for the mission								
○ Take photographs of today's traffic jams for an art exhibit								
○ Become a engineer or mechanic in the automotive field								
○ Be a grade-school teacher to prepare students for the future								

(continued on next page)

SUBJECT MATTER INTERESTS AND ACTIVITIES	INTEREST RANKING							
Scenario 8. You've been assigned to be a professor for one year at a university. What cluster of courses would you enjoy teaching?	Rank your selections (5, 4, 3, 2, 1) in the white boxes below to prioritize your level of interest. Use each ranking only once.							
Select exactly five from the subjects below (put a check mark in circles at left)	A	B	C	D	E	F	G	H
○ Astrophysics, molecular biology, paleontology								
○ World history, political science, human behavior								
○ Journalism, public relations, screenwriting								
○ Accounting, finance, business management								
○ Anatomy, nutrition, physical fitness								
○ Furniture making, cooking, interior design								
○ Mechanical engineering, information technology, masonry								
○ Child development, nursing, special education								
Total the points in each column and enter here								
Circle the letters of your top two highest scores	**A**	**B**	**C**	**D**	**E**	**F**	**G**	**H**

4. Add up your points for each vertical column and enter the totals at the bottom of the chart (add up all of column A, column B, and so on, from the top of this inquiry to the bottom). Each lettered column represents a different group of career fields. Your highest scores indicate general career fields you may want to explore in more depth. Circle the letters corresponding to your top two highest scores.
5. Go to the charts at the end of this chapter for descriptions of career field categories that match your high scores in the interest ranking columns. First check out the category indicated by your highest score, followed by your second highest score. Then explore the additional career field combinations of your top two highest scores in the Subject Matter Interest Combinations Chart. If none of the categories stands out from the others, it may be that subject matter will not provide any especially strong clues. It could also be because your areas of interest are not covered in this inquiry. People with careers they love do not necessarily work in a subject area they are passionate about. For example, a salesperson may simply love the art of selling and not much care about the subject matter.
6. Any definite career components? If so, add them to your Definite Career Design Components list. Put clues in your Work Strong Clues list.
7. If any of the listed careers seem worth looking into, add them to your Careers to Explore list.

Subject Matter Interest Profiles

Interest Profile Categories

A = Physical and life sciences

B = Social sciences and humanities

C = Arts, entertainment, and media

D = Business and financial

E = Body kinesthetic and sensory acuity
F = Designer and artisan
G = Engineering, technology, and trades
H = Education, hospitality, and health care

A = Physical and life sciences: professions that scientifically study the physical, geological, and biological world
Main attraction: to understand the physical mysteries of the world and universe, shift paradigms, and develop scientific theories about and technological solutions to complex spatial and tangible problems

B = Social sciences and humanities: the study of people, human behavior, society, and culture
Main attraction: to understand the mysteries of human behavior, society, and culture; shift social paradigms; and develop scientific theories and solutions to complex social problems

C = Arts, entertainment, and media: inspiring, entertaining, and informing others through multimedia, storytelling, and art
Main attraction: to inspire, entertain, and inform others and foster an understanding and appreciation for the wider world of people, society, and diverse cultures

D = Business and financial: the management, administration, and operation of organizations that produce and offer products and services
Main attraction: to work as part of a team effort in maximizing the efficiency and economic growth of business operations with the goal of satisfying others' needs and desires with high-quality products and services

E = Body kinesthetic and sensory acuity: professions and fields that engage the human body, where strength, endurance, balance, agility, flexibility, and manual dexterity are key aspects of the daily activity (also includes career fields and activities that engage a keen sense of sight, sound, smell, touch, and taste)
Main attraction: to be active and on the move, applying the human body in capacities that engage one's physical and sensory talents, including acuity for the sensual pleasures, personal taste, and style

F = Designer and artisan: professions and fields that entail hands-on designing and crafting of artistic and functional objects and employ an eye for visual design, color, style, and a keen sense of spatial acuity
Main attraction: to delight and bring joy and comfort to others in the aesthetic and functional realm; to engage a discerning eye for style to transform, shape, and craft living

spaces, arts, and practical living needs; to bring beauty and form to functional objects used in daily life

G = Engineering, technology, and trades: professions and fields that design, build, operate, and maintain all types of technological, electronic, and mechanical equipment, including computers, networks, digital technology devices, heavy equipment, tools, and machinery
Main attraction: to provide practical problem solving and make the world a better place for others through hands-on technology design and application

H = Education, hospitality, and health care: professions and fields that involve working directly with people a significant part of the day in providing educational, retail, travel and fun, personal services, and health care
Main attraction: to help people solve practical problems with the human touch, applying a natural propensity for understanding, listening, hosting, serving, empathizing, socializing, educating, promoting, and selling, as well as administering, planning events, and managing and supervising people, projects, and organizations

SUBJECT MATTER INTERESTS CHART

Physical and Life Sciences	Social Sciences and Humanities	Arts, Entertainment, and Media	Business and Financial	Body Kinesthetic and Sensory Acuity	Designer and Artisan	Engineering, Technology, and Trades	Education, Hospitality, and Health Care
alternative energy research	archaeology	acting	accounting	bartender	advertising art	auto repair	allied health technician
artificial intelligence	art history	advertising	actuarial science	border patrol	architecture	carpentry	alternative medicine
astrochemistry	behavioral economics	art direction	applied mathematics	clothing retail	art restoration	clothing alteration and repair	amusement park attendant
astrophysics	behavioral intelligence	brand management	auditing	Coast Guard	arts and crafts	computer programming	animal welfare and rescue
atomic physics	career coaching	broadcast journalism	banking	construction	automobile design	construction management	B&B innkeeper
biochemistry	cognitive psychology	campaign strategy	budgeting	emergency medicine	bicycle design	data mining	bartender
biogeography	counseling psychology	cartoonist	business administration	farming	bookbinding	data warehousing	camp counselor
biology	criminology	columnist	business consulting	federal law enforcement	cinematography	database administration	catering
biomedical engineering	cultural anthropology	comedian	buying	firefighter	cosmetology	database design	chef
biophysics	demography	comedy writing	cost estimating	fishing	costume and set design	diesel mechanics	children's health
biotechnology	economics	commercial arts	entrepreneurship	food critic	culinary arts	drafting	correctional education
botany	educational psychology	communications	finance	forestry	decorative painting	dressmaking	day care
climatology	Egyptology	creative writing	financial planning	furniture moving	desktop publishing	electrical	dental health
computer architecture	equity research	documentary film	forensic accounting	heavy equipment operator	exhibit design	electronics technician	disability studies
computer science	ethnic studies	educational TV		homeland security	fashion design		

Physical and Life Sciences	Social Sciences and Humanities	Arts, Entertainment, and Media	Business and Financial	Body Kinesthetic and Sensory Acuity	Designer and Artisan	Engineering, Technology, and Trades	Education, Hospitality, and Health Care
cryptography	ethnography	entertainment news	franchise ownership	housewares retail	fashion photography	engineering	early childhood education
ecology	ethnomusicology	fiction writing	general management	hunting	feng shui	ergonomics	ESL
evolutionary biology	evolutionary psychology	film producing	human resources	industrial scuba diving	flower arranging	facial recognition systems	event and party planning
forensic anthropology	forensic psychology	film scoring	industrial engineering	interior decorator	flower gardening	gunsmith	flight attendant
forensic art	gender studies	film studies	information systems	lifeguard	footwear design	heavy equipment operation	geriatrics
forensic pathology	gerontology	filmmaking	international business	logging	furniture design	home remodeling	guidance counseling
genetics	history	fine arts	inventory control	manufacturing	game art and design	human-computer interaction	health administration
geology	history of science	freelance writing	investment	military	graphic design	HVAC technician	hospitality management
geophysics	human evolution	graphic arts	management science	mining	green architecture	information architecture	hotel concierge
human-computer interaction	human geography	illustration	marketing research	National Guard	hairstyling	information technology	hotel management
hydrology	independent scholarship	marketing	merchandising	oil drilling	ikebana	ironworking	instructional design
inorganic chemistry	law	mediation	operations management	packing and assembling	industrial design	jeweler	K-12 teaching
marine biology	library science	music performance	operations research	paramedic	interactive media design	kitchen and bath	men's health
marine geology	life coaching	news editorial		park ranger	interior decorator		mental health
medical research	linguistics	performing		perfumer			midwifery
		photojournalism		pilot			
		playwright		police officer			

medicine
meteorology
microbiology
military intelligence
molecular biology
nanotech-nology
neuroscience
oceanography
organic chemistry
paleontology
plate tectonics
robotics
seismology
space physics
sustainable development
theoretical mathematics
theoretical physics
virtual reality

literature
new urbanism
organization development
organizational behavior
personality studies
philosophy
political science
pop culture studies
population studies
primatology
psychology
public policy
serious nonfiction writing
sexology
social biology
social history
sociology

poetry
political pundit
print journalism
product development
product management
public affairs
public relations
radio and TV news
screenwriting
sitcom writing
social satire
Web content writing

process improvement
process reengineering
program management
project management
quality assurance
quality control
retail management
sales
sales management
statistical process control
statistics
stock brokerage
strategic planning
total quality management
training and development

search and rescue
Secret Service
security guards
special forces
sports
trapping
veterinary medicine
wildlife conservation
wildlife management
wine steward

interior design
jewelry design
knitting
lacemaking
landscape design
lighting design
media arts and animation
park and recreation design
photography
printmaking
quilting
residential planning
retail space design
sewing
tapestry
textile manufacturing
typography
urban design

locksmith
masonry
material science
mechanic
metalworking
management information systems
mining
motorcycle repair
network administration
network engineering
object-oriented programming
PC repair
plumbing and pipefitting
roofing
shoe repair
systems engineering

nursing
nutrition
occupational therapy
pet health
physical therapy
public health
recreational therapy
reproductive health
restaurant hostess
school administration
short-order cook
social work
special education
teen sex education
tour operator
travel agent

Physical and Life Sciences	Social Sciences and Humanities	Arts, Entertainment, and Media	Business and Financial	Body Kinesthetic and Sensory Acuity	Designer and Artisan	Engineering, Technology, and Trades	Education, Hospitality, and Health Care
zoology	theology		venture capital		video production	welding	waiter
	urban policy studies				visual effects	woodworking	weight/health issues counseling
					Web page design		wine steward
							women's health
							workplace safety

SUBJECT MATTER INTEREST COMBINATIONS CHART

The following chart lists careers that may combine your two strongest areas of interest. Find your highest subject matter interest area across the top of the page and then look up your number two area of interest down the left-hand column. Then check out the careers in the box where the two areas intersect.

	Physical and Life Sciences	Social Sciences and Humanities	Arts, Entertainment, and Media	Business and Financial	Body Kinesthetic and Sensory Acuity	Designer and Artisan	Engineering, Technology, and Trades	Education, Hospitality, and Health Care
Physical and Life Sciences		evolutionary psychology neuroscience social biology economic geography epidemiology history of science patent law	science film/education anatomy illustrator science illustrator nature photographer science journalist	pharmaceutical sales medical instrument rep high-tech entrepreneur	zookeeper agriculture science horticulture forestry organic farming	glass blower sword smith gunsmith nature photography science photography exhibit design	green technology chemical engineering materials science science lab technician structural engineering aerospace engineering electrical engineering	science education health education adventure education ecotourism adventure travel
Social Sciences and Humanities	evolutionary biology behavioral genetics ecology		filmmaking documentary film photojournalism	tax accountant business law CPA	law enforcement military intelligence animal training	art restoration urban design concert hall design	urban planning human-computer interaction ergonomics	public health counseling social work

	Physical and Life Sciences	Social Sciences and Humanities	Arts, Entertainment, and Media	Business and Financial	Body Kinesthetic and Sensory Acuity	Designer and Artisan	Engineering, Technology, and Trades	Education, Hospitality, and Health Care
Social Sciences and Humanities (cont.)	sustainable development biopsychology cognitive psychology		art history comedy screenwriting fiction writing	labor relations human resources employment law ad account exec marketing research	real estate agent car sales makeover consulting feng shui design interior design	park design exhibit design	civil engineering	special education library science
Arts, Entertainment, and Media	forensic art art restoration science curator science documentary	documentary film photojournalism creative writing acting entertainment law		entrepreneur film producer talent agent business manager for artist business journalism marketing	acting performance war photography	instrument maker industrial design product design	industrial design architecture graphic arts graphical user interface AutoCAD/drafting	art therapy music therapy art education music education
Business and Financial	pharmaceutical sales	organization development	advertising art		personal services	retail product design	automotive executive	school administration

Business and Financial (cont.)	medical instrument rep high-tech entrepreneur	executive coaching management consulting marketing research advertising psychology corporate training	copywriting Web content writing commercial art music production brand management		personal training personal chef product entrepreneur restaurateur	workspace planning commercial architecture industrial design	manufacturing management freelance tradesperson IT consulting mechanical engineering industrial engineering	university dean human resources health care management hotel management staffing/ recruiting
Body Kinesthetic and Sensory Acuity	wildlife biology marine science geology agriculture forensic science kinesiology	sports law FBI criminology primatology archaeology	dance choreography circus performance	retail sporting goods retail personal products		sportswear design sports gear design park design landscape architecture	biomedical engineering prosthetics occupational therapy	movement therapy recreation therapy occupational therapy kinesiology chiropractic medicine Outward Bound
Designer and Artisan	cartography prosthetics science photography	art restoration historical restoration art history	feng shui design set design costume design	product development brand management	fashion modeling stunt acting body building		architecture human-computer interaction industrial design	chef restaurant design interior design

	Physical and Life Sciences	Social Sciences and Humanities	Arts, Entertainment, and Media	Business and Financial	Body Kinesthetic and Sensory Acuity	Designer and Artisan	Engineering, Technology, and Trades	Education, Hospitality, and Health Care
Designer and Artisan (cont.)		antique appraisal	makeup art		winemaking chef display design color specialist		auto body repair pet grooming dressmaking jewelry design and repair	dermatology cosmetic surgery
Engineering, Technology, and Trades	robotics artificial intelligence nanotechnology genetic engineering supercomputing computational science evolutionary algorithm	new urbanism urban planning and design architecture human-computer interaction	auto design landscape architecture interior design Web site design video game design	operations research industrial engineering production ops management IT consulting sales engineer	sound technician TV/radio production acoustic engineering	eyewear design prosthetics cinematography photography		trades education allied health general surgery physical therapy PC help desk tech tech customer service

Education, Hospitality, and Health Care	textbook writing	education psychology	art education	medical record tech	fitness training	trades education	occupational therapy
	science professor	curriculum design	drama coaching	health care finance	massage therapy	organic chef	lab technician
	medical research	public health	music education	health insurance	physical therapy	aromatherapy	allied health technology
	neuroanatomy	reproductive health	children's book writing	health care PR	nurse's aide		engineering education
	medicine	family law	textbook illustrator	sales	dental hygienist		vocational education
	pharmacology research	malpractice law	art therapy	school administration	yoga instruction		technology education
	psychiatry	clinical psychology	music therapy	university dean	martial arts instructor		
	forensic pathology	counseling	humor therapy		EMT/ paramedic		
	microbiology	career coaching					

CHAPTER

23 REWARDS AND VALUES

REWARDS

At the most basic level, we go to work to get rewards. Like any critter, we want to feel good and avoid bad consequences. We work to fulfill physical needs such as food and shelter. If those are met, we then seek security rewards, such as safety from danger, job security, benefits. Then if those are met, we seek the next level of rewards—things such as symbols of success, power, self-esteem, approval. Finally, at the top of the heap are rewards such as self-expression, achievement, fulfillment, recognition, creativity, fun, freedom. A secret to having a career you love is to have a job that rewards you on all levels. (Personally, I'm for both self-expression and food.)

This first inquiry lets you take a look at what rewards you want from a job.

Inquiry 23-1 **MY REWARDS**

1. Go through this list of rewards. Mark each reward that is very important for you to get from your work. Remember, in Detective mode, you look for strong clues, so mark only the ones that you personally consider important. Don't mark rewards you think you *should* care about if you really don't. If something important to you isn't on this list, add it.

Rewards

- Be able to afford all the creature comforts
- Be able to fully express my natural talents at work
- Be admired for making the world better
- Be appreciated and acknowledged
- Be financially independent
- Be financially successful
- Be motivated and love the job I do every day
- Be permitted to work odd hours, at my own pace
- Be the top dog, be in charge
- Be creative most of the time
- Be creative some of the time
- Complete projects and see tangible results
- Create enough wealth to be a philanthropist
- Feel good by making others look good

- Feel proud of what I do
- Feel secure, not worried about losing my job
- Fitting in, being liked and respected
- Four weeks of paid vacation every year
- Freedom to come and go as I please during the day
- Gain recognition for being a natural at what I do
- Get pay raises for my efforts
- Get the company to pay for advanced education
- Get a pat on the back for a job well done
- Have a cool boss who thinks I'm the greatest
- Have a fan club at work that adores me
- Have challenging problems to solve
- Have control of my schedule
- Have fun at work most of the time
- Have people hang on my every word
- Have power and influence
- Have fame and fortune
- Have symbols of success
- Have the influence to get what I want done
- Have the power to create my own job
- Become invaluable to my colleagues
- Get to be a star
- Get to be a visionary leader
- Get to be in the spotlight
- Get to be inventive
- Get to solve practical problems and be useful
- Get to work with people most of the day
- Look good to others
- Lead a balanced lifestyle
- Leave a legacy
- Make a contribution that I care about
- Make a difference that matters to me
- My work contributes to my physical fitness
- Opportunity to change scenery during the day
- Opportunity to dress up
- Opportunity to wear casual clothing
- Others commend me for my brilliant ideas
- Others praise me for my loyalty and sense of duty
- Personally passionate about my work
- Prestige
- Recognized as the best at what I do
- Take an early retirement
- Time during the workday to go to the gym
- Time for family
- Time to play during the workday
- When I speak, people listen to what I have to say

2. Once you have gone through the whole list, spend some time thinking this through over several days, then go through your selections and highlight the ones you really, really can't live without.
3. Any definite career components? If so, add them to your Definite Career Design Components list. Example: "My career will make full use of my talents, I'll have autonomy, which means I can work when and where I want so long as the job gets done, and get paid enough to live in a house like the one I grew up in."

VALUES

What Is a Value?

What is important to you, what matters, what do you care about? Those are values. They define your perspective, attitude, motivations, and whole way of life, including whom you want to associate with on a daily basis. For example, people who identify with a certain political party or religion have values that line up with that specific tribe of people, and will often go to great lengths to promote and protect the tribe's shared values. Everyone lives by a specific set of values. Some are more important than others. We will sacrifice a lower value for one we consider to be more important. Obviously, to have a career you love, you want one that reflects your values. For some people, their career needs to be entirely about furthering some value. For others, it is enough that their career does not conflict with their values. At Rockport, we have worked with thousands of clients who found themselves in a job that conflicted with their values, such as the corporate vice president who valued honesty but worked for an organization that cut ethical corners to make more money for the stockholders, or the young woman who strongly believed in merit-based advancement but worked for a company dominated by politics and the old-boy network.

How to Tell What Your Values Are

Your values show up constantly in your life, but they're so much a part of you, you might not see them. You can see signs, however. Your choices (about anything) can provide strong clues. Signs of your values are everywhere: whom you hang out with, what stuff you have, how you spend your time and money, how you interact with people, and what attracts you all have been shaped by your values. For example, if you value being creative, you probably do things that involve creating something new or unusual. If you value challenging the status quo, some of your best friends might embody that attitude. If being secure is very important to you, chances are you don't take many risks. If social status or looking good to others is a value, you probably have and want certain physical symbols (car, clothes, gadgets, club memberships, friends) that announce your status to the world around you. At every moment, much of who you are has been sculpted by your values. The following inquiry will show you how to sort out your values.

Inquiry 23-2 **MY VALUES**

1. Identify the most important values in your life. See which values have been guiding your life up until now. Explore the values that guide your choices and actions in four main areas of your life: personal, social, achievement, and physical.

- **Personal values.** Go through this list of personal values. Mark those values you strongly identify with. Remember, you are in Detective mode, looking for strong clues, so just mark the ones you feel strongly about. Add any other personal values you have that aren't listed here.

Personal Values

Values That Guide My Personal Conduct

- Accepting
- Adventurousness
- Aliveness, vitality
- Autonomy
- Be extraordinary
- Be liked
- Candor, frankness
- Careful, cautious
- Caring, understanding
- Change agent
- Cleverness
- Compassion
- Creativity, innovation
- Critical thinking
- Curiosity
- Deliberate, intentional
- Do the right thing
- Do what you should do
- Empathy
- Excellence
- Factual, literal
- Feel good
- Friendship
- Fulfillment, joy, fun
- Honesty, integrity, trust
- Independence, solo
- Justice, rules, order
- Leadership, stewardship
- Levelheaded
- Look good, appearance
- Loyalty, dutiful
- Mastery, learning
- Objectivity, logical
- Open-mindedness
- Play by the rules
- Play it safe
- Playfulness, laughter
- Practical, pragmatic
- Respect
- Responsibility
- Say it like it is
- Security, stability
- See the big picture
- Seek truth
- Self-development
- Self-discipline
- Self-awareness
- Subjectivity, see nuance
- Tactful
- Tradition
- Truthfulness
- Use my natural talents
- Wisdom, wit
- Work first, play later
- Work is play

- **Social values.** Go through this list of social values. Mark those values that guide your choices in the social realm. Just mark the ones that you feel strongly about. Add any other social values of yours that aren't listed here.

Social Values

Values That Guide My Choice of People and Culture

- Alternative
- Be in control
- Be who you are
- Belong to the group
- Blend in, be accepted
- Challenge status quo
- Companionship
- Conservative, traditional
- Consume, benefit from
- Democracy
- Diversity
- Empowerment
- Equality, equity
- Family, marriage, children
- Freedom

- Getting ahead
- Global-minded
- Have less or have more
- Independent
- Intellectual
- Interdependence
- Intuitive, outside the box
- Keep things the same
- Keep up with the Joneses
- Liberal, freethinking
- Local-minded
- Meaningful
- Meritocracy
- Moderate, fair, sensible
- My way or the highway
- No kids by choice
- Obey higher authority
- Obey inner authority
- Passion, emotion
- Patriotism
- Practical-minded
- Progressive morals
- Rational, logical
- Restitution, forgiveness
- Retribution, punishment
- Seek authority
- Seek competition
- Seek cooperation
- Seek partnership
- Sexually expressive
- Social responsibility
- Social status
- Supremacy
- Systems thinking
- Take care of others
- Take care of your own
- Team spirit, tribal
- The strong deserve more
- Tolerance of differences
- Traditional morals

- **Achievement values.** What values motivate you to achieve? In other words, what carrot makes your horse go? Go through this list of achievement values. Mark those values that galvanize you into action. Remember, you are in Detective mode, looking for strong clues. Just mark the ones that you feel strongly about. Add any other achievement values of yours that aren't listed here.

Achievement Values

Values That Motivate Me to Reach My Goals

- Analysis
- Be happy
- Be masterful
- Be the best
- Be world-class
- Big changes start small
- Change the world
- Daring
- Depend on others
- Disobey
- Do more with less
- Do something important
- Do what it takes
- Efficiency
- Enlightenment
- Entrepreneurship
- Fame
- Finish what you start
- Happiness is a way of life
- Happiness is earned
- Have the most
- Humor
- Improve, enhance
- Interdependence
- Invent, create
- Leave a legacy
- Live to the fullest
- Make a contribution
- Make a difference
- Make history
- Make lots of money
- Make others look good
- Make the world better
- New possibilities
- Obey, get rewarded
- One small step at a time
- Overcome the odds
- Peace
- Perseverance
- Personal comfort
- Philanthropy
- Quality

- Reliability
- Serve mankind
- Shift a paradigm
- Simplify
- Solving problems
- Spiritual development
- Start a revolution
- Stick-to-itiveness
- Synthesis
- Take a stand
- Usefulness
- Work hard
- Work smart

- **Physical values.** Go through this list of physical values. Mark those values that strongly guide your choice of physical things. Remember, you are in Detective mode, looking for strong clues. Just mark the ones that you feel strongly about. Add any other physical values you have that aren't listed here.

Physical Values

Values That Guide My Choice of Physical Things

- Adventure
- Aesthetics
- Artful
- Beauty
- Bigger is better
- Bright, sunny
- Casual
- Classical
- Close to home
- Comfort
- Conserve, protect earth
- Die with the most toys
- Dominate, rule earth
- Ecological
- Elegance
- Entitled, get my due
- Fairness
- Fashionable
- Financial security
- Fix broken things
- Functional
- Get my share
- Get what I deserve
- Holistic
- I'll show them
- Interesting experiences
- Luxury
- Maximize wealth
- Modern
- More is better
- Natural
- Nature
- Noisy, busy, bustling
- Organic
- Plan, simple
- Pleasure, sensuality
- Rural, countryside
- Safety
- Saving, investing
- See new places
- Seek conservation
- Seek development
- Seek quality
- Seek quantity
- Simple living
- Small is beautiful
- Solitude, privacy
- Stylish
- Success symbols
- Survive
- Sustainability
- Unique
- Urban, metropolitan
- Utilitarian
- Wealth

2. There's one more place to look for values. Go back to Inquiry 23-1, where you identified the rewards you "couldn't live without," and see if they point to any other important values you have that you haven't previously recognized in this inquiry.
3. List all your most important values in the Work Strong Clues section of your notebook.

Inquiry 23-3 **MY TRUE VALUES**

According to the dictionary, a value is a principle, standard, or quality held by an individual, group, or society. The definition doesn't say anything about actually living those values. When people do values assessments, they often wind up with a completely useless list that reads like the Boy Scout oath—trustworthy, loyal, helpful, friendly, courteous, kind, obedient, cheerful, thrifty, brave, clean, and reverent. Of course, these are all wonderful values, but you are looking for values you actually live, the ones that rule your everyday life. We have to do a little slash-and-burn work to get your list down to your true values, the values you actually live by every day. For example, if the list above was my values list and I was honest about which values I actually live every day, I would have to dump obedient right away. And if I were really honest, I would have to add something like nonconforming, unruly, and iconoclastic to my values list.

Some things muddy the picture of your true values. They appear to be values but aren't necessarily how you actually live your life from day to day. Your next step is to separate your standards, ideals, wants, and preferences from your true values.

IDEALS

An ideal is a conception or model of something perfect that exists only in concept, not in reality. It is the ultimate aim, not how we actually live. Extraordinary people strive in the direction of their ideals. Many of us do little more than complain about how other people don't live up to the ideals that we don't live up to either.

Having ideals gives us a vision of a perfect life to strive for. We can use our ideals as a reference point to pull us in the direction of living an ideal life. They act as a pointer, not a destination. Ideals are to strive for. You will find yourself in big trouble when you expect yourself or others to live up to your ideals, because no one ever will. You're not supposed to. That's why they are called ideals. If you demean your present reality by comparing it with your ideals, you nullify the opportunity that having ideals offers. If you are a musician, what is the point of selling yourself short by comparing yourself with Mozart or Bob Dylan?

STANDARDS

A standard is a judgment or conclusion that something should be another way than it actually is. For example, many people subscribe to a standard that "life should be fair." Whenever life isn't fair, they get upset. They feel that something is wrong. But, in fact, life is unfair. It has never been fair. The good guys don't necessarily finish first, except in the movies. Bad people don't usually get their comeuppance. We have standards about almost everything else—standards about how people should look, dress, and behave, how the government should work, how people should raise their children. We have standards about haircuts and bread, music and manners. We have standards about ourselves, our work, our relationships. The only things we don't have standards about are the things we haven't thought about yet.

How do you recognize a standard? Simple—it always contains a "should." If you think you should be taller, better-looking, further along in life, better-educated, younger, older, more successful, richer, more caring, and so on, you are face-to-face with a standard. If you think the world should be more peaceful, more just, or less polluted, there's a standard lurking about. There is always some sort of complaint attached to standards. The problem is that nothing is ever the way it should be. It's always the way it is. "Should" exists only when something doesn't measure up to your standards. If you want a less polluted world, give up your standards and dedicate your life to contributing to this goal.

WANTS AND PREFERENCES

Some "values" may simply be wants and preferences instead of important values. For example, you may have marked adventure as one of your values in the previous inquiry. This may simply be something that you think would be nice to have rather than something you are committed to.

LOOKING AT YOUR IDEALS AND VALUES

1. Go through the list of values in your notebook. Consider which of your values are actually ideals. Mark them with the letter *I*.
2. Go through the list of values in your notebook. Consider which of your values are actually standards. Mark them with the letter *S*.
3. Go through the list of values in your notebook. Consider which of your values are actually wants. Mark them with the letter *W*.
4. Now that you have separated and categorized the very different concepts we often lump together as "values," the ones you have left are very likely your *true* values. Make sure all the values left on your list are ones you are willing to live by, every day. If one of your most important values is not on the list, write it in. Don't mark the ones you think you should have, or the best or most noble ones. Mark only the ones that actually, truly guide your life.

   Here's how you can tell. If saving for a rainy day is one of your top values, you will be actively engaged in saving or you will be consistently striving to change your circumstances to make saving possible. If you get upset that you are not saving and you're not in action to remedy the situation, then saving is only a standard or an ideal.

   This is not the time to attempt to look good to yourself by selecting idealistic values that do not actually drive your life. For example, advertising psychologists say five things motivate people to buy what they buy and do what they do. These powerful motivators are: looking good, feeling good, being right, feeling safe, and avoiding pain. When we make up values lists, we tend to "forget" these powerful background motivators because we don't want to admit these things drive our behavior. If you do not have at least some of these in your true values list, you are probably fooling yourself.

5. Once you have sorted out the true values you actually live by and from, you may want to create some new ones. Look to see if you want to add any new values to your list. Please, no New Year's resolutions! See if there are any values you have not been living from but that you now want to adopt fully as your own. For example, you may have recognized that saving for a rainy day has been a standard, not a true value. You can forge it into a true value now by choosing it and then taking action consistent with that value from this moment on. There may also be values that you have lived by in one area of your life, but not at work, that you are now willing to forge into work values as well.
6. Prioritize your true values. Values are hierarchical. People will always sacrifice a less important value to protect or uphold a higher value. Some basically honest senior government officials have in the past resorted to lying when faced with a choice between loyalty to their administration and honesty. That's because loyalty, job security, or some other value was higher on their scale than honesty.

   Go over your true values. Which is your number one, most important true value? Which value would you never sacrifice under any circumstances? Move it to the top of your list. Which is next most important? Move it to second on the list. Which are third and fourth? Continue to prioritize your top values. Don't worry if you can't absolutely prioritize them all. Just do the best you can.

   If your top values are all noble and high-minded, you may be fooling yourself. Can you be counted on to be completely honest even if you will be terminally embarrassed by telling the truth? What if you will lose your job if you tell the truth? What if you will lose your life? For many people, job security is a higher value than honesty. That does not mean they are people devoid of integrity. They may always be honest except when confronted with the possible loss of their job. For many of us, avoiding embarrassment may be a higher value than honesty. Dig in and come face-to-face with your top values now. You may want to take a few days to work on this exercise.
7. Consider your top true values as they relate to a career. What do you mean by each of them? If security is a value, what do you mean specifically? Does this mean a secure job in an industry that will never shrink, in a company that provides full benefits? Write your own short definition for each of your true values.
8. Here's the creative part of sorting out your values: you get to promote or demote values on your values hierarchy. You may have security as your top value. It doesn't have to stay there. You can move any value up or down. Also, you can redefine what a value means. If you value security and what it means to you now is "a secure job in an industry that will never shrink, in a company that provides full benefits and a generous pension," you can either keep that definition

or make up a new one. You could redefine security as "growing in a field over my lifetime, so I become so proficient and effective that companies compete to have me work for them."

9. If your values are important to you, you probably have some things to add to your Definite Career Design Components list. Are you ready to commit to having all or some of your true values fulfilled in your new career?
10. Any clues? If so, put them in your Work Strong Clues list.

CHAPTER 24

MEANING AND MISSION

Even if your work fits everything we have discussed so far, it isn't going to be satisfying unless you are interested in the work you do. For some people it is enough that the subject matter is interesting or that talents, functions, and environment fit. But many people want to do something they consider meaningful, or make a contribution to other people or the world around them. This chapter gives you an opportunity to sort out what that meaning might be.

WHAT'S MEANINGFUL?

If you stood on the moon and watched humanity at work through a big telescope, we would look like a bunch of ants scurrying around. You would be able to detect the use of different talents, different functions, and different objectives. You couldn't detect much meaning from the actions of humankind, because meaning is personal. It is not a universal phenomenon. What's meaningful to you might not be so to your next-door neighbor. While goodness might be meaningful to you, badness could be more meaningful to him.

You can tell what is meaningful to you by looking at how you spend your time. Pay more attention to your actions than to your words. I do very little to alleviate the plight of homeless people. I will give a little spare change to an occasional residentially challenged individual. But that's about it. I am not actively engaged in dealing with this problem. I can tell that street musicians mean something to me, however, because I always go out of my way to honor them with money and appreciation. I also care about sailboats and guitars and making a difference in the quality of people's lives. I can tell I'm passionate about these things because I'm actively involved in doing, not just talking.

When I was designing my own career, one of my first commitments was to have my work be about making a difference in people's lives. It was so important that I made it the center of my career. You may want to do something similar. If that is the case, you have to figure out what's really important and meaningful to you—not what anyone else says you should care about. It isn't more noble to care about ending poverty than it is to care about fixing cars. It isn't better to care more about making money than it is to care about beautiful design. We need people who are passionately committed and gifted working to end poverty, fix cars, make money, and design beautiful things.

Which is more meaningful, tennis or reducing the use of fossil fuels? You might actually be more interested in tennis. I had a client once who thought that teaching tennis was the most meaningful activity a person could do. I had another who was in love with hydras—you know, those microscopic sea monsters you studied in ninth-grade biology. Though hydras may not butter your muffin, she just loved those little guys. She wound up designing her career around them. The lesson is that your satisfaction depends on doing what you consider meaningful.

Inquiry 24-1 **MEANINGFUL WORK**

If you want to know what matters to someone, just ask them. It's right there on the surface, not hidden in the murky depths of the unconscious. Let's take a look. Answer as many of these questions as you can. If you have difficulty with one, just mush on and come back to it later.

1. In regard to your future career, how important is it to do meaningful work?
2. What do you mean by "meaningful"? Before we get specific, look at this question in a general way. Which of the following general areas rings true for you in terms of what is likely to be worthy of spending your life engaged in?

   - In service to some important principle or value, such as making the world a better place
   - Subject matter that is a personal passion of yours or is at least interesting
   - A sense of mission—engaged in building or moving something forward
   - Solving certain types of problems

Some folks are happy without special meaning in their work. They may get enough from using their talents and working in an environment that feels like home territory. It that's the case for you, go on to the next chapter.

3. Make a list of everything that is most meaningful to you. Include things you might consider doing for a living as well as things you consider to be highly significant, important, or meaningful but unlikely to be the centerpiece of your career. Be specific. "Everything" could include specific fields of endeavor, problems that need to be solved, social ills, things you like to do, places you like to go, activities you are especially passionate about, functions you love to perform, and anything else that falls within the range of what you consider to be meaningful. Notice if any particular theme emerges.

4. Edit this list so it contains only items that you might consider as the centerpiece of your career. You could list different job names, specific fields of endeavor, things that you feel would be good to accomplish, or whatever else you think fits. Remove items that don't belong on this more refined version of this "what's meaningful to me" list.
5. Reorganize this list so that the most meaningful items are at the top.
6. Go through this list one more time. See if you can shorten the list. Are there any entries on the list you know in your heart you would never really pursue as a career? Do your best to trim your list down to as few entries as possible, but don't throw away anything that truly belongs on the list.
7. Find out more about your top contenders. Do some research, talk with people. What do you need to know to decide or to further narrow down the range of possibilities? What questions do you need to ask and answer in order to make a final choice?
8. Anything to add to your Definite Career Design Components list or to your Work Strong Clues list?

Inquiry 24-2 MAKING A DIFFERENCE

For those of you who want your career to make a difference in your world in some way, here are a few more questions.

1. For some people, it is vitally important that their work be the direct expression of their highest ideals. Other folks don't feel it's necessary to work in furthering one of those ideals. For them, it's enough to work in a field that does no harm. How important is it that your work make a positive difference in the world or in the lives of other people?
2. If you want to make a direct impact or contribution in an area important to you, what kind of an impact? How much of an impact? Could you work at a job that does not directly make a contribution even though the organization does?
3. What stands in the way of actually doing meaningful work? Write down all important obstacles. For example, two common yeah-buts are "I will have to work long hours for very little money" and "There are many jobs for people who want to pillage and loot but few for people who want to do something meaningful." Afterward, consider each obstacle separately. Brainstorm possible ways of handling the obstacle. Do not listen to your yeah-buts. Write down everything, even possibilities that seem far-fetched. After you have finished brainstorming, go over all the possible solutions, considering carefully: "Would this work? Is it possible? How could I make it happen?"

Inquiry 24-3 A MISSION IN LIFE

Some people find meaning in being on a mission of some sort. Being on a mission differs from doing meaningful work in that a mission drives toward some tangible goal in the world, whereas a career with meaning doesn't necessarily involve working toward some goal. The mission might be ending world hunger, creating tools to help educate people in poor countries, or making better razor blades. If career as mission appeals to you, dig into the following inquiry.

1. How important is it to you that your work involves having a mission, directing your energy toward achieving specific goals?
2. Who are some people you admire who have or had a mission? If they were asked what that mission is or was, what do you think their answer would be?
3. What possible results or outcomes from a mission might be fulfilling to you? Use this question to brainstorm. Write down whatever surfaces. Don't edit out things that seem beyond your reach or impossible for some reason or another.
4. Go over the previous list and cross out whatever you know you will not actually dedicate yourself to. Be completely honest with yourself. You might cross some out because, as noble or interesting as they seem, they just aren't something you can see yourself dedicating your life to.
5. Ask yourself why you crossed out the ones you did. What about them made you take them off the list? This is important information. It may guide you to focus on which of the remaining ones best fulfill what is important to you.
6. Which of the remaining ones are most fitting, most attractive? Which ones sing your song loud and clear? Mark the ones that rise to the top like cream.
7. What are the elements that make the ones you just marked so attractive to you? Is it the subject matter, the furthering of an ideal, an elegant fit between aspects of you and the work the mission would entail, or something else?
8. Can you narrow down your selection to one or more top candidates?
9. Do you need to do some research, talk with people, or otherwise find out more about any of your top contenders? If so, what do you need to do? Be specific. What information do you need in order to decide or to further narrow the range of possibilities? What questions do you need to ask and answer? Go do the research and come back here when it's complete.
10. Anything to add to your Definite Career Design Components list or your Work Strong Clues list?

SECTION 6

Where You Work

CHAPTER 25

WORKPLACE ENVIRONMENT

Seek those who find your road agreeable, your personality and mind stimulating, your philosophy acceptable, and your experiences helpful. Let those who do not, seek their own kind.

—*Jean-Henri Fabre*

Where do you want to work? The right environment can be your personal playground, the wrong one a prison. The more you and your workplace environment fit each other, the more you'll flourish, have fun, and prosper. Every work environment offers a physical, social, and cultural setting that can either advance or thwart you. Spend your days in the wrong environment and you'll feel like a stranger in a strange land on the job every day.

A work environment in which you will thrive provides challenging work you care about, engages your strongest talents, allows you to be yourself, surrounds you with like-minded people, supports you to live a balanced lifestyle, and inspires and rewards you to live by your values and fulfill your goals. It is a place that feels like home, where you can let your guard down, where you can grow and excel. The more suited you are to your environment, the better you'll perform and handle any day-to-day stress on the job.

This chapter will help you design a workplace environment that suits you perfectly. All zookeepers know that creating the right natural environment for each species contributes immensely to their charges' physical and mental well-being. In this chapter you get to be both critter and keeper. Here are some key factors to consider when designing a low-stress, healthy work environment:

- **Physical environment.** What physical environments will be likely candidates to give you a life you love? Consider the large scale (city, suburban, or rural; the climate; the kind of people around you; how far you have to commute) as well as the smaller scale (type of workplace, such as office, factory, outdoors, store, your own home, beachside shack; look and feel of the workplace; health of the workplace environment; clothes you need to wear). What about stress level? Would you fit best in a calm place or in a setting more like a three-ring circus?
- **Social environment.** What sorts of people do you want to be around?
- **Meaning and values.** Do a particular organization's products, services, goals, and values align with your own?

Inquiry 25-1: **DESIGN YOUR WORKPLACE ENVIRONMENT**

There are several major environmental components to consider. The following inquiry will help you in your Detective role.

1. **Look for clues.** Consider this list of questions. Mark the questions that stand out as important to you. Only mark questions that are the most important for you to consider, and then work them as clues. (This is a very long list to make sure you don't miss any important aspect of the workplace environment.) After you have marked the most important questions, go back over the items you checked and pick the best of the best—those clues that zero in on your major requirements for a working environment. If you find it difficult to make definite commitments, this inquiry will still be useful in helping you paint a mental picture of what you prefer.

Geographic Location and Lifestyle

___ What country?
___ What state?
___ What city?
___ Urban, suburban, or rural?
___ What climate? Mostly hot, seasonal, or mostly cold?
___ What kind of terrain? Near a body of water, mountains, plains, etc.?
___ East Coast, West Coast, Southwest, Midwest, etc.?
___ How long a commute to work?
___ Will you use public transportation, drive to work, bike, walk, or work at home?

Physical Setting

___ Will you work indoors or outdoors? If some of both, how much of each?
___ If outdoors, what will this look like in specific detail?
___ If indoors, what will this look like in specific detail?
___ If an office setting, will you have a cubicle, a bullpen, or an office with a door?
___ Will your setting be businesslike, casual, artsy, educational, medical, laboratory, scientific, retail, in a kitchen, on a construction site, ocean oil rig, etc.?
___ How important are the aesthetics, colors, windows, style of furniture, etc.?
___ What specific physical features will you need to feel comfortable all day long?
___ How much sitting, standing, walking, running, or driving during the workday?
___ Do you prefer a quiet workspace, hustle and bustle, high or low energy, noisy?
___ Do you prefer a workplace with an in-house cafeteria, or will you bring a bag lunch or go out to eat most of the time?
___ Do you prefer a workplace that provides an exercise or workout facility?
___ What other amenities are important to have as part of your daily workplace?

PHASES IN THE LIFE OF AN ORGANIZATION

Like people, all organizations go through phases of life, from infancy through childhood and adulthood. We have periods of growth, stability, and decline; so do all organizations. You may fit better in one life stage of an organization than in another. Here are the different stages:

Start-up. The first phase of growth, equivalent to infancy in humans. Everything is new and in a formative period. Zero stability. Highly innovative people are valued. Problem solving is a daily, if not hourly, occurrence.

Entrepreneurial. Equivalent to childhood and teen years in humans. Characterized by rapid growth of capacity and competence. Favors highly creative people who like change. Not much fun for traditional people who value established policies and stability.

Settling down. Similar to young adulthood. Still growing, but the goal is to create stability (building policies and procedures). Still a lot of experimentation, but less than in earlier phases. Particularly good for people who want to bring order and discipline to unruly environments.

Stability. Middle age in humans. Most companies are in this phase. Think of well-known corporations that are profitable and stable. Usually a conservative environment with traditional values. Managed with established policies and procedures. If you are high in diagnostic reasoning or passionate about change and improvement, stay away.

Decline. Old age in people. Nothing lasts forever. Think of huge old slow traditional corporations past their prime, or the later days of the Roman Empire. These organizations sometimes seem like attractive places for passionate problem solvers, but beware. They are led by stability-phase people who resist change and rarely rise to do what is necessary to revitalize their organization. As I write this, the American auto industry is a perfect example. By the time you read this, you might be teleporting to work.

Organizational Structure

___ Will you work in a field or industry that is new, growing, mature, or declining?

___ What industry or sector will you work for? Business, retail, financial/banking, manufacturing, construction, trades, energy, real estate, governmental, defense, educational, media, academic, publishing, science, technology, health care, travel, arts, entertainment, or nonprofit environment?

___ Will the organization be start-up, entrepreneurial, settling down, stable, or in decline?

___ Do you prefer a management structure that is hierarchical (vertical chain of command) or horizontal and democratic?

___ Will you be self-employed, a freelance consultant, or an employee of a company?

___ Will you have a set schedule, flextime, be on call, work at odd hours, work weekdays or weekends?

___ How much travel are you willing to do? How flexible are you?

___ What kind of benefits do you need, medical, dental, educational, paid vacation, etc.?

___ What salary range do you require? How flexible is this? How much is enough? What's the lowest you are willing to go to start your career?

___ How important is job security? What is your definition of security?

Human Environment

___ What kind of colleagues? How many, what age group, level of education, etc.?

___ What type of clients or customers? The general public, professionals, businesses, government, international, etc.? What level of education, age, and gender are your clients or customers?

___ How many people in the company: thousands, hundreds, fifty, twenty-five, ten, or fewer?

___ How much extroversion comes naturally to you on a daily or weekly basis? In other words, how many hours a day can you comfortably interact with people to get your job done? How much is too much?

___ Do you prefer to interact with one person at a time, small groups, large groups, on the telephone, etc.?

___ How much introversion comes naturally on a daily or weekly basis? In other words, how many hours a day can you comfortably work internally or in solitude? How much is too much?

___ How much autonomy? Do you prefer to control your schedule and amount of contact with others, be available upon request, or let someone else schedule your day for you?

___ How much break time do you need each day?

Cultural Environment

___ Do you prefer a conservative, moderate, or liberal workplace culture?

___ Do you prefer a competitive or cooperative culture, or something in between?

___ Do you prefer artistic, scholarly, casual, blue-collar, professional, or businesslike culture?

___ How much cultural diversity is important to you?

___ Do you prefer a serious or playful workplace?

___ Do you prefer a workplace culture that is innovative and visionary or stable and secure?

___ What style of attire do you prefer to wear to work? Business suit, uniform, casual, anything goes, etc.?

___ What are the values, ideals, and guiding principles you need to have in common with your coworkers? Does this matter to you?

___ Do you have a preference for traditionally religious, spiritual, or nonreligious coworkers?

___ Do you prefer to work with risk takers who challenge the status quo or people who live by socially accepted conventions and norms?

___ Do you prefer a team-oriented culture where people collaborate to get the job done or a soloist culture where people work independently most of the time?

Personal Work Style

___ Do you prefer to be your own boss or report to a supervisor?

___ Do you prefer minimal, moderate, or frequent supervision?

___ How much autonomy do you need? Are you independent or rely on others most of the time?

___ Do you work better on a regular schedule, or your own time schedule at odd hours of the day?

___ Do you prefer well-defined work tasks using preestablished methods to solve familiar problems?

___ Do you prefer to rely on your creativity to invent solutions for ambiguous, unique, or unpredictable tasks?

___ Do you prefer to design your own projects and tasks or have someone else assign them to you?

___ What timeline do you prefer to see results from your work? Short-term (hourly/daily), near-term (weekly/monthly), long-term (quarterly/yearly or longer)?

___ What kind of work pace do you prefer? Fast-paced with lots of change (e.g., journalism, emergency medicine), moderate-paced with some change (e.g., small business, consulting), slow-paced with very little change (e.g., big business, government, military, farming)?

___ Do you require lots of time to ponder and mull over your work or do you zip through your tasks quickly? Are the fields you are considering supportive of your natural work pace?

___ How much control and decision making do you prefer? Do you prefer to call the shots, support those in charge, or follow orders and instructions?

___ How integrated or separate will your workplace be in relation to the rest of your life?

___ What kind of relationship will you have with your coworkers? With customers? Do you prefer intimate, friendly, or strictly professional relationships at work?

Personality Fit with Environment

___ What other important aspects of your personality do you need to express in your daily workplace environment? Are you figurative or literal? Empathetic or logical? Cautious or spontaneous? Outgoing or reserved? Do the work environments you are considering require constant or regular use of your stronger personality traits?

___ What type of work environment does your Rockport Personality Type Indicator suggest?

___ Examine the career paths you are considering. Do these industries, sectors, and organizations typically attract people with your personality type and demeanor? Would your personality type be most common or least common in those fields?

___ What type of work culture suits your personality type? If you are creative and artsy, would you thrive in a top-down, military culture? If you're conservative and seek security, would you fit in an innovative culture like Google?

MEANING AND VALUES FIT WITH ENVIRONMENT

In addition to a physical and social environment, workplaces have different reasons to exist. Some are dedicated to making the world a better place; others are committed to innovation; some just grind out products or services mechanically as a habit; still others are mainly concerned with fattening their own bottom line. At Rockport we constantly hear stories of employees, even senior-level people, who have been chewed up and spit out by organizations whose only goal is to please their stockholders. Other people feel completely at home in these companies. The difference in workplace culture is enormous. Some organizations treat employees like family, while in others you are just a number. As you consider career fields and workplaces, consider how they correlate with your values so you don't wind up in a place where you won't thrive and be proud to work.

Americans used to work nine to five. Employees had time for a life outside of work. Only doctors and lawyers worked ridiculously long hours. One of the more unfortunate effects of single-minded dedication to the growth of stock valuation is corporations' mistaken belief that increased productivity requires longer work hours. Studies show there are better ways to increase productivity. A wise company values its employees as its heart and soul and demonstrates commitment to their well-being and self-expression. Other companies use employees as pawns in another game. It is easy to tell which is which. Ask a bunch of employees. If most of them say, "This is a great place to work," it probably is just that. If they don't, it probably isn't.

Other Environmental Factors

___ What is the supply and demand for people in the fields you are considering? If the supply is high and the demand is low, do you have what it takes to make the cut? Are you willing to make the stretch or play the games required to succeed in highly competitive environments?

___ What geographic locations are typical of the industry, sector, or profession you are considering? Certain career paths are less portable than others. For example, the hot spots for film careers are Los Angeles, Vancouver, and New York City. Public policy and nonprofit careers are clustered in Washington, D.C. On the other hand, careers in health care and education are very portable; cities of all sizes and locales have hospitals and schools.

___ What are the typical career advancement opportunities and paths available within the fields and professions you are considering? Do you like what you see at the end of the rainbow? To investigate this further, talk to at least five people who are at midcareer or have ten to fifteen years of experience in the fields you are most curious about. Do what it takes to get the inside scoop; see what your future will look like by talking to people who have already gone down that road. Date your career before you marry it.

WORKPLACE POLITICS

Politics has been around for a long time. The term comes from the ancient Greek word meaning "citizen." We have come to think of it in negative terms: scheming and forming alliances to gain some advantage. Wherever three or more people are gathered together, you will find politics. It's unavoidable. Each of us is born with personal tendencies that shape how we play politics. Some of us are fiercely politically competitive, while others behave in a more cooperative fashion.

Wherever you go, there will be politics. If your approach is to avoid conflict, that's your way of playing the game and you had better find a place to work where that approach will fit. If you get kicks from being the top dog and love to compete and win no matter whom you step on to get there, you aren't going to be happy in environments where this is frowned upon. A smaller percentage of people are individualists; much less political, they walk through life as soloists and don't rely on networks and alliances. Given that humans are predominately a tribal species, the traditional workplace is usually tough going for those with a maverick, independent demeanor.

Workplace Politics

___ What kind of politics are you most comfortable with playing at work? Are you naturally more competitive, cooperative, or somewhere in between?

___ If you are competitive, whom do you want to compete with? Your teammates, other teams, other organizations, other nations, etc.?

___ If you are cooperative, whom do you want to cooperate with? Your teammates, other teams, other organizations, other nations, etc.?

___ Do you seek conflict, seek to create harmony, or avoid politics altogether?

___ How important are power and status to you?

___ What is your definition of power? Running the company, being in charge of a project, being recognized as the best at what you do, being honored and adored by others, making billions, being able to influence public opinion, to be sought out for your advice, etc.?

___ What is your definition of status? For some people status is displayed as material wealth, while others gain a sense of status from being known by the public or the people in their field, solving a big problem, making the world a better place, contributing as a proud parent of a healthy family, being loved by many friends, etc.

___ What is your definition of success? How is it related to your power and status needs? What do you need to see as a result in your life to feel successful? Would you consider yourself a success if you had power, status, and material wealth but found your job dull, boring, or unfulfilling?

2. **What's important to you?** Go over the work you have done in this inquiry and identify the most important factors in regard to workplace environment. What matters most to you?

    - What environmental factors are absolute must-haves? Consider aspects of the workplace environment that stand out as important or critical to build into your career early on.
    - What environmental factors would be nice to have but not critical in the short-term?
    - What environmental aspects are you willing to work toward achieving over several years?

3. **Any definite career design components?** You know where to put them.
4. **Clues?** I'm sure you found several strong clues to work somewhere in these long lists.

SECTION 7

Making the Final Choice

You have finally reached the place where the rubber meets the road—where you actually design your future career. So far, you have been playing the roles of Detective and Decider. Now you are going to assume a completely different role, that of the Designer. Using the definite career design components you chose as specifications, you will create a list of careers that fit those specifications. Then you will research each of those careers, comparing and contrasting them until you can make a final choice.

Depending on your age and situation, it may be premature for you to go all the way through this final part of career design now. Ideally, career choice is done in stages. At first the compass needle swings in wild circles. As you learn more about your talents, personality, and other traits, the swing narrows considerably. As you continue your career design project, the swing of the needle narrows still further until it points unwaveringly in one direction.

If you must make a decision now, by all means complete this section, choose your career, and be done with this project. Back in Chapter 4 we talked about how long it would take to go through this process. Those guidelines still hold true. For example, if you are an undergrad student and drawn to professions where your postgrad years serve as a trade school, such as engineering or medicine, it makes sense to take this process all the way to the final goal in the near future. The same may be true if you are in grad school or out in the real world. Choosing the perfect career may be a long-term project, however, that requires more experience (and sometimes maturity) than you have now. If possible, take your time and make sure you get it right. Narrow the swing of the compass needle as much as possible. You may need to put on your Detective hat again. You may have to let some time pass while you learn more. It may be appropriate to gain actual experience through an internship or a summer job in a field you are seriously considering before you make the final choice.

CHAPTER 26

CAREERS TO CONSIDER AND RESEARCH

You are now in the home stretch. The goal of this chapter is to come up with a new list: Final Careers to Consider and Research. This list will be completely reality-based because it will be built from the specifications you selected as definite elements of your future career.

This is different from the possible Careers to Explore list you have been adding to as you worked your way through this book. The list you already made is a very rough one; those careers were based on a momentary appeal or a guess that they might prove interesting. It's still a useful list, however, since it may give you some good ideas as you create your Final Careers to Consider and Research list in this chapter.

Inquiry 26-1 MY FINAL CAREERS TO CONSIDER LIST

In this inquiry, you will start to create your Final Careers to Consider and Research list by using your Definite Career Design Components list. If possible, you want your career to fit all your specifications (career design components). By now, however, you probably have quite a few specifications, and you could burn out your brain trying to think of careers that fit them all. So the first job is to narrow your career components. Don't worry—you aren't killing off any components, just focusing on a few that will be useful in this inquiry.

Look over your Definite Career Design Components list and select a few components that point most directly to specific careers. Some point more directly than others. For example, "working in an ethical organization" or "wearing casual clothes" may be absolutely vital to you, but those components won't help point to actual careers. Thousands of different careers fit those specifications, including mucking out horse stalls.

So look for those elements on your Definite Career Design Components list that point most directly to specific careers. If you have difficulty with this or don't have a lot of experience out in the world, get help from others, older people with wide experience in the working world, family, or experienced friends.

1. Mark any items on your Definite Career Design Components list that point directly to a career or a few potential careers. Here are examples of design components that point directly:

Talents and Job Functions	Subject Matter, Meaning, Goals	Workplace Environment
· Manage day-to-day operations of a business	· Medicine	· Start-up dot-com setting
· Work with animals	· Education field	· Physical work outdoors
· Software development	· Financial services	· Live in small rural village
· Hands-on-trade	· Music business	· Work in a hospital
· Sales	· Robotics	· Academic setting
· Work with abstract, theoretical ideas	· Politics	· Think tank
· Focus on real 3-D objects	· Solve long-term global problems that engage my love of the sciences	· Work on ship or boat
· Use my sense of design	· Information technology	· Hospitality industry
· One-on-one coaching	· Make 300K	· Military
· Create works of art	· Business management	· Work in science lab
· Writing as primary job function	· Focus on creating beautiful environments	

Notice that all the entries in this list are specific enough that you can read one and then imagine a small number of specific careers that would fit it. That's what to look for—specifications that point toward as specific a direction as possible. If you don't have any definite components that point to this specifically, just go on to number 2 below. The following components don't point quite as directly to specific careers as the list above. But if you don't have components as specific as in the above list, you will have to do the best you can and pick ones that are somewhat less specific.

2. Go over your list of career design components again and mark any that may not be quite as specific as the last group but still point to a reasonably small number of career areas. Here are some examples.

Talents and Job Functions	Subject Matter, Meaning, Goals	Workplace Environment
· Spatial problem solving as my main function	· My main goal is to nurture and support others	· Large stable corporation
· Teaching is a major component	· Strong psychological component	· Work from home
· Fits my ENFP personality	· Humanities	· Involves extensive world travel
· Entrepreneurial	· Sciences	· Work in government

Important note: If you discover that your best, most specific career design components aren't specific enough to suggest a small number of careers that fit them, you need to go back into Detective mode and do more work. You can't come up with a Final Careers to Consider and Research list unless you have components that are fairly specific. For example, let's say your most specific components are "have an office window that opens" and "work mainly by myself." Those components won't help you come up with a good, strong Final Careers to Consider and Research list. That's like trying to pick a vacation destination based on "planet Earth" and "warm."

3. Pick three to five of the most useful, most specific components you chose in steps 1 and 2. Write them on a clean page as your Short List of Specifications. This short list will keep you from going nuts trying to juggle all your components. You are going to use this Short List of Specifications to make your Final Careers to Consider and Research list more specific.
4. Use your Short List of Specifications to come up with as many careers as you can that might fit all the components on that short list. Once again, don't do this off in a corner by yourself. Unless you have vast experience of the wide world around you, get some help from others, especially older people with wide experience in the working world. Tell them you want some help in thinking of careers that might that fit *all* the specifications on your Short List of Specifications. This process is like brainstorming. The participants should save any instant critiques or cautions for later. Right now you are just thinking of careers that fit the short list. (See the section on brainstorming in Chapter 14.)

   Now would be a good time to check out your original Careers to Explore list one more time. It is often a great place to look for careers that fit your specifications but which you might not have seriously considered. Do any of the careers fit your Short List of Specifications? Your intuition or gut instinct may have already come up with some careers that fit your specifications. If so, transfer them to your Final Careers to Consider and Research list.
5. Keep working on your Final Careers to Consider and Research list over several days, weeks, or months. Show your Short List of Specifications to many people and get their input and ideas. Contact people in fields your components point to. For example, if components point to education or financial services, talk with some people in those fields and ask them which careers and specific jobs might fit your Short List of Specifications.

   If you have trouble coming up with a list of careers to consider, go back to your main Definite Career Design Components list and try out various combinations of components to see if they yield more specific career ideas. For example:

   - I am going to use my strong analytical problem-solving ability.
   - I am going to use my strong 3-D spatial ability.
   - I am going to work with computers and similar high-tech gear.

Notice that when you combine multiple components, like the three examples above, the combination of components points much more specifically than any of the individual components. Sometimes combining components can narrow down your list of fitting careers to a very few. Not too many careers fit "performing" plus "lions."

CHAPTER

27 MAKE YOUR CHOICE

You're almost at the finish line. It is time to make sense of all the hard work you've done. In this last stage of your career design project, you compare your Final Careers to Consider and Research List with your Definite Career Design Components list to see which careers fit you best. Then you investigate and research the best-fitting careers to narrow them down to the final choice.

Inquiry 27-1 HOW WELL DO MY FINAL CAREERS TO CONSIDER FIT MY COMPONENTS?

The goal of this inquiry is to check out how well your Final Careers to Consider and Research list fits your Definite Career Design Components list.

1. For this inquiry, you need worksheets similar to the example on the next page. Create one you can make copies of. Make sure you have as many spaces down the page as you have career design components (as shown in the far-left column of the sample worksheet).
2. Across the top of the page, list careers you think might be the best fit with most of your definite career design components. If you have more careers to consider than will fit across the top of one page, make up as many worksheets as you need. Write in your definite career design components vertically down the left side of the worksheet. If you want, you can group them into the three main categories: "Who You Are," "Why You Work" and "Where You Work."
3. Starting with the first career, go down the column of components and check all the spaces under that career where you think the components match the career. Do the same thing for the other careers. Notice that in the abbreviated sample, brain surgeon fits all the components listed, whereas burger flipper does not. Don't guess. If you don't know whether or not something fits, put a question mark in the space and do some research. It may take time to do this inquiry. The quality of your entire life may depend on doing this well rather than trying to get through it quickly.

CAREER COMPARISON WORKSHEET

Career Design Components	Brain Surgeon	Burger Flipper	Career #3	Career #4	Career #5	Career #6
	Mark columns to show where components match up with a career					
3-D spatial	✓	✓				
Make 400K	✓					
Use my hands	✓	✓				
Respected	✓					
Total check marks	4	2				

4. Total the check marks to see which careers fit your specifications best.
5. Do your best to come up with several careers that fit or mostly fit your Definite Career Design Components so you have several to compare and contrast in the next inquiry.
6. It is possible that no careers fit all your specifications. If that is the case, slap that Detective hat back on your head and do some more research. Or you might decide to drop a component or two that aren't in the "can't live without" category. There is no guarantee that any career will fit absolutely everything.

Inquiry 27-2 **EIGHT GREAT CAREERS**

At this stage, it is time to further narrow down the list of careers that fit you. You are going to compare and contrast the careers on your list. You have seen people do something similar in a grocery store when they're selecting apples from a bin. Few people just grab apples and throw them into a bag. They look at each one, one by one, comparing and contrasting so they get the best. That is exactly what you will do in this inquiry. Before you begin, read all the way through the instructions and then read the next inquiry, 27-3, which concerns research. Use that inquiry to help you with the research you will need to do to complete this one.

1. From the results of the last inquiry, pick approximately eight careers that are as close as possible to being a perfect fit with everything important to you, making sure to include any careers you are now seriously considering. If you have already narrowed the list down to fewer than eight, that's fine.
2. Write the name of each career at the top of a clean page in your notebook. Allow two pages for each career. Work on one career at a time, doing all the steps of the inquiry with one career before moving on to the next. Repeat the process until you have done all eight (or however many you have) completely.

3. On the first page of each two-page spread, write a description of the career you are considering in a way that brings it to life for you, so you are actually able to see yourself, in your mind's eye, in the midst of this career. You want to be able to see, feel, hear, and touch it. Write down exactly what you would probably do each day, how often and how long you would do it, the nature and purpose of the work, functions performed, the physical location, the abilities and traits you would make use of, the kinds of people you would come in contact with, how much money you would make, and so forth. The more multisensory you make your description, the more real it will be for you.
4. If you don't know what's involved in a career, don't guess. You will probably need to do lots of research to understand the real nature of the careers you are describing. You will waste your time trying to do this inquiry based on anything less than sure and certain knowledge of the careers you are considering. If you can't accurately describe these careers in depth, you aren't ready to narrow down. As I've said, I recommend that you do this inquiry along with the in-depth research described in the next inquiry. One reason so many lawyers say they hate their job is that they didn't do this step. They based their decision on inaccurate impressions of the legal profession from TV and movies.
5. Draw a vertical line down the middle of the second page for each of the eight careers. Above the left column, write "Hot," and write "Not Hot" above the right-hand column. Then begin to look critically at all aspects of the career. First, figure out what's hot. Write down everything positive about the career—what is attractive to you, what fits, what feels good, what fulfills your goals, and so forth. Dig deep. Don't just take the obvious, easy answers. Consider everything about this potential career and how it might contribute to you, and you to it. The point of this is to mine all the gold from every possible vein. If one of your "hots" involves working with people, ask yourself other questions concerning people: "How many people? How often? What sort of people? Why be with them? What's the result of our interactions?" Next, do the same thing with everything that is not hot about the potential career. This inquiry will take some time to do well. Spend enough time to explore each fully.
6. Go back over the eight careers. Compare and contrast the "hots" and "not hots" of each with the others. In terms of fit and appeal, which careers rise to the top? Which sink to the bottom? See if you can narrow the list down to fewer final careers to consider. Ask yourself, "What further questions does this inquiry bring to light?"
7. Keep with it until you have narrowed the candidates down to a very few career finalists. Keep using this inquiry and more in-depth research until you make your final choice. Use the next inquiry to help you with your research.

Inquiry 27-3 **IN-DEPTH RESEARCH**

The average American male spends more time researching and considering his first new car purchase than he does in designing his career. Remember, you are going to be driving this career for a long, long time. So please, put in the time to do sufficient research.

Since you are reading this, you should now have a short of list of great careers that are ready for more research. (If you don't, go back to Inquiry 27-2, "Eight Great Careers.") In-depth research will be a very thorough reality check that is best applied to your top few contenders. This stage of research is more extensive. Think of it as dating your career before you marry it.

The point of this research is twofold: to find out enough about a career to be able to predict how well it will fit, and to move beyond any romantic fantasies to the real deal. Will the career satisfy all or most of your career design components? It's going to take some time to turn over all the rocks and learn everything you can about a career. Work to see what each career is really like; flush out all the details down to the hour-by-hour flow of a typical workday. You may be able to do this with research, or you may need to spend some time as an intern in the top fields you are considering.

This last inquiry can take anywhere from a week to months. Put your Detective hat back on. Get your questions answered and prepare yourself to make the final choice.

1. **List your unknowns.** To find out if the careers you turned up with all your hard work are actually a good fit, you need solid information about all aspects of each possible career. To make sure you've covered all the bases, take a look at what you *don't* know. Identify the major unknowns you have for careers you need to research. You probably have incomplete knowledge, missing information, distorted generalizations, and flawed understandings about the careers you are considering.
2. **Ask sharp questions.**

   - The main question to ask is: "What do I need to know in order to make a final choice?" If you can answer this, you will know exactly what research you still need to do.
   - Ask *who, what, when, why,* and *where* questions. Sharpen your questions to make them more specific.
   - Break down your unknowns into specific parts. For example, the question "Will I like to do what doctors do?" is far too general to answer intelligently. First you need to know: "What kind of doctor am I thinking about? What are the day-to-day activities of various medical specialists, especially the one I'm considering? Are my personality and abilities more suited for preventive or acute medical care?" If you're considering joining an organization such as Doctors Without Borders, you'll want to take other things into account, including the strength of your commitment to air-conditioning.

3. **Compile resources and research to-do list.** Determine the best resources to help you gather information to answer your questions. Then do the research. Take a clue from the research you've done before and search three places:

   - *Look inside.* In some cases the best answers are internal. For example, only you can answer a question such as "Should I follow my talents and do something I love or go for a more practical option that has more security?" You can ask other people what they think, but in the end, you get to say.

- *Look outside.* In many cases you need external information. Use all the resources you can come up with, including Internet searches, libraries, company Web sites, college professors, people who do what you are considering, networks of alumni associations, seminars and conventions in the field, professional associations, professional journals and trade magazines, and anything else you can think of. Talk to as many people in the field as possible. Pick their brains. Ask them to be frank about what they like and dislike and exactly how they spend their day. Make sure your questions are razor-sharp.
- *Make up an answer.* In some cases you won't find the answer internally or externally, so you need to invent the answer. (Remember, making up an answer is not guessing because it is based on all your detective work and research.) For example, the question "Can I make 200K as a green architect?" may be hard to answer definitively; there may be no "right" answer out there. In cases like this, you can invent an answer and make a commitment to act on it, such as, "I will do what it takes to become one of the world's best green architects and take home at least 200K per year." Obviously, before you can make a bold statement like that, it pays to do some preliminary external research to make sure your bold promise is within the range of what you deem possible.

4. **State answers and findings.** Sift through all the information you gathered, take notes on what's hot and what's not, and then state your answers.

You could make up a table in your notebook like the following example to manage your in-depth career research effort. Create a chart like this for each career you research fully. For each career, investigate the three major design areas: "Natural Gifts," "Subject Matter and Meaning," and "Workplace Environment" (as shown below). Once you've gone through this process for each career you're considering, use this along with Inquiry 27-2, "Eight Great Careers," to compare and contrast your answers and narrow it all down to your final career choice.

	CAREER TITLE: MECHANICAL ENGINEER		
Research Steps	**Natural Gifts and Job Functions**	**Subject Matter and Meaning**	**Workplace Environment**
1. Unknowns	Not sure if I have the right talents to excel in this field	Not sure if I care about the problems that mechanical engineers solve	Not sure what kinds of companies hire mechanical engineers
2. Questions	Whom can I talk with to learn what talents are needed in this field?	What are the major problems they solve and niche areas they work in?	Which are the innovative companies and where are they geographically?

(continued on next page)

Research Steps (*continued*)	Natural Gifts and Job Functions	Subject Matter and Meaning	Workplace Environment
	How do I know whether I have the right talents? What kinds of people go into this field, and am I like them? What job functions do they typically perform? Am I into building things?	What industries hire mechanical engineers? Why am I attracted to this field? What am I trying to get out of it? Do I care about this subject matter enough?	What type of company do my talents and personality traits fit best with? What kind of human and work culture setting would be best for me? What is the typical pay and benefits?
3. Resources and Research to Do	Talk to three college professors and at least five engineers. Find a career coach, get my aptitudes professionally measured. Read engineering journals and Web sites. Visit an engineering library on campus.	Find professional associations: get recommendations for books to read. Read books to learn about the niches and problems solved in this field. Think about my true motivations; get clear why I would care to do this kind of work. What are my meta-goals here?	Read online blogs about engineering companies and their work environments. Volunteer to work in an engineering company, apply for an internship. Talk to recent grads near my age to get an insider's perspective.
4. Answers and Findings	Mechanical engineers are high in spatial orientation and analytical reasoning. Most are strong introverts with logical, practical mind-sets. I am exactly like this; I would be in my element in this field.	A large percentage of jobs in this field are in the aerospace, defense, home appliance, and automotive industries. I love cars and am very excited about helping to develop on alternative-fuel engine.	Work environments vary widely; it depends on whether they are innovating new products or mass-producing them. I am an innovator, so a small, dynamic firm that designs new products is where I would fit best.

WHAT IF NOTHING FITS ALL MY SPECIFICATIONS?

It may turn out that there aren't any careers that fit all your specifications. It happens all the time. We're always working with at least one client whose ideal career does not fit reality. The root problem is usually one of the following:

1. **"I can't uncover any careers that match all my definite career components."** Stay loose and open-minded. Don't be discouraged if you can't find the perfect match right away. Remember, you are defying the odds with your commitment to have a great career. The taller an order your career components add up to, the more challenging it's going to be to find everything you want instantly.

   Sometimes you have to build up to the perfect career. What you want may not be available until you have jumped up several levels. If you want to be a senior-level executive for a big corporation, you have to work your way to that level. Just starting out, for example, some people buy a "fixer-upper" house, knowing they can work on making it the house of their dreams. If a career matches up with much of what you want but still comes up a little short in some respects, don't throw it out right away. Consider if you can add to it, improve it over time. But be wary! Many folks have conned themselves into careers that don't fit by hoping things will work out later. Regularly check to see if the path upward is actually leading where you want.

   Keep an eye out for ways you can add on the missing components a little further down the road along your career path. Great careers are usually built up over many years. As long as you have a clear vision of where you are headed and launch your career path in the right general direction, you can enjoy the journey as you go about incorporating all your career design components over time.

   You might have to give up on having a "regular job." Most jobs may be too narrow in scope for you. If that's the case, you are just going to have to design your own career as some sort of entrepreneur, whether that means starting a business or working for yourself. This is by far the best way to fit a lot of components together that don't normally correlate with traditional endeavors.

   If you are a big dreamer, are willing to shoot for something extraordinary, and have discovered that all the jobs out there are not interesting enough, don't worry: you're *not* going crazy. These days many people want more than is offered by the cookie-cutter job world, and they're willing and able to generate a career by design. No standard-issue career path fit the guys who created Google. There was nothing out there for them to find, so they made up a career to fulfill their career design components. If you can't find a career that has everything you're committed to, you'll have to make one up. If appropriate, you might want to do another "Eight Great Careers" inquiry focusing on careers you have custom-designed that do not fit into the regular job mold.

2. **"I'm not qualified."** Sometimes people lack the qualifications to do what they want. If you want to be president of the United States and you weren't born in the United States, it isn't going to happen. You need to get yourself a new dream. Most of the time, however, when people say they aren't qualified, the real problem is that they aren't willing to do what it takes. If you want to play NBA ball and you can't shoot well enough, practice. If you want a tenure-track job teaching Ping-Pong, you'll have to become a pioneer and convince the world that Ping-Pong is a worthy college-level subject.

3. **"I'm not willing to do what it takes to make the dream come true."** Whenever anyone says "I can't," I wonder whether they are really saying "I won't" or "I'm not willing to step beyond my beliefs about what I can and can't do." If you catch yourself making a case for why you can't do what you would love to do, you're just having an attack of the yeah-buts. Go back to Chapter 13 and read about the yeah-buts and get those suckers under control.

DECLARE YOUR PROJECT COMPLETE AND CELEBRATE!

You did it! I know how much you have put into this project, all the time, energy, and hard work. I know you kept going when the going got rough, when there was no light at the end of the tunnel, when the yeah-buts were doing their best to shoot you down. You persisted through all of it to arrive here. Congratulations! I wish you the best—a life you love, a passion for your own personal growth and development, and most of all, a commitment to make your world a better place for everyone.

Remember, the final step is to celebrate. Go have yourself an amazing party. You deserve it!

PART 3

The Career Finder

SECTION 8

Additional Tools and Charts

The chapters in this section are tools to help you sharpen up your understanding of your personality and talents and begin to identify careers that might fit you. In order to use them, you must have already done at least some of the inquiries in Section 4, "Natural Gifts." The present section delves deeper and gets more specific as you go through it. I suggest that you start with Chapter 28 and continue all the way through to the end. If you are not sure of your personality type or you are not completely clear about your natural talents, this section will be less useful to you because all of the information in this section is based on your knowing your personality and talents.

You are too complex to find your perfect career on any list. Lists can give you a sense of the kinds of careers that might fit your combination of talents. You want to use the lists to get ideas for further investigation, not as a prescription.

CHAPTER

28 ROCKPORT TYPE AND TALENT INDICATOR

This powerful new approach to the "Who am I?" aspect of career choice integrates personality types with some key natural abilities. It combines your personality type with the Maestro/Tribal indicator and with the spatial/nonspatial scale. For example, if you are an ENFJ, it has a list of careers that fit Maestro ENFJs and another for Tribal ENFJs. Then it takes it a step further and divides those lists into careers that fit spatial, tangible, and nonspatial people. So if you are a spatial Maestro ENFJ, you will find a list of careers that might be a good fit for you.

It works only if you know your personality type and whether you are Maestro or Tribal. And it works best if you know where you fit on the spatial/nonspatial scale. If you aren't sure, I suggest that you go back to chapters 16 and 17, get absolutely certain about your personality and natural talents, and then come back to this chapter.

The best way to use this chapter is to check out the list of careers that fit your type and talents. Notice what the careers have in common. Notice which ones are attractive to you and ask yourself why. Notice which ones are not attractive to you and figure out what it is that makes them unattractive. The game here is to find some great clues. For example, if you notice that the careers in your category that appeal to you involve solving abstract puzzles or using your hands, you might have found a powerful clue. This also might provide some good ideas for your Careers to Explore list.

Very important note: The career lists are no more than suggestions to help you understand yourself. Do not take any of this too literally. The goal is to give you ideas, not a list to pick from. More than one type and talent profile fits each career. You may fit careers that are suggested for other types. Study the whole set of careers for your personality type. For example, if you are a spatial Maestro ENTP but don't like the careers suggested in the spatial column for your type, see what you find interesting in the tangible Maestro ENTP column. Get to know what fits people somewhat like you. You may be attracted to careers that fit combinations closely connected to your own. For example, a Maestro ENTP may feel an attraction to some Tribal ENTP careers. Ask what makes these careers attractive to you.

MAESTRO ENFP

Nonspatial	Tangible	Spatial
actor: theater	adventure education: program designer, instructor	alternative medicine practitioner
coach: personal growth, career change, life planning	alternative therapist: biofeedback, virtual reality therapy	primatologist
consultant: communications, education, HR	cognitive scientist: personality, psychobiology	evolutionary biologist, sociobiologist
drama coach	documentary filmmaker	film director: independent production
law: entertainment, media	Outward Bound guide	fine artist
motivational speaker, self-help seminar leader	photojournalist	holistic medicine: naturopath
organizational development consultant	professor: humanities, film, arts	life sciences professor
psychologist: relationship, spiritual, career	psychologist: sports psychology	neuropsychologist
social entrepreneur	theater director	performing arts: dance instructor
social scientist: emphasis on teaching	therapist: neurolinguistic programming (NLP)	physician: family, psychiatry, preventive
		yoga and meditation instructor

TRIBAL ENFP

Nonspatial	Tangible	Spatial
admissions counselor: college	buyer: educational products, arts, books, music	art therapist
activist: education reform, health care reform, peace	film producer: feature films	athletic coach
agent for actors, artists, writers	internal consultant: HR, organization development	dance/movement therapist
clergy in low-dogma faiths	music therapist	design arts (team leader): set design, new urbanism

counselor: career center staff, outplacement firm	nonprofit director: public health, international development	film director: Hollywood production
diplomat: senior level	nurse: counseling, psychiatric	neurotherapist
journalist: human interest	passenger service representative	nurse: midwifery, psychiatric
fund-raiser	political campaign manager	physician assistant: family practice, preventive
lobbyist: social causes	recreation leader	teacher: spatial arts, computer graphics, dance
marketing/communications director	recreation therapist	team leader: life sciences, technology projects
marketing research	religious activities director	trainer: technology fields, sciences, engineering
meeting facilitator	teacher: high school social studies, history, English	
nonprofit director: social issues, arts/culture advocacy	trainer: applied social sciences, counseling, education	
ombudsman: corporations, universities, government agencies		
public relations director		
school psychologist		
social marketer		
training and development: program designer, trainer		

MAESTRO INFP

Nonspatial	Tangible	Spatial
actor	cognitive scientist: personality, psychobiology	alternative medicine practitioner: naturopath, bodywork
attorney: social change, international human rights	documentary filmmaker	archaeologist
coach: career, life, personal growth	evolutionary biologist	architectural historian

Nonspatial	Tangible	Spatial
consultant: education, organizational behavior	fine artist: impressionist, abstract	choreographer: dance, performing arts
counselor: relationship, spiritual, career change	forensic psychologist	dancer: jazz, improvisational
creative writer: poet, novelist, playwright	historian: history of science	engineer: human-computer interaction, ergonomics
cultural anthropologist, ethnographer	life scientist: wildlife biology, sociobiology	fine artist: sculpture
curriculum designer	photojournalist	industrial designer
drama coach	psychologist	music video filmmaker
economist: family, public, labor, health, education	science journalist	performer: Cirque du Soleil, acting
historian: social, art	software designer: educational application	physical anthropologist
humanities scholar	software developer: graphical user interface	physician: psychiatrist, family, holistic
independent scholar: social sciences, humanities	survey methodologist	primatologist
law professor: psychology of human emotions		screenwriter: independent feature
linguist		set designer
mythologist		somatic psychologist
nonfiction writer: self-help, personal growth		symphony conductor
professor: humanities, social sciences		yoga and meditation instructor
psychologist: evolutionary, educational, organizational		
researcher: social sciences, humanities		

social entrepreneur		
social scientist: sociology, social policy, regional studies		
songwriter/musician		

TRIBAL INFP

Nonspatial	Tangible	Spatial
activist	commercial artist: greeting card designer, advertising	architect: green design, monuments, memorials
advertising: copywriter, Web content writer	foreign service officer: U.S. State Department	artist: 3-D animation, spatial arts
campaign strategist	human-computer interface designer	athletic coach (mental and physical game)
clergy in low-dogma faiths	human factors engineer	design artist: feng shui, interior design, historic parks
fiction writer: historical novels, memoirs, romance	IT: database designer, graphical user interface	screenwriter: educational, sitcom, TV, Hollywood
human resources: training specialist, career coaching	military: human intelligence, psychology ops specialist	set designer: theater, film, costume
journalist: editor, staff writer, freelance	nurse: psych, counseling	urban planner: new urbanism designer
librarian: specialized in social science, arts, humanities		video game designer
mediator		Web site designer: graphic design and information architecture
nonprofit researcher: societal issues		
speechwriter: politics		
training and development: program designer, trainer		

MAESTRO ENFJ

Nonspatial	Tangible	Spatial
career coach	art historian: emphasis on teaching	alternative medicine practitioner
communications consultant: meeting facilitator	art therapist	athletic coach, college level
communications director	documentary filmmaker	film director: independent production
consultant: HR, training program design specialist	music therapist: neurobiological disorders	naturopath
drama coach	professor: life science, medicine	neurotherapist
humanities professor	sports psychologist	physician: family, holistic, preventive
lawyer: mental health, race relations, disability rights		professor, instructor: architecture, design
life coach: personal development, relationships		yoga instructor
psychologist		
public speaker: social causes		
sex therapist		
social sciences professor		
social work counselor: addiction disorders		
trainer: leadership development, team building		

TRIBAL ENFJ

Nonspatial	Tangible	Spatial
administrator: health care, adult education	camp director	athletic coach, high-school level
admissions counselor: college	nurse manager	design arts manager
advertising account executive	outplacement counselor	film director: Hollywood production
agent for actors, artists, writers	producer: films, TV programs, television promotions	military officer: broadcasting director
association executive	speech pathologist	physician assistant
clergy	supervisor, manager, team leader	urban planning: project manager
counselor: career, public health, student advisor	Web site producer	
dean, university president	teacher: visual arts, graphic arts	
diplomat: senior level	information architect: project manager	
fund-raiser		
human resources director		
marketing director		
mediator		
newscaster: human interest		
nonprofit director: social causes, arts promotion		
political consultant: campaign strategist		
politician: state senator, U.S. senator		
public relations consultant		

Nonspatial	Tangible	Spatial
recruiter		
sales manager		
teacher: high school English, history, music		

MAESTRO INFJ

Nonspatial	Tangible	Spatial
coach: career, life, personal growth	art appraiser	acupuncturist
consultant: education, human resources	art historian	alternative medicine practitioner: naturopath
counselor: relationship, spiritual, career	composer: film scores	archaeologist
drama coach	information science specialist	architectural historian
entrepreneur: education- and human-development-related	IT: database designer	artist: sculptor
humanities scholar: history, literature, musicology	playwright	challenge course designer: outdoor adventure
law professor	training and development: program designer, presenter	computer game designer
lawyer: art, civil, employment, comparative family law	Web site design: information architect	engineer: human-computer interaction, ergonomics
nonprofit: director of writing and research		geographer: economic, political, cultural, historical
organizational behavior and development specialist		holistic therapist: mind/body connection
politician: U.S. senator		organic farmer: environmental educator
psychologist/therapist: narrative therapy, neurolinguistic programming		screenwriter: feature-length screenplay
researcher: political think tank		symphony conductor

social scientist		
social work: researcher, program development		
songwriter/musician		
writer: biographer		

TRIBAL INFJ

Nonspatial	Tangible	Spatial
activist	commercial artist: graphic arts, advertising	architect: sustainable development, green
advertising: copywriter, Web site content writer	film editor	design artist: sets, monuments, historic parks
clergy in low-dogma faiths	human-computer interaction designer	exhibit designer: museums, living history exhibits
director: education or social service nonprofit	human factors engineer	industrial design artist
editor: book, magazine, newspaper journalist	information architect	physician assistant: psychiatric, preventive
grant writer	jury consultant	screenwriter: TV, sitcom
human resources: career planning and leadership trainer	marketing research analyst	software development: graphical user interface designer
meeting facilitator, mediator	nurse: psych, counseling, midwife	urban planning: landscape architect
paralegal: researcher, law librarian	physician: psychiatrist, family, preventive	
public policy analyst	reference librarian: college library	
public relations/communications: writer, researcher	script reader: film	
researcher/writer: advocacy, nonprofit, policy think tank		

Nonspatial	Tangible	Spatial
social marketer		
speechwriter		
strategic planner		
TV sitcom writer		
resume writer		

MAESTRO ENTP

Nonspatial	Tangible	Spatial
academic professor: law, social sciences, public policy	academic professor: mathematics, computer science	architecture: sustainable development consultant
consultant: change management, social change projects	consultant: MIS, telecommunications, business systems	academic professor: engineering, physical and life sciences
foreign service officer: U.S. State Department	documentary filmmaker	consultant: engineering, medicine, science applications
humanities scholar	entrepreneur: new technologies, scientific research	ecologist
investment fund manager: emerging markets	epidemiologist	evolutionary scientist
lawyer: constitutional, intellectual property	executive coach	inventor
political pundit, columnist	math tutor: coach high schoolers how to pass SATs	life and physical scientist: chief researcher
political scientist	social entrepreneur	neuropsychologist, neuroscience, neurology
social critic		physician: medical scientist, preventive medicine
social policy researcher: think tank, nonprofit		

Nonspatial	Tangible	Spatial
social scientist: emphasis on teaching		software and engineering design: technical team leader
venture capitalist		space exploration: NASA scientist

TRIBAL ENTP

Nonspatial	Tangible	Spatial
agent: literary, film	advertising, creative director	architect: marketing role, educator
campaign strategist	business systems analyst	construction manager
journalist: investigative reporter	CEO, high-tech companies	design engineer: research and development (all fields)
lobbyist	corporate executive: special-projects developer	industrial designer: new-product innovation
manager: leading-edge company	design arts: project manager	instructor/professor: medicine, science, engineering
marketer	film producer	physician assistant: neurology, cardiology
political analyst	intelligence agent: U.S. homeland security, CIA, FBI	project manager: physical sciences, engineering
politician: U.S. senator, U.S. congressman, U.S. president	intelligence analyst: CIA, FBI, DIA, NSA, DEA	real estate developer: green buildings
public relations publicist	military officer: counterintelligence, interrogator	science/math teacher: high school AP courses
strategic planner		

MAESTRO INTP

Nonspatial	Tangible	Spatial
comedian: comedy writer, performer	artificial intelligence research	archaeologist
cultural anthropologist	bioinformatics	biologist: all subspecialties
economist: international, development, game theory	computer programmer	biomedical engineering: virtual-reality engineer

Nonspatial	Tangible	Spatial
historian: prehistory, ancient, world	documentary filmmaker	chemist: all subspecialties
independent scholar: social sciences, humanities	economist: environmental and natural resource	computer scientist
judge: federal courts and Supreme Court	epidemiologist	design engineer: research and development (all fields)
lawyer: constitutional, intellectual property	evolutionary scientist: sociobiology	ecologist: global warming research
linguistic scientist	fiction writer: sci-fi, horror, screenwriter	film: special effects and animation artist
mathematician: theoretical, operations research	fine artist	forensic artist
musician: jazz/classical guitarist, violinist, pianist	lawyer: international environmental law	forensic paleontologist
musicologist	political cartoonist	forensic scientist: biochemist, geneticist
nonfiction writer: sciences, politics, technology	psychologist: psychometrics, cognitive science	geneticist
philosopher	researcher: computer science, new technology	inventor
political pundit, columnist	social entrepreneur: new technologies	lawyer: patent
political scientist		life and physical scientist: emphasis on research
psychiatrist		nanotechnology scientist
researcher: social sciences		neuroscientist, neuropsychologist
social critic		optical engineer: lasers, holography
social policy researcher: think tank, nonprofit		physician: medical scientist, academic research
social science professor		physicist: all subspecialties
		researcher: life science, physical science

sociologist		robotics researcher
statistician		software architect, designer, developer
		surgeon: plastics, neurology, cardiology

TRIBAL INTP

Nonspatial	Tangible	Spatial
editor: social sciences, public health, public policy	advertising artist	architect: green technologies, new urbanism
financial analyst	environmental planner	industrial designer
grant writer	intelligence agent: U.S. homeland security, CIA, FBI	interior design, interior planner
investment analyst: mutual fund, stock/ bond analyst	intelligence analyst: CIA, FBI, DIA, NSA, DEA	physician assistant: surgery, oncology, neurology
journalist: media criticism, politics, science, health	military officer: counterintelligence, interrogator	urban designer
lawyer: researcher, district attorney, military lawyer (JAG)	technical writer	video game animator
marketing researcher	urban planner	yacht and marine designer
public policy: researcher, analyst		
strategic planner		

MAESTRO ENTJ

Nonspatial	Tangible	Spatial
college professor: economics, law, political science	college professor: IT, MIS, computer science	architectural consultant
credit investigator	consultant: management, business systems, IT, MIS	college professor: engineering, physical sciences
economic consultant	engineering executive	computer security specialist

Nonspatial	Tangible	Spatial
Federal Reserve: economic analyst, board member	entrepreneur	engineering consultant
financial planner	epidemiologist	medical specialist: environmental, virology, immunology
judge: federal courts and Supreme Court	executive coach	sales rep: pharmaceutical, medical equipment
lawyer: ethics, health policy, trial		
lobbyist		
military officer: lawyer, judge		
mortgage banker		
SEC analyst		
stockbroker		
strategic planner		

TRIBAL ENTJ

Nonspatial	Tangible	Spatial
administrator: college dean, university president	business manager: high-tech, engineering	architect: project manager
corporate leader: CEO, board of directors	business systems analyst	athletic coach
journalist: reporter	chief information officer (CIO)	computer systems analyst
manager: sales, marketing	federal agency director: FEMA, EPA, FDA, FCC	construction manager
mutual fund manager	general manager, senior level	design engineer: technical team leader
mutual fund trader	intelligence agent: U.S. homeland security, CIA, FBI	manufacturing executive
nonprofit: director, program designer		patent agent, attorney
		project manager: engineering, software, IT

politician: U.S. president, U.S. senator	intelligence analyst: CIA, FBI, DIA, NSA, DEA	shop foreman: auto repair service
project team leader	lawyer: public defender, district attorney	U.S. foreign service: medical officer
public policy analyst	salesperson: high-tech	U.S. surgeon general
sales: banking, securities		

MAESTRO INTJ

Nonspatial	Tangible	Spatial
curriculum designer	artificial intelligence scientist	acoustic engineer: concert hall, recording studio designer
economist: financial, business, history of economics	bioinformatics expert	biologist: all subspecialties
forensic accounting expert	computer programmer: software development consultant	biomedical engineer
historian	consultant: business, information technology	chemist: all subspecialties
journalist: technology, political columnist	forensic psychiatry	computer forensics specialist
judge: federal courts and Supreme Court	information technology: network and database design	computer hardware engineer
law professor	lawyer: housing, criminal, health care, public health	computer security specialist
lawyer: constitutional, immigration, international finance	mathematician: applied problem solving	design engineer: all fields
musicologist	psychologist: research, psychometrics, cognitive science	economist: urban and rural, agricultural, development
political science professor	science writer	environmental engineer
psychiatrist		forensic scientist: biochemist, geneticist
social policy researcher: think tank, nonprofit		genetic engineer
sociologist		inventor
statistician		lawyer: patent, antitrust, technology, land use, cyberlaw

Nonspatial	Tangible	Spatial
		pharmacologist
		physician: neurology, cardiology, facial reconstruction
		physicist: all subspecialties
		robotics engineer
		software architect, designer, developer

TRIBAL INTJ

Nonspatial	Tangible	Spatial
CEO, high-tech	computer programmer: banking, financial applications	architect
financial analyst	electronics engineer, technician	computer programmer: engineering, manufacturing applications
grant writer	environment planner	computer systems analyst
investment analyst: mutual fund, stock/ bond analyst	intelligence analyst: CIA, FBI, DIA, NSA	industrial designer
journalist: editor, staff writer	lawyer: public defender	landscape architect
loan officer: banking, mortgage, small business	military enlisted: electronic technician	patent agent, examiner
marketing researcher	urban planner	physician assistant: cardiovascular surgery
military officer: lawyer, judge		structural engineer
public policy analyst		transportation planner
SEC analyst		urban designer
strategic planner		

MAESTRO ESFP

Nonspatial	Tangible	Spatial
actor	animal trainer, pet psychologist	art appraiser
comedian	athlete	athlete: gymnast
entrepreneur: specialty products and services	botanist	chiropractor
language professor	Outward Bound instructor	cinematographer
music teacher	public health scientist	dance instructor, choreographer
pharmaceutical sales representative	recreational therapist	dermatologist
singer, performer	restaurant manager, host, hostess	makeup artist
social worker: young adults, teens at risk	sport psychologist	midwife
	wellness and fitness nutrition expert	naturopathic doctor
	wine steward, sommelier	sports medicine practitioner
		wildlife biologist

TRIBAL ESFP

Nonspatial	Tangible	Spatial
advertising account executive	B&B owner, manager	athletic coach
communications director: associations, nonprofits	entrepreneur: restaurant, hospitality, retail	cheerleader
diplomat	health promotion manager	chef
foundation manager	health spa manager	firefighter
fund-raiser	merchandiser, product buyer	gym teacher
marketing director	personal shopper, image consultant	hairstylist

Nonspatial	Tangible	Spatial
mediator	personal trainer	kindergarten teacher
military officer: public affairs officer, broadcast manager	police officer	nurse: emergency, sexual assault forensics
newscaster	politician: city council, mayor	paramedic
press secretary	sales rep: manufacturers, distributors, service providers	physical therapist
producer/promoter: film, TV	salesperson: housewares	U.S. foreign service: health practitioner
public relations, public affairs specialist	teacher: elementary school, science, physical education	
salesperson	travel: agent, tour guide, TV program host	
talk show host: travel, food, entertainment	Web site producer	

MAESTRO ISFP

Nonspatial	Tangible	Spatial
actor	animator: film, video games, cartoons	animal rescue officer
animal trainer, pet psychologist	art therapist	art and antiques appraiser
entertainer	body builder	art conservator
meditation and relaxation teacher	botanist	artisan, craftsman
music teacher	cartoonist	athlete
musician, performer, singer	cheese maker	baker, cake maker
occupational/vocational counselor	color specialist	chef
social worker: teens at risk, inmate rehab	dietitian	cinematographer
songwriter	fashion model	dancer, ballerina, figure skater, gymnast

special education tutor

training and development specialist

travel writer

fitness trainer

graphic artist, multimedia specialist

nutritionist: clinical specialist

painter: ornaments, fine wood, home interiors

pastry chef

perfumer artisan

photographer: fashion, nature, advertising, travel

poet

public health scientist

wildlife biologist: nature photographer, conservationist

wine and cheese shop owner

wine steward, sommelier

yoga instructor

fine artist: portrait, mural, landscape, sculpture

forester

gardener, plant nursery, landscaper

luthier: instrument maker/repairer

makeup artist

massage therapist: sport, Rolfing

military: plastic surgeon, dietitian, counselor

naturopathic doctor, holistic medicine

performer: Cirque du Soleil gymnast, acrobat

performing arts medicine: musician injuries

physician: plastic surgeon, audiologist, emergency, sports medicine

potter, glassblower, stained-glass maker

restoration specialist: historical homes and buildings

stonemason, woodworker

veterinarian

TRIBAL ISFP

Nonspatial	Tangible	Spatial
communicator: PR, public affairs, public outreach	advertising artist: photography, 2-D art	advertising artist: 3-D graphics
customer service representative	bartender, waiter/waitress	aerobics instructor
editor	child care provider: day care center	bodyworker: massage, Rolfing, etc.
employment counselor	children's book writer, artist	drafting technician: computer-aided design
guidance counselor	entrepreneur: retail, personal services, B&B owner	dressmaker: wedding, special occasions
interpreter	fashion buyer, sales	firefighter
language teacher	interior decorator	hairstylist
matchmaker: dating service	personal assistant	interior designer
mediator	police officer	jewelry designer
recruiter, staffing adviser	product buyer	landscape architect
student adviser, admissions counselor	secret shopper	nurse: emergency, psych, first assist
teacher: preschool, K-12, ESL	U.S. foreign service: health practitioner	set designer, costume designer, film location scout

MAESTRO ESFJ

Nonspatial	Tangible	Spatial
genetic counselor	antiques dealer	animal rescue officer
hospice counselor	caterer	chiropractor
job counselor: unemployment office	food service specialist	medical technologist: allied health
language professor	health educator	personal trainer

religious educator	nutritionist	physician: gynecologist, obstetrician, pediatrician
social work counselor: mental health, drug rehab	recreation therapist	physician: palliative care, pain management, geriatrics
special education teacher	sales rep: manufacturers, distributors, service providers	physician's assistant
trainer: customer service, sales	shopkeeper: specialty items	space planner: retail, grocery, commercial
weight management counselor	special event designer	sports physician
		veterinarian (primary care)

TRIBAL ESFJ

Nonspatial	Tangible	Spatial
account executive: sales, marketing	assisted-living attendant	athletic coach
administrator: social services, public health	bartender, host/hostess, waiter/waitress	dental hygienist
advertising sales: hospitality, human resources, health	funeral home director	engineering manager
concierge	grocery store manager	food service manager
customer care liaison	hospitality manager: hotel, restaurant, innkeeper, health spa	general contractor
diplomat	interior decorator	hairstylist
health care administrator	nurse manager	health club manager
human resources manager	office manager	hospitality manager: restaurant, hotel, B&B, resort
marketing manager	personal shopper	household/holiday crafts maker
military: public affairs officer, personnel manager, recruiter	politician: city mayor, municipal government council	nurse: gerontology, midwife, pediatric
news reporter, broadcaster	real estate agent	occupational therapist
		physical therapist: recreational, pediatric

Nonspatial	Tangible	Spatial
personal secretary	retail management	police officer
receptionist	sales engineer	property manager
recruiter	teacher: preschool, kindergarten, elementary, ESL	window display designer: retail
retail salesperson	travel agent, planner	
sales party host: cookware, cosmetics, jewelry	wedding planner	
school principal		

MAESTRO ISFJ

Nonspatial	Tangible	Spatial
counselor: drug rehab, hospice, geriatric, crisis hotline	animal trainer	acupuncturist
language professor	art and antiques appraiser	animal rescue officer
lawyer: family, divorce, human resources, tort and accident	art therapist	art restoration specialist
librarian: information science specialist	baker	artisan, craftsman
mediator	botanist	chef
meditation teacher	calligrapher	curator, conservator
religious educator, scholar	cheese maker	dentist: orthodontics, endodontics
special education tutor	color specialist	food scientist
training and development specialist	entrepreneur: retail, personal services, B&B owner	forester
	gardener	furniture maker
	nutritionist: clinical specialist	industrial designer
	organic farmer	instrument maker

	perfumer artisan	medical technologist: allied health technician
	sport psychologist	midwife
	technical sales support person	military: plastic surgeon, dietitian
	trainer: hardware/software technologies	nurse: research
	wine and cheese shop owner	optometrist
		pastry chef
		physician: family practice, pediatrician, internist

TRIBAL ISFJ

Nonspatial	Tangible	Spatial
administrative assistant, secretary	child care provider: day care center	anesthesiologist
customer service representative	children's book writer	dental hygienist
editor	clinical dietitian: home health, rehab facility	fashion designer
educational administrator	dietetic technician	firefighter
guidance counselor	health service worker	graphic artist, multimedia specialist
human resources administrator, generalist	innkeeper	hairdresser, cosmetologist
insurance agent	interior decorator	interior designer
interpreter, translator	IT network administrator	jewelry designer
librarian, archivist	librarian: multimedia management	landscape architect
magazine editor	manager: restaurant, retail, personal services	massage therapist
	PC technician: help desk	nurse: generalist, rehab, hospice, occupational

Nonspatial	Tangible	Spatial
matchmaker: dating service	personal chef	occupational therapist
medical transcriber	pet groomer	paramedic
paralegal	police officer	physical therapist, exercise physiologist, kinesiologist
personal assistant	product buyer	respiratory therapist
priest, minister, rabbi, monk, nun	retail store clerk, cashier	speech pathologist
receptionist	teacher: preschool, K-12, ESL	veterinary assistant
social work administrator: adoption, foster care		Web site designer
student adviser, admissions counselor		zookeeper

MAESTRO ESTP

Nonspatial	Tangible	Spatial
business consultant	athletic coach	astronaut
corporate lawyer	auctioneer	athlete
entrepreneur: specialized products and services	ecotourism guide	driver: tank, truck, construction and heavy equipment
financial planner	fitness instructor	earth sciences: geology, volcanology, seismology
negotiator	lawyer: military, sports	explorer
stockbroker	outdoor-challenge course guide	home inspector
tax consultant	pharmacist	IT: PC and network troubleshooter, problem solver
	photographer: adventure, wartime correspondent	physician: intemist, oncologist, physiatrist
	retail store owner: specialty products	

		pilot: military training
		racer: auto, boat, motorcycle
		real estate developer
		resource extraction engineer: mining, petroleum
		special forces: Navy SEAL, Green Beret, special ops
		stunt actor
		surgeon: emergency medicine, battlefield
		veterinarian

TRIBAL ESTP

Nonspatial	Tangible	Spatial
actuarial manager	agriculture: farm manager	air traffic control manager
auditing manager, supervisor	bicycle tour guide	construction manager
broadcast news reporter	drug enforcement agent (DEA)	firefighter: urban, forest fires
lawyer: corporate	engineering manager: all specialties, field and test	food service manager
marketing presenter	executive: hands-on, operations, manufacturing	forestry: land manager
retail business manager	field agent: CIA, FBI	mechanic supervisor
sales manager	insurance adjuster: natural disaster claims	military officer: artillery, missile systems, tank
tax manager	law enforcement: detective, CSI, police officer	paramedic: ambulance driver, EMT, helicopter pilot
white-collar crime investigator	project manager: business, technical	physical therapist: sports medicine

Nonspatial	Tangible	Spatial
	real estate agent: commercial	search and rescue worker: FEMA, National Guard
	recreational therapist	trades: carpenter, plumber, HVAC technician
	Secret Service agent	
	teacher: math, physics, chemistry	
	technical salesperson: engineering, medical, heavy equipment	
	travel tour manager	

MAESTRO ISTP

Nonspatial	Tangible	Spatial
accountant: forensic, auditing, forecasting, tax	agriculture: organic farmer, beekeeper, farm manager	adventure education: outdoor challenge course designer
actuary	animal scientist	astronaut
business consultant	diplomatic security: special agent	athlete: golf, baseball, basketball
entrepreneur: practical products and services	ecotourism guide	chef
financial planner	horticulture: botanist, winemaker, gardener	construction: surveyor, landscaper
lawyer: mergers and acquisitions, securities regulation	IT: PC and network troubleshooter, problem solver	dentist: emergency surgeon, forensic dentistry
statistician	operations research scientist	driver: tank, truck, construction and heavy equipment
stock analyst	Outward Bound guide	earth scientist: geology, volcanology, seismology, geomorphology
tax consultant	personal services: barber, personal chef	forestry: forester, arborist, ecologist, land manager
technical writer	pharmacist	

venture capital analyst	photographer: news, wartime correspondent	gemologist
	soil scientist	home inspector
		hunter, fisherman
		lifeguard
		martial arts instructor
		mechanic: general, race car, motorcycle, aircraft
		military: fighter pilot, infantry officer, machine gunner
		mining engineer, mineralogist
		mountain medicine practitioner: altitude illness, hypothermia, frostbite
		nurse: ICU, emergency room
		optometrist
		petroleum engineer: offshore drilling, geochemistry
		physician: ophthalmologist, orthopedic surgeon, forensic pathologist
		pilot: military, news, stunt, recreational
		racer: auto, boat, motorcycle
		scuba diver: industrial underwater welder
		special forces: Navy SEAL, Green Beret, special ops
		sport physician

Nonspatial	Tangible	Spatial
		stunt actor
		surgeon: ER, military flight or field surgeon
		surveyor/mapper

TRIBAL ISTP

Nonspatial	Tangible	Spatial
chief financial officer (CFO)	athletic coach	dental assistant
chief information officer (CIO)	bicycle tour guide	engineer: all specialties, field and test, Army Corps
chief operations officer (COO)	drug enforcement agent (DEA)	firefighter: urban, forest fires
corporate executive (all levels)	executive: hands-on, operations, construction	paramedic: ambulance driver, EMT, helicopter pilot
executive secretary	insurance adjuster	search and rescue worker: FEMA, National Guard
financial analyst	intelligence field agent: CIA, FBI	teacher: high school physics, geometry, shop
lawyer: corporate, contracts, copyright	law enforcement: detective, CSI, police officer	trades: carpenter, electrician, plumber, mason
	production operations analyst	
	project manager: business, technical	
	recreational attendant	
	Secret Service agent	
	teacher: math, biology, chemistry	
	technician: allied health, lab, IT, telecom, TV/radio	
	video camera technician	
	white-collar crime investigator	

MAESTRO ESTJ

Nonspatial	Tangible	Spatial
auditor	computer programmer: technical team leader	chef
business consultant: accounting, auditing	dietitian	computer security analyst
business systems analyst	FBI field agent	computer systems analyst
certified public accountant (CPA)	funeral director	conservationist
entrepreneur: practical products	industrial engineer	earth scientist: geologist, hydrologist
financial planner	IT consultant	engineering consultant (all specialties)
insurance agent, broker, or underwriter	pharmaceutical sales representative	field technician: HVAC, telecom, cable TV
IRS agent	technical salesperson: engineering, medical, heavy equipment	medical equipment representative
judge: municipal court		physical therapist: speech pathologist, occupational
lawyer: corporate, tax, real estate, estate planning		physician: oncology, urology, orthopedics
stockbroker		quality inspector: USDA, FDA, EPA, indoor air, safety
		space planner

TRIBAL ESTJ

Nonspatial	Tangible	Spatial
actuarial manager	business operations manager: all industries	construction manager
administrator: health, school, government	engineering manager	dental hygienist
audit supervisor	event planner	engineer: team-centered
bank manager	food service manager	firefighter, paramedic, EMT

Nonspatial	Tangible	Spatial
cashier	homeland security analyst	general contractor
chief executive officer (CEO)	immigration officer	manufacturing foreperson, supervisor
chief information officer (CIO)	insurance adjuster	military manager: communications, supplies
chief operations officer (COO)	project manager: all industries	nurse: RN, case manager, rehab manager
corporate executive (all levels)	office manager	patent agent
executive assistant	purchasing agent	physician assistant: orthopedics
loan officer	police chief	production operations manager
mutual fund trader	real estate agent	shop foreperson: auto repair
sales manager	real estate manager	
school principal	retail store manager	
stock broker	sales rep: manufacturers, distributors, service providers	
tax manager	teacher of practical material: math, gym, shop, technical	
	travel tour manager	

MAESTRO ISTJ

Nonspatial	Tangible	Spatial
actuary: health, life, annuities, property, pensions, insurance	computer programmer	adventure guide
auditor	conservationist	airline pilot
business consultant	defense intelligence analyst	applied mathematician
business systems analyst	dietitian	chemist: inorganic

certified public accountant (CPA)	electrical engineer	computer security analyst
compliance analyst	entrepreneur: practical products	dentist: general, periodontist
financial planner	historian: military, Civil War	earth scientist: geologist, hydrologist
forensic accountant	industrial engineer	engineering consultant: civil, mechanical, reliability
lawyer: business, tax, real estate, estate planning, mergers	IT: database and network administrator, PC technician	entomologist
mutual fund accountant	operations research scientist	environmental engineer
statistician	pharmacist	farmer, hunter, fisherman
stock analyst	compliance specialist: pharmaceuticals, biotech, chemistry	field technician: HVAC, telecom, cable TV
tax analyst	quality assurance specialist: engineering, biotech	forest ranger
technical writer: business-related	technical writer: computer, software related	green architecture specialist
		heavy equipment operator
		historic restoration specialist
		lawyer: patent, property, land use
		machinery operator
		metallurgist
		meteorologist
		physical therapist: speech pathologist, occupational
		physician: surgeon, pathologist, podiatrist, radiologist
		technical writer: engineering-related
		woodworking specialist: furniture maker

TRIBAL ISTJ

Nonspatial	Tangible	Spatial
accountant: general	chef: short-order cook, line chef	athletic coach
administrator: public health, school, health care, government	clinical research librarian	autoCAD technician
bank teller	event and travel planner	combat engineer: U.S. Army
business manager: Fortune 500	FBI analyst	computer systems analyst
chief financial officer (CFO)	homeland security analyst	construction manager
chief information officer (CIO)	immigration officer	engineer: all specialties, field and test
chief operations officer (COO)	insurance adjuster	engineering manager
corporate executive (all levels)	manager: retail store, operations, projects	firefighter, paramedic, EMT
executive assistant	property manager	materials engineer
financial analyst	purchasing manager, inventory control, supply chain	mechanic: aircraft, auto, diesel, heavy equipment
government employee	quality inspector: USDA, FDA, EPA, indoor air, safety	military: resource management analyst, aircraft navigator
IRS agent	real estate manager	nurse: OR, radiology, generalist
lawyer: corporate, business law, bankruptcy	reference librarian: business research	patent examiner
librarian	security engineering officer: U.S. State Department	police officer: civil servant, military police
office manager	security guard	production operations manager
paralegal	summer camp director	roadway engineer
school principal	teacher: math, gym, shop	teacher: shop, vocational
		technician: lab, science, engineering, health, TV/radio
		trades: carpenter, electrician, mason, plumber
		wastewater/drainage engineer

CHAPTER

29 THE FOUR TEMPERAMENTS

All of us are born with a disposition or temperament that plays a big role in shaping our personality. A useful way to learn about your temperament is to combine the middle two elements of your Rockport Personality Type Indicator. Refer to your personality type in Chapter 17; the middle two elements of your personality type make up your temperament.

There are four temperaments: NF, NT, SF, and ST.

THE BASICS ON TEMPERAMENT

As you go about your daily life, the way you perceive the world and behave largely depend on how your brain is wired. Each of us is born with preset perception and decision-making styles. We are largely predisposed to see the world through the lens we were born with. Our innate temperament is a big part of what makes us who we are.

PERCEPTION—SENSOR OR INTUITIVE?

Some people perceive the world through a more literal lens; they were born with a sensing style. These people are called Sensors (S). Your eyes, ears, nose, mouth, and sense of touch are continuously receiving factual input from the external world. Others perceive the world through a figurative lens; they were born with an intuitive style, and are called Intuitives (N). Intuition gives your perceptions context and personal meaning.

Sensors are usually very observant of their physical surroundings. Many of them love to engage in tangible activities that rely on some specialized use of the five senses. Most of the U.S. population, about 70–75 percent, measure as Sensors. On the other side of the perception system are strong Intuitives, who are typically attracted to explore hidden meaning in situations. They like to dream up or add new meaning to the facts, such as the poet who sees the universe in a grain of sand. About 25–30 percent of the U.S. population measure as Intuitives.

DECISION MAKING—THINKER OR FEELER?

Some people make decisions objectively and logically by emphasizing the thinking style. These people are called Thinkers (T). Others make decisions subjectively and personally by emphasizing the feeling style; they're called Feelers (F).

Thinkers fit well in fields such as law, business, and engineering, where they can logically size up situations using rational and quantitative decision making; in making decisions, they tend to emphasize empirical truth over tact and compassion. Feelers fit well in fields such as psychology, advertising, and design arts, where they can use their empathy or sense of personal style to read the emotional needs and desires of others; in making decisions, they tend to give more weight to tactful diplomacy than to logical truth and established procedure.

The following tables provide a breakout of the four temperaments, as well as how they combine with the four Core Personality Types, described in Chapter 18.

NF (INTUITIVE FEELER) PERSONALITY TEMPERAMENT CHART

Type Indicator	Traits/Talents	Style	Key Job Functions	Main Motivations	Work Environment	Quirks	Pet Peeves
ENFP	Idealistic	Affirming	Initiate new projects	Originality	Entrepreneurial	Perfectionist	Hierarchies
ENFJ	Emotional	Supportive	Change agent	Be authentic	Leader in field	Easily bored	Bureaucracies
INFP	Warm	Cooperative	Create new vision	See all sides	Innovative	Too many ideas	Greedy Fortune 500 companies
INFJ	Creative	Positive	Dream	Seek meaning	Scholarly	Indecisive	Status quo
	Imaginative	Open	Design	Change the world	Intellectual	Anything's possible	Complacent people
	Original	Multifaceted	Imagine	Personal growth	Think tank	Head in the clouds	Traditional religion
	Artistic	Sensitive	See new possibilities	Make a difference	Academia	Too nice	Accounting
		Compassionate	Mentor	Understand people	Pioneering	Too sensitive	Conspicuous consumption
			Coach	Improve society	Change agent	Overly understanding	Power mongering
			Counsel	Beauty		See the positive side of everything	Unimaginative leadership
			Facilitate	Elegance		Unrealistic	Tribal politics
			Advise	Simplicity		Space cadet	
			Guide			Odd	
						Unrealistic	

NF PERSONALITY TEMPERAMENT (COMBINED WITH CORE PERSONALITY GROUPS)

Personality Group	Traits/Talents	Style	Key Job Functions	Main Motivations	Work Environment	Quirks	Pet Peeves
Extroverted Maestro	Enlighten Invent	Enthusiastic Expressive	Direct Teach, advise	Pass on a legacy	Entrepreneurial Innovative	Big ego Always evocative	Most corporations Working for others
Introverted Maestro	Inspire Illuminate	Deep, quiet Poetic, artistic	Write Design	Personal expression	Solitude Autonomy	Overly idealistic Eccentric, odd	Commercialism Pop culture
Extroverted Tribal	Encourage Facilitate	Zestful Responsive	Manage Present, promote	Share new ideas	Socially responsible	Overly outgoing Easily hurt	Logical arguments Mathematical fields
Introverted Tribal	Insightful Caring	Intellectual Intense	Research, edit Write, train	Help others grow	Entrepreneurial	Very private Passive, shy	Noise Arrogant people

NF PERSONALITY TEMPERAMENT (COMBINED WITH PERCEIVING AND JUDGING)

Attitude	Traits/Talents	Style	Key Job Functions	Main Motivations	Work Environment	Quirks	Pet Peeves
Perceiving	Improvise Perceptive	Playful Versatile	Conceptualize	Seek new possibilities	Start up	Lots of dreaming, not much doing	Mediocrity, shortsighted-ness
Judging	Tactful Careful planner	Thorough Accommo-dating	Design	Heal, encourage	Entrepreneurial	One foot on the gas, one on the brake	Closed-minded people

NT (INTUITIVE THINKER) PERSONALITY TEMPERAMENT CHART

Type Indicator	Traits/Talents	Style	Key Job Functions	Main Motivations	Work Environment	Quirks	Pet Peeves
ENTP	Objective	Independent	Design	Seek perfection	Entrepreneurial	Lose interest after newness wears off	Daily operations
ENTJ	Inventive	Improviser	Invent	Pursue objectivity	Leader in field	Despise incompetence	Routine
INTP	Insightful	Witty	Simulate	Challenge status quo	Innovative	Bored with routine	Repetition
INTJ	Visionary	Quick-minded	Conceptualize	Intellectual mastery	Scholarly	Can be intimidating	Bureaucracy
	Forward-thinking	Rebellious	Strategize	Demonstrate logic	Intellectual	Sharp-tongued	Production
	See the big picture	Perfectionist	Research	Find the truth	Think tank	Ambitious	Positions that require constant empathy
	Problem solver	Clever	Analysis	Understanding the root cause	Academia	Impersonal	Ignorance
	See new possibilities	Lifelong learner	Critique	Exploring new possibilities	Pioneering	Argumentative	Irrational thinking
	Architect of new ideas	Precise	Find flaws		Change agent	Geeky	Inefficiency
	Imaginative	Deep, cerebral	Improve systems			Brainy	Stupidity
		Skeptical	Plan ahead			Bookworm	Dogma
		Questioning	Change agent				Blind faith
		Critical					
		Open-minded					
		Tough-minded					
		Questioning					
		Curious					

NT PERSONALITY TEMPERAMENT (COMBINED WITH CORE PERSONALITY GROUPS)

Personality Group	Traits/Talents	Style	Key Job Functions	Main Motivations	Work Environment	Quirks	Pet Peeves
Extroverted Maestro	Educate Enlighten	Gregarious Visible expert	Teach and mentor Visionary leader	Communicate new vision	Entrepreneurial Consultative	Controlling Intimidating	Tribal politics Managing people
Introverted Maestro	Question Find the truth	Deep Scientific	Write and research Pioneer	Develop the perfect theory	Autonomy Scholarly	Annoyed by people Knows everything	Everything but innovation
Extroverted Tribal	Decisive Competent	Be in charge Tough	Lead Supervise	Run the show	Vanguard edge, leader in field	Bossy Argumentative	Slackers, losers
Introverted Tribal	Thorough Resourceful	Precise Skeptical	Analysis Design and plan	Design and improve everything	Solitude Constant challenge	Impersonal Realist	Incompetence

NT PERSONALITY TEMPERAMENT (COMBINED WITH PERCEIVING AND JUDGING)

Attitude	Traits/Talents	Style	Key Job Functions	Main Motivations	Work Environment	Quirks	Pet Peeves
Perceiving	Improvise Adaptable	Break rules Open-ended	Invent new models	Logical purity	Start up	Cerebral, speculative, overly conceptual	Routine, one-sided ideas
Judging	Organize Plan	Strategic Efficient	Innovate, make perfect	Efficiency	Entrepreneurial	Argumentative, reserved, detached	Irrational thinking

SF (SENSOR FEELER) PERSONALITY TEMPERAMENT CHART

Type Indicator	Traits/Talents	Style	Key Job Functions	Main Motivations	Work Environment	Quirks	Pet Peeves
ESFP	Helpful	Warm	Hands-on	Seek harmony	Service-oriented	Too nice	Abstraction
ESFJ	Common sense	Giving	Practical problem solving with people	Nurture people	Aesthetically pleasing	Passive	Theory
ISFP	Observant	Friendly	Nurture people	Live and let live	Harmonious	Too kind	Conflict
ISFJ	Service-oriented	Accepting	Relationships	Go with the flow	Easygoing	Easily hurt	Complexity
	Tactile	Generous	Heal	Please people	Task-oriented	Too emotional	Logic
	Loyal	Considerate	Beautify	Smell the roses	Practical application	Too sensitive	Mathematical models
	Dutiful	Thoughtful	Empathize	Seek comfort	Sensual	Shortsighted	Shades of gray
	Caring	Uncomplicated	Mediate	Be sensual	Beautiful	Air-headed	Poor manners
			Entertain	Seek pleasure		Obsessed with appearances	Immorality
			Host			Narrow-minded	
			Sell				
			Promote				
			Market				
			Customer service				

SF PERSONALITY TEMPERAMENT (COMBINED WITH CORE PERSONALITY GROUPS)

Personality Group	Traits/Talents	Style	Key Job Functions	Main Motivations	Work Environment	Quirks	Pet Peeves
Extroverted Maestro	Mentor	Zestful	Perform Present	Spread the good news	Creative Autonomous	Big ham Steals the spotlight	Quiet contemplation
Introverted Maestro	Tactile	Quiet Modest	Craft Heal	Mastery of craft	Creative Autonomous	Happily invisible	Commercialism
Extroverted Tribal	Nurturing	Gregarious Affirming	Sell Host Manage	Please others Social acceptance	Conventional Traditional	Mothering Self-sacrificing	Rule breakers
Introverted Tribal	Loyal	Gentle Devoted	Observe details Administer	Do your duty	Stable Hierarchical	Too trusting Charlie Brown syndrome	Pushy bosses

SF PERSONALITY TEMPERAMENT (COMBINED WITH PERCEIVING AND JUDGING)

Personality Group	Traits/Talents	Style	Key Job Functions	Main Motivations	Work Environment	Quirks	Pet Peeves
Perceiving	Holistic	Fun-loving Adventurous	Explore Entertain	Love life Enchant people	Entrepreneurial Liberal-minded	Impulsive Risk taker	Routine
Judging	Practical	Dutiful Reliable	Teach Enforce	Follow rules Do what you should	Stable Conservative	Rule-bound Inflexible	Immorality

ST (SENSOR THINKER) PERSONALITY TEMPERAMENT CHART

Type Indicator	Traits/Talents	Style	Key Job Functions	Main Motivations	Work Environment	Quirks	Pet Peeves
ESTP	Objective	Realistic	Project management	Seek security	Stable	Rule-bound	Immorality
ESTJ	Logical	Practical	Administering	Follow the rules	Structured	Rigid	Far-left liberals
ISTP	Analytical	Dutiful	Analyzing	Duty	Hierarchical	Hardheaded	Abstraction
ISTJ	Observant	Loyal	Taking action	Defend tradition	Traditional	Militant	Theory
	Decisive	Down-to-earth	Operating systems	Honor	Leveling off	Type A	Inaction
	Efficient	Hands-on	Building	Protect	Declining	Shortsighted	Rule breakers
	Detailed	Uncomplicated	Repairing	Survive	Bureaucratic	Inside the box	Cheaters
		Monotone	Production operations	Get results	Governmental	Too serious	People's emotions
		Utilitarian	Implementing	Take action	Fortune 500	Too literal	Performance reviews
		Function over form	Executing plans	Do, then think	Outdoors	Unemotional	Vision statements
		Plain	Getting results	Simplicity	Hands-on	Too traditional	Touchy-feely seminars
		Stark	Maintaining systems		Factory floor	Unaesthetic	
						Plain Jane	
						Miss the forest for the trees	
						Stuck in the details	

ST PERSONALITY TEMPERAMENT (COMBINED WITH CORE PERSONALITY GROUPS)

Personality Group	Traits/Talents	Style	Key Job Functions	Main Motivations	Work Environment	Quirks	Pet Peeves
Extroverted Maestro	Pragmatic	Aggressive	Commanding	Take charge	Professional	Macho	Disorder
Introverted Maestro	Analytical	Sincere	Improve quality	Efficiency	Autonomous	Very private	Fluff
Extroverted Tribal	Objective	Competitive	Operations management	Lead the tribe	Military-like	Rule-bound	Ambiguity
Introverted Tribal	Observant	Loyal	Detailed Thorough	Duty to tribe	Structured	Black-and-white view	Starting from scratch

ST PERSONALITY TEMPERAMENT (COMBINED WITH PERCEIVING AND JUDGING)

Personality Group	Traits/Talents	Style	Key Job Functions	Main Motivations	Work Environment	Quirks	Pet Peeves
Perceiving	Spontaneity	Laid-back	Practical design	Do the impossible	Adventurous	Easily bored	Desk work
Judging	Systematic	Efficient	Administration	Get the job done	Chain of command	Inflexible	Rule breakers

CHAPTER

30 CAREER PATH—GENERAL DIRECTION

The world is a big place. When choosing your career path, be sure you're headed in the right general direction for your natural abilities. Clarifying a general direction will help you ask more useful questions. If you head east when your path lies west, you'll never get on the right road. I often hear people ask "Should I be a doctor or a lawyer?" as if those two careers lie in the same general direction. This question is a sure sign that the speaker isn't even on first base in getting to know him- or herself as a unique individual. It makes as much sense as asking "Should I teach Plato or design chairs for people with bad backs?"

For example, if you are spatial-oriented, you have an aptitude that "wants" to be constantly engaged in solving three-dimensional problems and situations. Many people who excel at spatial reasoning have mistakenly become lawyers. Law is a very nonspatial field, and most spatial people become very bored and unhappy in the legal profession because one of their strongest aptitudes is left high and dry all day long.

On the other side of the coin, a nonspatial-oriented person in a spatial career will find it difficult to excel and impossible to enjoy work. Surgeons who don't have spatial talent typically suffer from high stress caused by a constant fear of making mistakes. A lack of spatial talent creates a lack of confidence in their ability to visualize and work with 3-D anatomical problems. Here's a quote from Ben Carson, chief of pediatric neurosurgery at Johns Hopkins: "I became acutely aware of an unusual ability—a divine gift, I believe . . . encompassing the ability to understand physical relationships, to think in three dimensions. Good surgeons must understand the consequences of each action, for they're often not able to see what's happening on the other side of the area in which they're actually working. For some reason, I am able to 'see' in three dimensions. . . . It's just something I happen to be able to do. However, many doctors don't have this natural ability, and some, including surgeons, *never learn* this skill. Those who don't [have this innate talent] don't develop into outstanding surgeons, frequently encountering problems, constantly fighting complications."

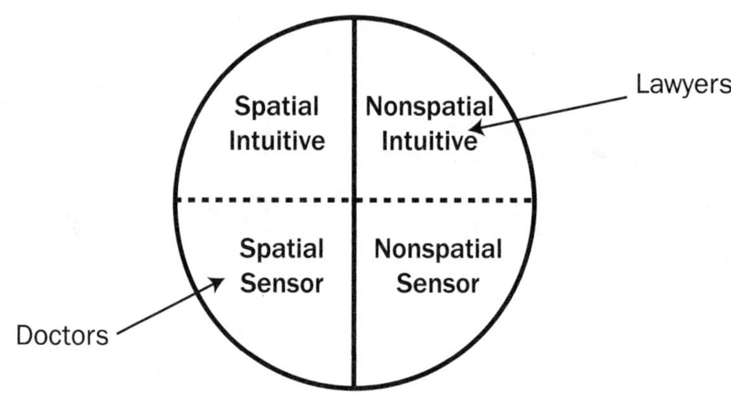

The left half of the pie consists of careers that require more tangible and spatial (3-D) orientation, and the right half consists of nonspatial, non-3-D orientation. The solid vertical line cuts the pie into spatial and nonspatial career fields. The horizontal dotted line cuts the career pie in half again; the top half is intuitive (N) and the bottom half is sensing (S). Each of the four quadrants represents a general career path direction.

You were introduced to these discrete talents and abilities earlier in this book. As a recap, the diagram below illustrates the two talent continuums, represented as pairs of opposites. Recall your self-ratings in these areas; for example, if you lean toward spatial and intuition, this may predict your general career path to be spatial intuitive.

Spatial (3-D Objects) ________________________________ **Nonspatial (Ideas)**

Intuition (N) ________________________________ **Sensing (S)**

THE FOUR GENERAL CAREER PATHS

- **Spatial intuitive (N).** Physicists, geneticists, technology inventors, and filmmakers use the combination of spatial orientation and intuitive perception to imagine or invent spatial possibilities and solve complex systemic, three-dimensional problems. Together these abilities work as a talent for 3-D imagination, which is the aptitude toolkit for scientific discovery, technological innovation, spatial design, and creative problem solving in the physical world. People with this aptitude combination excel at designing and conceptualizing in 3-D and can work comfortably on projects with a long-term time frame, often on a global scale. Great inventors and physical scientists are members of this club.

Spatial 3-D imagination career fields:

- Physical, earth, and life sciences
- Scientific research and development
- Sustainable development and urban design
- Fine arts, design arts, film directing
- Advanced technology innovation
- Medical research

- **Spatial sensor (S).** Surgeons, occupational therapists, mechanics, craftspeople, and virtual reality programmers use the combination of spatial orientation and sensing perception for solving practical, concrete 3-D problems. People with this talent combination excel in the world of 3-D application, which is the aptitude toolkit for physically building tangible and useful objects and things in the immediate or near-term time frame. Great doctors and engineers are in this club.

Spatial 3-D application career fields:

- Engineering and information technology
- Acute and emergency medicine
- Allied health care, nursing, physical therapy
- Construction, trades, and craftsmanship
- Farming, agriculture, and forestry
- Hairstyling

- **Nonspatial intuitive (N).** Economists, poets, psychologists, and historians use the combination of nonspatial orientation and intuitive perception for dreaming up new ideas, theories, and concepts to understand and solve complex social problems and situations. People with this talent combination excel in the career world of concept imagination, to include working imaginatively with ideas, data, knowledge, and information. Great novelists and visionary leaders are in this club.

Nonspatial concept imagination career fields:

- Social sciences and humanities research
- Advertising and marketing research
- Creative writing, acting, documentary film
- Law, geopolitics, international diplomacy
- Journalism and publishing
- Entrepreneurship and business strategy
- Management consulting

- **Nonspatial sensor (S).** Bankers, business executives, stockbrokers, and kindergarten teachers use the combination of nonspatial orientation and sensing perception for practically applying information and concepts in the operation and administration of daily life in all types of organizations. People with this talent combination excel in the career world of information/data application, to include working practically with concepts, information, ideas, and knowledge. Great tax accountants and project managers are in this club.

Nonspatial data application career fields:

- Business administration, sales
- Public relations and communications
- Accounting and finance
- K-12 education
- Social work
- Operations research, statistics
- Actuarial in science

MORE SPECIFIC CAREER PATHS

Recall your personality temperament (NF, NT, SF, or ST). In the illustration below, the career path pie chart incorporates temperament to create more specific career directions, eight in all.

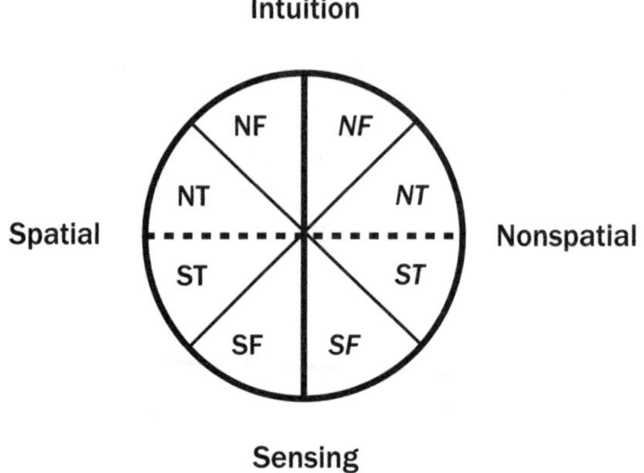

In the left half of the career pie we now have four spatial career paths, and in the right half of the pie we now have four nonspatial career paths.

Spatial Career Paths		Nonspatial Career Paths	
Spatial NF	Spatial NT	*Nonspatial NF*	*Nonspatial NT*
Spatial SF	Spatial ST	*Nonspatial SF*	*Nonspatial ST*

The detailed pie chart on the next page illustrates a few example subject areas for each slice of the career pizza pie.

If you find more than one segment of the circle that describes you, that's fine. Many people are a mix of these descriptions. For example, someone with an SF temperament who

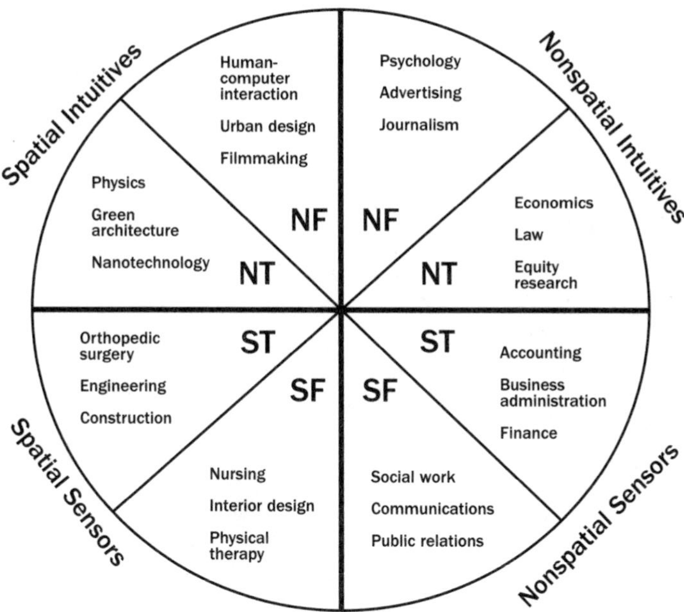

is in the middle of the spatial-to-nonspatial continuum, also called "tangible," may find suitable career fields in both the spatial SF and nonspatial SF general areas.

CAREER PATH CHARTS

The charts on the following pages further expand the list of career path possibilities you can explore.

The first chart lists the four spatial career paths, which correspond with the left side of the pie diagram above; the second chart lists the four nonspatial career paths, corresponding with the right side of the pie. The leftmost column in the charts, "Major Categories," is a simplified breakout of the major career subject areas, roughly aligned with our economic sectors or industries. It's a good idea to skim both charts; this will give you a sense of how the career world is divvied up into general natural talent categories.

Read down the vertical column to see the recommended career paths in each category for your mix of talents and personality temperament. Note the darker shaded areas, which indicate the more obvious "sweet spots" or best-fit career fields for the personality temperaments in each vertical column. The lighter shaded areas are also good fits for each temperament but are less obvious.

SPATIAL CAREER PATH CHART

Major Categories	The Four Spatial Career Paths			
	Spatial NF	**Spatial NT**	**Spatial SF**	**Spatial ST**
Physical/Earth and Life Sciences	Behavioral life sciences Ecology	Physics Biology Chemistry Geology Ecology	Botany Horticulture Marine science Cartography	Agricultural science Forestry science Soil/food sciences Geology Chemistry
Social Sciences and Humanities	Sociobiology Physical anthropology Demographics Urban planning	Primatology Archaeology Anthropology Economic geography	Geography Public health	Criminology
Arts, Entertainment, Media	Performance arts Filmmaking Screenwriting Set design	Documentary film Game design Film animation	Graphic arts Photography Cinematography Performance/dance Choreography	TV/radio tech Sound/lighting tech
Business and Financial	Entrepreneurship	Entrepreneurship	Technology management	Technology management
Body Kinesthetic and Sensory Acuity	Athletics Sports coaching	Athletics Sports coaching	Athletics/coaching Organic farming Law enforcement Exercise physiologist Fashion modeling	Athletics/coaching Firefighting Law enforcement Search and rescue Military

			Dance Vintner	Stunt acting Organic farming
Artisan, Craftsman, Designer	New urbanism Green architecture Web site design Design arts	Industrial design Architecture Design arts	Artisan Fashion design Interior design Art restoration Art appraisal	Craftsman Masonry/trades
Engineering, Technology, Trades	Human-computer interaction Human factors engineering	Emerging technology Engineering/R&D Computer science Artificial intelligence Robotics	PC technician Help desk tech Manufacturing	Engineering Construction/trades Information technology Computer science Mechanics Pilot/heavy equipment operator
Health Care	Holistic medicine Preventive medicine Family medicine Cognitive psychology Yoga, healing arts	Medical research Forensic science Cardiology Neuroscience Genetics	Family medicine Dermatology Nursing Allied health Physical therapy Holistic medicine Yoga, healing arts Veterinary medicine	Surgical medicine Emergency medicine Optometry Podiatry Gastroenterology Dentistry Orthopedics Urology Pathology

Major Categories	The Four Spatial Career Paths			
	Spatial NF	**Spatial NT**	**Spatial SF**	**Spatial ST**
Educational/Teaching	Life sciences Adventure education Arts/performance Drama Design arts Holistic medicine	Physical sciences Medicine Engineering Architecture/design	Technology training Elementary science Holistic medicine Dance Commercial arts	Vocations/trades Mathematics Engineering Athletics
Hospitality/Travel	Specialty travel: arts, architecture	Specialty travel: archaeology	Culinary arts Pastry chef Baker Innkeeping/B&B Specialty travel: equestrian, garden tours	Culinary arts Specialty travel: ecotourism, scuba diving, cycling

NONSPATIAL CAREER PATH CHART

Major Categories	The Four Nonspatial Career Paths			
	Nonspatial NF	**Nonspatial NT**	**Nonspatial SF**	**Nonspatial ST**
Physical/Earth and Life Sciences	Science journalism	Science journalism	Science photography	
Social Sciences and Humanities	Psychology Sociology Anthropology History Literature Public policy Diplomacy	Economics Political science Philosophy Public policy Law	Social work Family law Mediation	Statistics Tax law Business law Public administration
Arts, Entertainment, Media	Creative writing Theater/film acting Journalism Music Art	Journalism Political commentary	Broadcasting Communications TV acting Entertainment TV Music Art	
Business and Financial	Advertising Branding/marketing Public relations Organizational development Management consulting	Marketing research Financial analysis Strategic planning Investing Entrepreneurship	Management Human resources Public relations Marketing	Accounting Actuarial science Business administration Operations management Production management Operations research Banking

Major Categories	**The Four Nonspatial Career Paths**			
	Nonspatial NF	**Nonspatial NT**	**Nonspatial SF**	**Nonspatial ST**
Body Kinesthetic and Sensory Acuity	Adventure education		Wine tasting Perfumer Food critic	
Artisan, Craftsman, Designer				
Technology, Information Sciences	Information architecture	Informatics	Library science	Management information systems Informatics Technical writing
Health Care	Counseling Career coaching Clinical psychology Meditation	Psychiatry Public health policy Epidemiology	Psychiatric nursing Hospice counseling Social work Public health education	Pharmacy
Educational/Teaching	Educational methods Social sciences Humanities Arts	Social sciences Humanities Law Public policy	Child day care Teaching K-12 Special education Training and development Library science	Mathematics Business Library science
Hospitality/Travel	Educational travel	Educational travel	Hotel management Restaurant management Spa/resort management Concierge/host	Hospitality management Tour operator

Gather Your Self-Ratings

Rockport Personality Type Indicator: _____

Core Personality Type: _____

Temperament: _____

General Direction: _____

Specific Career Path: _____

Legend: N = Intuitive, S = Sensor, F = Feeler, T = Thinker, E = Extrovert, I = Introvert

Keep these results handy for when you explore the Rockport Major Aptitude Profiles in the next part of this section.

Example:

Rockport Personality Type Indicator: **INFP**

Core Personality Type: **Introverted Maestro**

Temperament: **NF**

General Direction: **Nonspatial N**

Specific Career Path: **Nonspatial NF**

CHAPTER 31 THE ROCKPORT INSTITUTE MAJOR APTITUDE PROFILES

At Rockport Institute, we use very sophisticated career testing to measure a complete suite of natural talents, abilities, and personality traits discussed throughout this book. Although it is quite difficult to self-rate yourself in these abilities, if you work through this book you will have a chance to get a rough estimate of your talents and traits. If you have had trouble self-rating, don't worry—we've tested many thousands of people in the last twenty-five years, and we've met only a handful who were able to accurately estimate their strongest talents. Even so, you can do some good detective work and gather clues to help get your career on course.

The aptitude profiles that follow are combinations of natural talents, abilities, and personality traits. You won't find these profile descriptions anywhere else; they are based on more than two decades of research and helping many thousands of people make wise career choices.

Don't get bent out of shape trying to box yourself into one of these profiles. This is an analytical approach to something that can't be completely defined or described analytically, so these categories and recommendations are a very broad and rough cut. You're a complex human being, and you won't find a magic formula here for designing your life. You may not fit perfectly into any of these groups. Take this information with a grain of salt, learn from it what you can, and do your best to use what you'll learn here to gather more good clues that will help you make a carefully considered and smart career decision. This is all about finding clues.

TRIBAL APTITUDE PROFILE 1: BUSINESS AND MANAGEMENT TRIBAL

Natural Talents and Traits	Profile Scores
Core Personality Type	Extroverted and Introverted Tribal
General Direction	Nonspatial Sensor*
Specific Career Path	All Nonspatial (ST and SF* are most common)
Spatial-Nonspatial Orientation	Nonspatial to Tangible
Abstract-Concrete Orientation	Concrete

Diagnostic Reasoning	Low-Mid
Analytical Reasoning	Mid-High
Rate of Idea Flow	Low-High
Visual Dexterity	Mid-High
Number Memory	Mid-High

* Ideal score for this profile, unless noted otherwise. See career path breakouts below for more detail.

Do you see yourself as part of a company, operating and maintaining the nuts and bolts of daily business activities, making the economic world hum like a well-tuned machine? If you think that being successful at business is just common sense, chances are you're a business and management Tribal.

Business Tribals love the idea of buying and selling products and services, and view the economic system as the lifeblood of the culture. Organizations of all kinds bring together teams of business Tribals to collaborate on projects that ultimately provide a wide variety of products and services.

Business and management Tribals often take one of the following career paths:

- **Senior manager.** Can you see the big picture, think strategically, and dream up new business ideas? Senior managers are often extroverted Tribal nonspatial NTs, and although you're just starting your career, you may be ready for visionary leadership roles sooner than you expect. Business and project managers who think strategically and exude confidence are quickly recognized as executive talent.
- **Middle manager and team leader.** Are you an outgoing person who needs to work through and with people to get the job done, rather than go at it alone? Businesses are "tribes" of people with common goals, all in service to satisfy the goals of their customers. Middle managers and team leaders are often extroverted Tribal nonspatial sensors who play a central role in a business endeavor; it takes like-mindedness with coworkers, and a desire to make decisions by consensus and lead people to adhere to common values.
- **Analyst and administrator.** Does working in solitude with spreadsheets sound like fun to you? The business disciplines of accounting, finance, administration, and operations management may be your area. Working with data and information in a practical and quantitative way is the real meat and potatoes of how business decisions are made. Accountants, financial analysts, and general office administrators are often introverted Tribal nonspatial STs, the most common type in the number-crunching side of the business world.
- **Persuader.** If you're practical and attuned to people's needs, you may fit the Tribal nonspatial SF career path. Extroverted Tribal nonspatial SFs are the natural "people persons" who excel as team managers and in customer care. If you are also mid to high in idea flow, sales may be a career that fits you.

- **Entrepreneur.** Maybe you are the kind of Tribal cut out for a creative and visionary business domain. If you happen to have high diagnostic reasoning, high intuition, and high idea flow, you have the key aptitudes for entrepreneurship, product innovation and invention, new business development, and start-up ventures. Google during its explosive growth period exemplifies the kind of organization where you would fit in and be appreciated for your natural ability to innovate and challenge the status quo.

CAUTIONS AND GENERAL RULES OF THUMB

- **Steady-mindedness.** Most large corporate workplace environments need people with a steady mind-set much more than creative innovators. Are you suited to large and bureaucratic work environments, where things move at a slower pace? Tribal nonspatial STs with low idea flow and high analytical reasoning are often geared to steadily work at detail with analytical rigor every day and get bottom-line results without getting bored. In most cases, businesspeople have a structured mind, with less desire for creativity and autonomy, and are best at keeping the ship on course without being overly tempted to change direction or redraw the strategic map.
- **Diagnostic problem solvers beware.** If you have high diagnostic reasoning, please be mindful that working for a large, well-established corporation may seem like going for a jog with a glacier. Unless you find urgent problems to troubleshoot or fires to put out, you'll feel like your brain is turning to mush. Diagnostic reasoning, with its insatiable curiosity and drive to innovate whether it's necessary or not, is one of the main factors behind job dissatisfaction among corporate executives, managers, and analysts in big organizations.
- **Maestros beware.** Are you a Maestro who is considering a career in the business world? You may find it difficult to thrive in the typical business setting. If you're a loner Maestro by nature, your need for autonomy, self-direction, specialization, and uncommon perspective may cause friction. Maestros are sometimes perceived by others as mavericks (i.e., not trusted to "get with the program") and often punished—or ostracized—for rocking the boat. However, midrange Maestros who have some Tribal tendencies can find a challenging spot that is honored by the corporate tribe but also makes them feel unique and special—a technology expert or information technology director, for example.

BUSINESS AND MANAGEMENT TRIBAL CAREER PATHS

The Senior Manager

- NT: visionary executive leadership: CEO (chief executive officer), CFO (chief financial officer), board of directors
- ST: operational executive leadership: CIO (chief information officer), COO (chief operations officer)

The Middle Manager and Team Leader

Diplomatic personality: general management, information management, inventory management, human resources management, team leadership

- ST, SF: small branch/division management
- NT, NF: large district/regional management

(Note: managers may need high idea flow, high extroversion, and high visualizing possibilities if managing in a growth or innovation stage.)

The Persuader

- SF, ST: sales, sales management, buying, purchasing, training
- NF, NT: literary agent, talent agent

The Analyst and Administrator

- ST, SF: office management, program management, project management, accounting, business financial analysis, inventory control, quality control, clerical, data management, secretarial

The Business Entrepreneur

- NF: adventure education, educational products, personal growth services, arts, health and nutrition
- NT: financial and investment services, technology products and services, commercial real estate
- SF: personal care, pet care, child care, senior care, health and fitness services, salons, B&B innkeeping, clothing retail, travel and hospitality, meal preparation services
- ST: self-service facilities (gas station, car wash), convenience stores, home improvement and maintenance services, electronics retail, appliances, automotive, real estate, household products, outdoor adventure and sports gear, retail franchise, fast-food franchise, printing and shipping services

(Note: entrepreneurs often have significantly higher scores in rate of idea flow, diagnostic reasoning, and/or analytical reasoning. Entrepreneurial types should also reference the Creative and Artistic Tribal Profile below for more on creative business career paths in advertising, public relations, marketing, and product development.)

Rate Yourself

How well does the Business and Management Tribal profile describe you?

___ Nails me perfectly
___ Mostly describes me
___ Partly describes me
___ Not at all

TRIBAL APTITUDE PROFILE 2: THE CREATIVE AND ARTISTIC TRIBAL

Natural Talents and Traits	Profile Scores
Core Personality Type	Extroverted and Introverted Tribal
General Direction	Nonspatial Intuitive*
Specific Career Path	Nonspatial NF and NT*
Nonspatial-Spatial Orientation	Depends on situation

Natural Talents and Traits	Profile Score
Abstract-Concrete Orientation	Depends on situation
Diagnostic Reasoning	Mid-High
Analytical Reasoning	Mid-High
Rate of Idea Flow	Mid-High
Design Memory	Mid-High, where needed

* Ideal score for this profile, unless noted otherwise. See career path breakouts below for more detail.

If your natural strengths are in dreaming up new ideas and possibilities, inventing new concepts and models, exploring the unknown, understanding what motivates human behavior, or creating aesthetically beautiful products and services, you may be a creative and artistic Tribal. Advertising, marketing, public relations, and commercial arts are the creative side of the business world. Also in this club are pop culture artists, journalists, and spatial designers who create commercial products.

Are you more interested in form over function, but enjoy making useful things too? Although much of the business world is dominated by practical-minded people with quantitative talents, they can't do the job alone; they need the help of the imaginative and creative people who bring insight, vision, creativity, possibility, and tastefulness to everyday life. For those of you who are intrinsically motivated by persuading, influencing, delighting, and inspiring others through your work, this may be your ballpark.

Creative and artistic Tribals often take one of the following career paths:

- **Influencer.** If you can accurately imagine what total strangers desire to have—and convince them to go buy it—you are a natural marketer. Tribal nonspatial NFs with high diagnostic reasoning and idea flow are gifted at the psychological side of doing business. The advertising activities of ad campaign design, marketing, communications, and public relations are their main stomping grounds. If you're a diagnostic Tribal NF, you're a born, practical sociologist. If you are a Tribal nonspatial NT, you will excel in the quantitative side of business development, including marketing research and strategic planning, happily applying your high diagnostic and analytical reasoning to make sound, logical predictions.
- **Commercial artist.** Do you find yourself doodling and dreaming up cool logos or rock band cover art in your free time? If so, you may be in the same group as advertising creatives, graphic artists, and Web site designers who bring their sense of style and flair to the visual side of advertising. If you're a Tribal spatial NF with high idea flow, you may be adept at communicating the spirit of a company vision in the form of a logo and tagline that says everything in a glance. If you are a Tribal spatial SF with lower idea flow, you may excel at the craftsman side of producing appealing graphics.

- **Pop culture artist.** Do you have the talent for creating pop culture art? If you're a Tribal SF with high idea flow, your type can create simple, sensual, sizzling, sexy works of art. If you dream of singing love songs or acting in TV sitcoms, where the message is right on the surface, all practical and pretty, this may be your world.
- **Tribal spatial designer.** Do you have the perfect combination of an eye for form and practical function? If you're passionate about designing cool things for people, such as houses, clothes, kitchens and bathrooms, gadgets, and furniture, this is a talent ballpark you'll thrive in. Introverted Tribal spatial SFs with high idea flow rule in the design world, from fashion to interior design. You crafty Tribal SFs know how to make our lives sparkle with color, functionality, and beauty.

CAUTIONS AND GENERAL RULES OF THUMB

- **Supercreative?** If so, beware of conventional business roles and settings. On the whole, highly creative and artistic people resist number crunching to improve the bottom line; this type considers practical tasks and goals drudgery. It is uncommon to find both practical and creative talent in a single individual, although it's not unknown. Generally, people with a creative and artistic profile flee the financial side of the business world once they realize what is required of them.
- **Creative Maestro?** If you are a Maestro considering a career in commercial art and design, proceed with caution. The more independent-minded Maestro SF and NF spatial designers often get heartbroken and frustrated in the Tribal mainstream design professions. Their personal vision and conviction correlates with the temperament of a fine artist; they don't like to bend to the customer's wants. Architecture, often mistaken as a Maestro profession, is really a design domain for spatial Tribals. Only the very rare Frank Lloyd Wright–type superstar architect can command the total direction of his or her design. Maestro artists are in it for the sake of their artistic expression, which is hard to sell in our bargain-priced big-box-store culture. See more on this in the Creative and Artistic Maestro profile.

CREATIVE AND ARTISTIC TRIBAL CAREER PATHS

The Influencer

- NF, NT (with high diagnostic reasoning): marketing, strategic planning, advertising, public relations, lobbying, communications and media planning, journalism, political spin doctor, talk show host, publishing, talent agent and publicist, professional service entrepreneur, business consultant, political campaign consultant
- NF, NT (with tangible or spatial orientation, and high diagnostic reasoning): product and brand management, new product development, product marketing, creative art director, high-tech product entrepreneur
- SF, ST (with tangible or spatial orientation, and high diagnostic reasoning): entrepreneur: retail home and office products, entertainment products, outdoor recreation, sports, health and fitness clubs, specialty foods and beverages, full-service restaurant, child care and educational development products

The Commercial Artist

- NF, SF (with midrange diagnostic reasoning, tangible or spatial orientation): Web site design, graphic design, advertising arts, production studios (TV commercials, radio, music videos, infomercials, animation), photography

The Pop Culture Artist

- NF, SF (with low diagnostic reasoning): sitcom acting and comedy, sitcom writing, pop performers, singers, and musicians

The Tribal Spatial Designer

- SF, ST (with tangible or spatial orientation): pastry chef, hairstyling, cosmetic specialist, fashion design, interior design, jewelry design, window display design, landscape architecture, kitchen and bath design, interior decoration
- NF, NT (with high spatial orientation): architecture, landscape architecture, industrial design, exhibit design, interior design/feng shui, urban design and planning, parks and recreation planning, historical preservation, ergonomics and human factors design and planning

Rate Yourself

How well does the Creative and Artistic Tribal profile describe you?

___ Nails me perfectly
___ Mostly describes me
___ Partly describes me
___ Not at all

TRIBAL APTITUDE PROFILE 3: THE TECHNOLOGICAL TRIBAL

Natural Talents and Traits	Profile Scores
Core Personality Type	Introverted and Extroverted Tribal
General Direction	Spatial Sensor*
Specific Career Path	Spatial ST and SF*
Spatial-Nonspatial Orientation	Tangible-Spatial
Abstract-Concrete Orientation	Concrete
Diagnostic Reasoning	Depends on situation
Analytical Reasoning	Mid-High
Rate of Idea Flow	Low-Mid
Visual Dexterity	Mid-High

* Ideal score for this profile, unless noted otherwise. See career path breakouts below for more detail.

Do you consider yourself a natural at fixing things and figuring out how things work, or doing things such as tinkering with your computer or installing a complex sound system? If you have the key mix of talents for this career category, Tribal spatial and high analytical reasoning, you are a technological Tribal. In today's workplace the business and technological Tribals usually work together in the same companies. For instance, in a software firm the business Tribals run the company and bring in the customers, while the technological Tribals apply specialized spatial problem-solving talents and knowledge to design and build the company's software products and services.

Technological Tribals often take one of the following career paths:

- **Engineer, family doctor, technologist.** Many doctors, engineers, and technologists are 3-D thinkers as well as hands-on, practical people. It may surprise you to learn that doctors and engineers often inhabit the same talent category—the key talents to accurately diagnose the anatomy are fundamentally the same abilities required to engineer and troubleshoot physical systems. In medical and technology domains most problems are immediate and tangible; real-world application is what drives the Tribal spatial SFs and STs.
- **Technical Extrovert.** If you happen to be born with both spatial orientation and extroversion, you may shy away from technology fields for fear of being too isolated behind a computer screen all day. Fortunately, there is a solution for you. At first glance it appears that most spatial problem solving is the domain of the quiet, spatial introvert. While it is true that most technical work requires focusing your attention on inanimate physical things and mathematical data on a computer screen, there are niches that require a more outgoing personality. For instance, doctors in most disciplines spend a large part of their day meeting with patients. These patients usually present the physician with physical symptoms and problems through face-to-face conversation. Many practicing physicians who love their jobs are extroverted and spatial diagnosticians. The same goes with extroverted technologists and engineers; if you're in this club, you can usually find your way into project management and technical team leadership roles, where you'll play the role of mentor, supervisor, and customer liaison in technology fields.
- **Health technologists and healers.** If you are a techie but have a warm, people-oriented nature, you may be an extroverted Tribal spatial SF. Healers who are good at figuring out physical problems often have high diagnostic reasoning ability, which is used in health fields and physical therapies to diagnose diseases or injuries. If you are a bit more reserved or ingoing, introverted Tribal spatial SFs fit in this club too, where you would concentrate more on the technology rather than the relationship with the patient.

CAUTIONS AND GENERAL RULES OF THUMB

- **The forest or the trees?** If you're spatial and imaginative, you may prefer to work on systems-level architecture and design engineering projects with a team, and think about how all the parts work together as an integrated whole—you see the forest. Contrary to popular wisdom, not all spatial people need to work with their hands, and many may never physically build or troubleshoot real, physical products. This is especially true for the introverted Tribal spatial NFs and NTs, the innovators in 3-D fields. If you're a spatial intuitive, much of the 3-D work you do happens in your mind's eye.
- **Should I climb the ladder to management?** If you've had a brilliant career as a highly technical professional, should you take that job offer to climb the ladder into an executive role? Be careful—it may give you prestige, but you may find yourself feeling like a duck out of water. As we discussed earlier, business management problems are conceptual, not spatial; there is little use for spatial problem-solving talents in analyzing data in financial balance sheets. If you're a spatial introvert, climbing your way to the top of the abstract management beanstalk may cause pain and pressure. The daily job tasks there no longer engage your strongest talents and will tax your weaker abilities. If you don't want to end up working fifteen-hour days to compensate for the talent mismatch, take heed. At the executive level, much time is spent in meetings; many introverts find this exhausting. This may be a stressful way to live for you, which all the money and prestige in the world won't cure.
- **Avoid the midcareer crisis.** If you're a spatial Tribal, the trick is to stay close to the spatial and tangible technology—the factory floor, so to speak. The best bet is to climb the technical ladder and lead technical teams, as well as mentor others in your technical specialty. Career fulfillment will come from being the technical guru at what seems most natural and interesting to you. However, if being a corporate executive is your dream, find a way to roll up your sleeves and hang around the technology where you can talk shop with like-minded people. At the same time, it's not uncommon for spatial Tribals with strong extroversion to rise to the top of a smaller engineering or high-tech firm. In smaller companies there is more flexibility to wear both the technical and business hats.
- **Too introverted to be the family doc?** If you're a strong introvert who is planning to become a doctor, seek specialized areas in medicine where there is less conversational contact with patients, such as radiology, anesthesiology, pathology, or surgery.

TECHNOLOGICAL TRIBAL CAREER PATHS

The Engineer

- ST: IT and network administration, database administration, quality assurance and test engineering, industrial engineering, civil engineering, environmental engineering, mining engineering, automotive engineering, chemical engineering, architectural engineering
- NT: software development and design, R&D engineering (all disciplines), computer hardware architecture, information architecture, system design engineering (e.g., telecommunications, electrical power)

The Family Doctor (Spatial Extrovert)

- SF, NF: family medicine, preventive medicine, internal medicine, OB/GYN, pediatrics
- ST, SF: family dentistry, chiropractic, physician's assistant, nursing, midwifery

The Information Technologist (Tangible-Spatial Orientation)

- ST, NT: computer programming, HTML programming, database design, database analysis, bioinformatics, statistical analysis, data warehousing system architecture, business process reengineering (BPR)
- NF, NT: organizational learning, knowledge management, total quality management (TQM), information architecture

The Technical Extrovert

- ST, NT: construction management, engineering management, nurse management, information technology (IT) management, U.S. military officer, sales engineer, pharmaceutical sales representative, manufacturer's representative, medical equipment sales representative

The Allied Health Technologist

- SF, ST: anesthesiologist, audiologist, blood bank technologist, cardiovascular technologist, dental hygienist, MRI technologist, X-ray technologist, surgical assistant, surgical technologist, perfusionist, optician, medical technologist

The Allied Health Rehabilitative Healer

- SF, ST: art therapy, music therapy, dance therapy, genetic counseling, physical therapy, massage therapy, kinesiotherapy, occupational therapy, therapeutic recreation therapy, nursing, respiratory therapy, speech therapy, exercise physiology, fitness training

The Technician (Mid-High Introversion)

- ST: technical drawing, surveying, computer network troubleshooting, TV/radio technician, air traffic control, PC/help desk technician, audio technician, electronics technician, medical laboratory technician, pharmacy technician, dental technician, enlisted military technician

Rate Yourself

How well does the Technological Tribal profile describe you?

___ Nails me perfectly
___ Mostly describes me
___ Partly describes me
___ Not at all

TRIBAL APTITUDE PROFILE 4:
THE EDUCATION, SOCIAL SERVICE, AND HOSPITALITY TRIBAL

Natural Talents and Traits	Profile Scores
Core Personality Type	Extroverted Tribal
General Direction	Nonspatial Sensor*
Specific Career Path	Nonspatial SF*
Spatial-Nonspatial Orientation	Nonspatial
Diagnostic Reasoning	Depends on situation
Analytical Reasoning	Mid
Rate of Idea Flow	Low-High

* Ideal score for this profile, unless noted otherwise. See career path breakouts below for more detail.

If you have a responsive, empathetic personality and love to be around people most of the day, you may be an extroverted Tribal nonspatial SF, since the bulk of work in this career category is about educating, counseling, caring for, and comforting people.

Do you have a heartfelt desire to help others in very practical and immediate ways? Educational, social service, and hospitality fields attract people who are naturally service-oriented and have the natural talent and ability to work with a broad clientele of people from all walks of life.

Education, social service, and hospitality Tribals often take one of the following career paths:

- **K-12 teacher.** If relating to students, on their level, is one of your gifts, you may have what it takes to be a great teacher. The K-12 teacher is often an extroverted Tribal nonspatial SF. Teachers at any grade level spend the bulk of their day in front of the classroom; there's little to no downtime during the workday. We recommend high extroversion for this career path; introverted Tribals quickly burn out in the teaching profession. Why is it important to be a strong Tribal in the K-12 education field? Many teachers say that at least half of their job is classroom management—keeping order, disciplining students, and so on.
- **The practical counselor.** Many happy social service counselors are extroverted Tribal nonspatial SFs. Are you cordial, understanding, and responsive to people's needs? If you like solving people's immediate problems, social service work is a good area for you. Both men and women with this profile have a natural "mothering" tendency, and from an early age are recognized for their warm nature.
- **Hospitality and customer care.** If you're a natural host or hostess, the hospitality industry may be for you. This area is a magnet for Tribal nonspatial SFs, and both introverts and extroverts can find a spot serving people. Hosting, greeting, pampering, educating, and providing physical comforts are roles and functions you would perform taking care of people who are traveling, va-

cationing, or visiting a spa. Travel agents, hotel managers, waitstaff, restaurant managers, resort hosts, managers, and entertainers often fit the Tribal SF profile. If you happen to be a Tribal nonspatial ST, the hospitality industry can use your talents to perform the quantitative business management activities.

CAUTIONS AND GENERAL RULES OF THUMB

- **Crisis problem solver?** In some situations where the root problems are less obvious or there's a greater sense of urgency that requires thinking on your feet, higher diagnostic reasoning and idea flow would be an added advantage. An example would be a school psychologist who needs to respond to a troubled student in the heat of the moment. Counselors and social workers who serve clients in drug and alcohol abuse situations also need to quickly diagnose critical problems.
- **Too scholarly to teach kids?** If you're in love with a subject area and don't have much patience for youthful shenanigans, beware of high school teaching. Disasters occur when you put a Maestro professor-like teacher in a grade-school situation. Maestro teachers often get the cold shoulder from colleagues who feel that the more intellectual and scholarly types just don't get it when it comes to dealing with students.
- **Worried about the money?** If you happen to be born with an aptitude profile that suits you to educational, social service, and hospitality work, you may not get rich, but fortunately your type usually is motivated by intrinsic rewards beyond financial incentives. Those who go into this career area are typically less motivated by money than other types. Serving others is their passion.
- **Too idealistic to be a social worker?** At Rockport we frequently meet unhappy social workers who measure as introverted Maestro NFs. Although these more visionary, scholarly counseling types enjoy the helping professions, their gift of imagination, academic study time, and desire for solitude is less useful to their clientele, who need more responsive, practical problem solving and hands-on tactics for immediate application. For more on the Maestro nonspatial NFs, see the profile for Social Sciences and Humanities Maestro.

EDUCATION, SOCIAL SERVICE, AND HOSPITALITY TRIBAL CAREER PATHS

The K-12 Teacher

- SF, ST: kindergarten, grade school, junior high; reading, writing, arithmetic, science, geography, history
- NF, NT: high school and advanced placement courses; history, social sciences, biology, calculus, physics, chemistry

The Special Education Teacher (with High Diagnostic and/or Analytical Reasoning)

- SF, NF: special education teacher and tutor, early childhood intervention, art and music therapy, speech therapy, developmental psychology, educational psychology, concentrative movement therapy

The Practical Counselor

- SF: juvenile delinquency prevention (substance abuse education, parenting education, family counseling, young mentoring), probation officer, social worker, caseworker, employment counseling, school social work, guidance counselor, military social work, hospice counseling, bereavement counseling, hotline crisis counselor, child welfare (adoption, child abuse, foster care), child day care, nursing home care, disability services, family planning, homelessness services, refugee and immigrant services, college admissions counselor

The Hospitality and Customer Care Attendant

- SF: hotel management, spa/resort and restaurant management, travel agent, tourism operator, tour guide, concierge, innkeeping, waiter, bartender, wine steward, receptionist, bellhop, doorman, bathroom attendant, butler, valet, housekeeper, customer service

Rate Yourself

How well does the Education, Social Service, and Hospitality profile describe you?

___ Nails me perfectly
___ Mostly describes me
___ Partly describes me
___ Not at all

TRIBAL APTITUDE PROFILE 5: THE PUBLIC SERVANT TRIBAL

Natural Talents and Traits	Profile Scores
Core Personality Type	Introverted and Extroverted Tribal
General Direction	Tangible, mix of Sensing and Intuition*
Specific Career Path	Nonspatial SF, NF, NT, ST
Spatial-Nonspatial Orientation	Tangible, depends on situation
Diagnostic Reasoning	Depends on situation
Analytical Reasoning	Mid-High
Rate of Idea Flow	Low-Mid
Visual Dexterity	Mid-High
Associative Memory	Depends on situation

*Ideal score for this profile, unless noted otherwise. See career path breakouts below for more detail.

Do you dream of making your local or state government work better? Maybe you're cut out for a career in local or state government. People who are well suited to be public and civil servants are similar to the business and management Tribals; they just do what they do in the public sector.

Public administration and municipal management are the main activities in the day-to-day operations of a local or state government agency. Similar to project management in the profit-making business sector, managing a city government also requires a strong dose of practical problem solving; this area is good for extroverted and introverted Tribal non-spatial SFs and NFs.

A key difference between the public servant Tribal and the business Tribal lies not so much in the talents but the values of the individual. It is likely, however, that you'll find more feelers in the public service sector, where they are more at home with catering to the general public's demands in a congenial manner.

- **Tribal politician.** If you are an extroverted Tribal with a levelheaded perspective, becoming a mayor or city administrator may be as natural as breathing. To do your job well and to even get elected in the first place requires knowing lots of people. City administrators, council members, school principals, agency directors, and program managers of all types get things done by building consensus, diplomacy, making deals, building relationships, and getting out there in the community to meet the people they represent.
- **Public administrator.** Most jobs in the public sector are administrative, with a heavy dose of nuts-and-bolts data processing. If you like playing by the rules as well as enforcing them, you are naturally suited to this environment. Attention to detail and adherence to policy and laws require an innate sense of loyalty and duty to serve the common good—Tribal SFs and STs with a steady, customary mind-set are often perfect for public service.

CAUTIONS AND GENERAL RULES OF THUMB

- **How's your memory?** Politicians and administrators of all types do well to remember people's names and faces; it's just part of the job. High associative and design memories are useful talents for anyone considering a career in public office.
- **Good with paperwork?** If you can concentrate on all the tiny details, you'll fit in here. An abundance of regulatory paperwork requires high visual dexterity and high number memory to quickly and accurately sift through the mounds of applications and forms that pass across the desk of a typical government administrator. Also very helpful are high memories for all the data, facts, and figures that make up the bulk of daily reality in a public sector office. Another aptitude valuable on the job is high manual speed and accuracy; the ability to type fast and accurately on a computer keyboard is a big plus.

PUBLIC SERVANT TRIBAL CAREER PATHS

The Tribal Politician

- SF, ST: local-level politicians: mayor, city council member, school board member
- NF, NT: state-level politicians: governor, lieutenant governor, state legislator

The Public Director

- ST: chief operating officer for the governor, senior policy officer for a foundation
- NF, NT: U.S. state and local level department and agency directors, nonprofit director, public research institute director, university dean, agency division director, federal regional administrator, director of regional development, circuit court judge

The Public Administrator

- ST, NT: city manager, school superintendent, county administrator, public university administration, benefits manager, community development manager, grants manager, research program manager, transportation manager, solid waste manager, director of parks and recreation
- SF, NF: library coordinator, communications coordinator, community education director, foundation relations associate, social marketer, community organizer, training manager

The Public Planner

- NF, NT: urban planning, community planning, community practice, park planning director

The Public Analyst (Introverted Tribal)

- ST, NT: policy analyst, financial analyst, research associate, bank examiner, budget analyst, quality assurance analyst, international trade analyst, field program supervisor

The Public Clerk (Introverted Tribal)

- ST, SF: circuit court clerk, deputy sheriff, bailiff, city clerk, postal clerk, mail carrier, file clerk, bookkeeper, secretary, police dispatcher

Rate Yourself

How well does the Public Servant Tribal profile describe you?

___ Nails me perfectly
___ Mostly describes me
___ Partly describes me
___ Not at all

MAESTRO APTITUDE PROFILE 1: THE PHYSICAL/EARTH AND LIFE SCIENCES AND TECHNOLOGY INNOVATOR MAESTRO

Natural Talents and Traits	Profile Scores
Core Personality Type	Introverted and Extroverted Maestro
General Direction	Spatial Intuitive
Specific Career Path	Spatial NT*
Spatial-Nonspatial Orientation	Tangible to Spatial
Diagnostic Reasoning	High
Analytical Reasoning	Mid-High
Rate of Idea Flow	Low-Mid-High (depends on situation)
Visual Dexterity	Mid-High
Associative Memory	Mid-High
Number Memory	Mid-High
Design Memory	Mid-High
Manual Speed and Accuracy	High (where needed)
Mathematical Ability	High-Very High

* Ideal score for this profile, unless noted otherwise. See career path breakouts below for more detail.

Are you a science whiz? You may have a gift for a career in the physical or life sciences if you like to use your 3-D intuition and high problem-solving abilities to imagine new solutions to complex spatial problems. Perhaps you dream up and construct prototype inventions and gadgets in your mind's eye, and even build them in your spare time.

If you consider yourself a bit of a scholar or "geek," and read physics or biology books for fun, you may be an introverted Maestro spatial NT with high problem-solving abilities. Maestros know from an early age that they are not like the rest of the kids on the block; auspiciously, they don't really care to follow the pack. If this sounds like you, you could be wired for a career path as a solo expert, rather than a Tribal team player.

Do you have fantasies of being a university professor or research scientist? Maybe you see yourself creating new theories for understanding the mysteries of the universe, or unraveling secrets of the origins of life on the planet. If so, this may be your talent area. Also in this group are Maestros who apply the sciences. If you think you're a spatial Maestro but a tad more practical, you may be cut from the same cloth as technology inventors, R&D engineers, highly specialized doctors, and high-tech entrepreneurs or scientific consultants.

Introverted and extroverted Maestro spatial intuitives (and occasionally sensors) often take one of the following major career tracks in the physical and life sciences ballpark:

- **Physical and life sciences research academic.** Do you have what it takes to be an academic? On top of being a brilliant Maestro spatial intuitive, you've got to be fiercely independent, be logically minded, and have a burning passion to solve a complex spatial problem that will take a lifetime of commitment to understand. If you think a career in academic research is just a clever way to set your own schedule and bask in your PhD status, you're barking up the wrong tree. You have to be persistent for at least a decade, for little money. Most importantly, to be a successful scientist in today's competitive higher education system will require a natural talent for seeing out-of-the-box solutions, and diagnostic ability to help you leap to new and accurate conclusions. Scientists such as Isaac Newton and Albert Einstein were in this group, as are most physical and life scientists who seek to understand and solve complex problems.

- **Applied life scientist.** If you are fascinated by biology and have a sense that you are bright but not quite abstract enough to be a professor in an ivory tower, there are career pathways for you as well. Not all spatial Maestros are abstract academics and researchers; many prefer to study the sciences and then find ways to apply their knowledge to real-world, tangible problems. Highly specialized physicians fit this category, including neurosurgeons and oncologists, as well as doctors working in medical research fields. Also in this group are real-world-oriented Maestro spatial STs and SFs, who work with more concrete, spatial problems, including specialized dentists, chiropractors, veterinarians, and physicians of all subspecialties.
- **Applied physical scientist.** Do you have a knack for dreaming up new technological ideas or thinking of ways to improve such things as household appliances, cars, and computers? If so, you might fit the same group as the physical scientists who become highly specialized engineers and technologists. They work in research labs out in the real world, in fields such as nanotechnology, biomedical engineering, robotics, and artificial intelligence. These specialized scientific technologists often find a comfortable fit in the research and development department of high-tech engineering firms and government laboratories.
- **The technology entrepreneur and consultant.** Got an inkling that you're a bit of a maverick, with an interest in both science and business? Another avenue for spatial Maestros is the start-up venture—the high-tech entrepreneur. Maestros with high idea flow, intuition, and high diagnostic reasoning may find traditional academic environments less exciting and opt to take their inventive ideas to the marketplace as high-tech products. Many of the R&D engineers behind technology inventions are PhD-level scientists who decided not to become research academics.

CAUTIONS AND GENERAL RULES OF THUMB

- **Are you misunderstood? Scientifically minded Maestros often spend years trying to figure out what makes them different. Midcareer Maestros tell stories of how their parents tried to socialize them by pushing them to join clubs or play team sports. Strong introverted Maestros can get the impression that they're not normal because they'd rather read a book than toss a football. If this is the case, recognize that your type is often misunderstood. If you have an independent streak, it likely won't fade and may even get stronger in later life. Most scientific Maestros are very passionate people, especially the NFs and NTs, who seem discontent until they are fully committed to a life's work in pursuit of a unique area of mastery.**

- **Abstract enough for a PhD?** If you rated yourself as a spatial SF or ST, think long and hard about whether to pursue a PhD. Once you get beyond a master's degree, things get pretty abstract; results are fewer and farther between. A PhD is a ticket to do research. Advanced degrees can overqualify you for practical work, which you may find more satisfying. Many academics seeking career-change advice are Maestro sensors who are bored with long-term, theoretical research.

PHYSICAL/EARTH AND LIFE SCIENCES AND TECHNOLOGY INNOVATOR MAESTRO CAREER PATHS

The Physical Sciences Research Academic (Abstract Orientation)

- NT: astronomy, physics, chemistry, geology, geophysics, soil science, hydrology, oceanography, volcanology, petrology, mineralogy, atmospheric sciences, meteorology, climatology, earth system science, systems theory, cybernetics, physical geography, topography, cartography, geomorphology

The Applied Physical Scientist (Mix of Abstract and Concrete Orientation)

- NT, NF, ST (with tangible or spatial orientation): applied physics, acoustics, fluid dynamics, medical physics, fiber optics, laser physics, space exploration and space flight, astrodynamics, nanotechnology, nuclear engineering, quantum electronics, semiconductors, superconductors, vehicle dynamics, materials science, alternative energy and photovoltaics, weather forecasting, global warming, climate modeling, renewable energy, hydroelectric power, irrigation, agricultural productivity, economic geology, urban drainage, flood and drought prediction, water supply, green architecture, FBI analysis (forensic science research and technology services units)

The Life Sciences Research Academic (Mix of Abstract and Concrete Orientation)

- NT, NF: biology, molecular biology, cell biology, developmental biology, genetics, physiology (anatomy), neurology, immunology, evolutionary biology, zoology, marine biology, botany, biodiversity, behavioral ecology, paleontology, primatology, sociobiology, biogeography, biogeology

The Applied Life Scientist (Higher Extroversion, Concrete Orientation)

- NF, NT: alternative medicine, integrative medicine, internal medicine, neurology, preventive medicine, holistic health, naturopathic medicine, meditation and yoga instruction, acupuncture, medical research, biomedical research, biomedical engineering, biomedical technology, bioinformatics, Human Genome Project, neurophysiology, psychiatry, spatial epidemiology, public health
- ST, NT: conventional medicine, clinical laboratory science, dermatology, anesthesiology, emergency medicine, pathology, radiology, urology, cardiothoracic surgery, orthopedic surgery, neurosurgery, forensic medicine, specialized dentistry, forensic odontology, pharmaceutical research, clinical pharmacology
- SF, ST: veterinary medicine and dentistry, emergency medicine, plastic surgery, pediatrics, palliative care, OB/GYN, sports medicine, exercise science, sports nutrition and conditioning, massage therapy, cosmetic dentistry, pedodontics (pediatric dentistry)

The Technology Entrepreneur and Consultant (Higher Extroversion and Mix of Abstract-Concrete Orientation)

- **NT, NF, ST* (with tangible or spatial orientation): agricultural technology, domestic technology, software technology, digital electronic technology, biotechnology, computer engineering, video game design, green architecture, sustainable development, new urbanism, renewable energy, alternative fuel, alternative transportation, military weaponry, social entrepreneurship, robotics, artificial intelligence, human-computer interface (HCI), cybernetics**

***STs with strong diagnostic reasoning and idea flow also fit into the entrepreneur's club, usually playing a "right-hand" role focused on the practicality of a new product or service.**

Rate Yourself

How well does the Physical/Earth and Life Sciences and Technology Maestro profile describe you?

___ Nails me perfectly
___ Mostly describes me
___ Partly describes me
___ Not at all

MAESTRO APTITUDE PROFILE 2: THE SOCIAL SCIENCES AND HUMANITIES MAESTRO

Natural Talents and Traits	Profile Scores
Core Personality Type	Introverted and Extroverted Maestro
General Direction	Nonspatial Intuitive
Specific Career Path	Nonspatial NT and NF*
Spatial-Nonspatial Orientation	Nonspatial-Tangible
Diagnostic Reasoning	High
Analytical Reasoning	Mid-High
Rate of Idea Flow	Depends on situation
Visual Dexterity	Depends on situation
Associative Memory	Mid-High
Intrapersonal Intelligence	High, where needed
Interpersonal Intelligence	High, where needed
Language Ability	High

* Ideal score for this profile, unless noted otherwise. See career path breakouts below for more detail.

Are you fascinated by what makes people tick? If you often find yourself observing people and seeking insight into their actions, you may be a behavioral Maestro. People with this profile are intensely curious about human motives. Rather than seeking to be like most people, they like studying people and culture and are often driven to understand *why* people do what they do. If you find yourself regularly reading self-help, poetry, history, or biography books for pleasure, you are much like the members of this unique group—the Maestro nonspatial NFs and NTs.

Social sciences and humanities Maestros often have heightened intuition and interpersonal intelligence; their ability to read what's going on inside someone else's head is sometimes uncanny. Strong introverts with these abilities can happily spend hours pondering their own thoughts and daydreams, and often have the poet's ability to see from a unique, personal perspective. If these powers of empathy and insight into people's moods and intentions are a big part of your life, the social sciences and humanities fields may be in your talent area.

Introverted and extroverted Maestro nonspatial initiatives (and occasionally sensors) often take one of the following major career tracks in the social sciences and humanities talent category:

- **Social science research academic.** Are you scientific, but more interested in social science than physical things? Many social scientists use the same intuitive thinking NT and diagnostic reasoning abilities as physical scientists, but aim their objective and quantitative curiosity to study the behavior of people.
- **Humanities scholar.** Do you like to look beyond the facts to explore the inner world of others? Behavioral Maestros use high problem-solving intuitive and diagnostic talents to gain insight into the internal life of others; their ability to read human behavior is a gift that is almost impossible to learn through formal training. For example, biographical historians who study Abraham Lincoln's life and inner motivations need to think beyond the facts to reach their conclusions.
- **Applied social scientist and humanities specialist.** Are you fascinated by people and cultural behavior, but driven to get results and solve current problems in the real world? Some nonspatial Maestros are more concrete, and even though most are quite conceptual, not all are cut out for abstract and theoretical research typical of the academic world; some prefer to apply their ideas in a more tangible way. For instance, an applied version of political science is law; attorneys are applied social scientists in the same way doctors are applied biologists. The same is true of humanities. The applied theologian would be the religious leader, the applied musicologist would be a music teacher, and the applied linguist would be a language teacher.
- **Applied mathematician.** Are you conceptual, but more interested in math than people? The mathematical Maestro also fits into the nonspatial expert problem-solving profile and sometimes works side by side with sociologists, economists, and psychologists. Statistics is an applied discipline in social science research think tanks, where heavy-duty number crunching is a key tool. Advanced mathematics is used to support scientific research, such as bioinformatics, epi-

demiology, and operations research. Most of these Maestros are nonspatial-tangible NTs and STs, and naturally more objective and quantitative.

- **Concept entrepreneur and consultant.** Do you love the social sciences but have an urge to be self-employed and run your own consulting practice? Many Maestro nonspatial intuitives (and occasionally sensors) bypass the academic world altogether and become entrepreneurs and consultants. For example, marketing researchers apply sociology, and public policy consultants apply political science. Psychotherapists, management consultants, and career coaches apply both sociology and psychology in their practices to help people and organizations reinvent themselves. Also in this group are independent scholars who operate outside the academic system—they are usually rare, brilliant maverick types who make new social science discoveries and write books that shift conventional social paradigms.

CAUTIONS AND GENERAL RULES OF THUMB

- **For parents and teachers of high school students.** How well are you steering your science-bound Maestro NFs and NTs? The human sciences are usually invisible to the typical high school senior getting ready to pick a college major. It's a rare high school student who recognizes that he may fit perfectly with one of the social sciences such as psychology, sociology, economics, and political science.

  If you are encouraging bright young Maestros to pursue careers in "science," which typically means physical sciences such as physics and chemistry, be extra thoughtful. On the nonspatial side of the science aptitude fence there's a whole world of sciences that are not physical or tangible—the social sciences, which deal with concepts and ideas about people, society, and culture.

- **For young Maestros.** If you're a Maestro and have an inclination to pursue a physical science path, proceed with caution—not all Maestros are born with strong spatial orientation. Statistically, 50 percent of males and 75 percent of females are nonspatial, which means that most female Maestros and half of male Maestros may be more naturally suited for the social sciences and humanities. At Rockport Institute we have tested the aptitudes of many unhappy engineers, technologists, biologists, chemists, and various other physical scientists. Well into their careers in 3-D science fields, they discovered that their natural talent and personality were geared more for the human behavioral and social science fields.

SOCIAL SCIENCES AND HUMANITIES MAESTRO CAREER PATHS

The Social Research Scientist (Abstract Orientation)

- NT: economics, political science, sociology, quantitative psychology, research methods, comparative psychology, public health, social statistics, demography, psychometrics
- NF: research psychology, personality psychology, social psychology, political sociology, law, social history, cultural anthropology, ethnology, ethnomusicology, linguistics, phonology, psycholinguistics, behavioral finance and economics, women's studies
- NF, NT (with tangible or spatial orientation)*: archaeology, geography, demographics, physical anthropology, psychobiology, primatology, human evolution, prehistory, paleontology, paleoanthropology, cognitive psychol-

ogy, neuroanthropology, evolutionary psychology, population genetics, neurolinguistics, science and technology studies, film studies, urban studies, econophysics, neuropsychology, biological psychology, developmental psychology

*Spatial orientation may be needed in niches of social science that combine with physical and life sciences.

The Applied Social Scientist (Mix of Abstract and Concrete Orientation)

- NF, SF: nonacademic research (think tank), science journalism, photojournalism, counseling psychology, public policy, demography, public health, educational psychology, health psychology, organizational psychology, school psychology, FBI analyst (behavioral analysis unit)
- NT, ST: nonacademic research (think tank), clinical psychology, forensic psychology, lawyer, judge, legal psychology, forensic accounting, biostatistics, marketing research, strategic and defense intelligence analysis, FBI analyst (counterterrorism unit)
- NF, NT (with tangible to spatial orientation): somatic psychology, neurotherapy, biofeedback therapy, psychiatry, art and music therapy for neurobiological disorders, yoga and meditation instruction, sports psychology, sex therapy, epidemiology, criminology, forensic anthropology, speech pathology, human factors psychology, industrial psychology

The Humanities Scholar (Abstract Orientation)

- NF, NT: classics, history, linguistics, literary scholarship, musicology, philosophy, mythology, art history, art criticism, creative writing, theater, comedy, opera, religion
- NF, SF, NT (with tangible to spatial orientation): architectural historian, history of painting, history of sculpture, history of performing arts (dance, choreography, magic, juggling, film)
- SF, ST (with tangible to spatial orientation): military history, performing arts history (marching arts, brass bands)

The Applied Humanities Specialist (Mix of Abstract and Concrete Orientation)

- NF, SF, ST: music education, music performance, music composition, dance education, language education, art education, film studies, film scoring, film directing, theater acting and directing, stagecraft, screenwriting, fiction writing, nonfiction writing, choreography, clergy, life coaching, counseling, art appraisal, nonprofit arts management, advocacy for the arts

The Applied Mathematician (Mix of Abstract and Concrete Orientation)

- NT, ST: statistics, probability, game theory, cryptanalysis, survey methodology, social statistics, opinion polling, marketing research, epidemiology, operations research, social informatics, statistical process control, actuary science, financial planning, computational finance, financial engineering, financial economics, experimental finance, investment management, derivatives and securities trading, investment banking

The Maestro Politician (Mix of Abstract and Concrete Orientation)

- NF, NT: U.S. president, senator, congressman, state governor, Supreme Court justice, appellate court judge, U.S. federal agency and department secretary

The Concept Innovator, Consultant, and Entrepreneur (Mix of Abstract and Concrete Orientation)

- NF, NT (with nonspatial to tangible orientation): career consulting, life coaching, motivational speaking, drama coaching, organization development consulting, change management consulting, training and development consulting, educational consulting, political campaign strategy, business strategy consulting, social entrepreneurship, documentary filmmaking, marketing consulting, economic consulting, legal consulting, jury consulting, speechwriting
- NT: investment broker, venture capitalist, constitutional lawyer, political pundit, political writer, economic consultant

Rate Yourself

How well does the Social Sciences and Humanities Maestro profile describe you?

___ Nails me perfectly
___ Mostly describes me
___ Partly describes me
___ Not at all

MAESTRO APTITUDE PROFILE 3: THE CREATIVE AND FINE ARTS MAESTRO

Natural Talents and Traits	Profile Scores
Core Personality Type	Introverted Maestro*
General Direction	All
Specific Career Path	All
Spatial-Nonspatial Orientation	Depends on situation
Abstract-Concrete Orientation	Depends on situation
Diagnostic Reasoning	Low-Mid*
Analytical Reasoning	Low-Mid
Rate of Idea Flow	Mid-High
Visual Dexterity	Depends on situation
Associative Memory	High for literary arts
Design Memory	High for visual arts
Manual Speed and Accuracy	High, where needed
Intrapersonal Intelligence	High, where needed
Interpersonal Intelligence	High, where needed
Musical Ability	High for musical arts

Language Ability	High for literary arts
Body Kinesthetic	High for performance arts

* Ideal score for this profile, unless noted otherwise. See career path breakouts below for more detail.

Do you have a flair for communicating through works of art or music? Fine arts fields attract committed introverted Maestro NFs, NTs, SFs, and occasionally STs, who have an obsessive quality that is the secret to their success. To excel in the arts requires a natural drive to spend many hours each day in solitude mastering an art or craft.

If you are driven to express something unique to the world, you may be one of these creative Maestro types. Arts are a form of personal commentary, and these highly eclectic Maestros use their powers of intuition and personal point of view to reflect what they see in culture—and often try to move culture in a new direction. If you rely more on your perceptive intuition, keen senses, and idea flow, rather than problem-solving talents, this may be your talent ballpark. The core aptitude profile is the introverted Maestro intuitive or sensor with high idea flow and low diagnostic reasoning.

Maestro spatial and nonspatial NFs, NTs, SFs, and occasionally STs often take one of the following major career tracks in the fine arts and creative performer talent area:

- **The artist.** Do you see the world through a unique aesthetic lens? Unlike the Tribal commercial artists and creatives who make art for business applications, Maestro artists are the painters, musicians, performers, and writers who make art for art's sake. Like most Maestros who dance to the beat of a different drummer, this is to your advantage in the fine arts; the greatest accolades go to those with a unique vision. There are differing specialized abilities that compliment the core creative introverted Maestro talent profile. The aptitudes that suit various art forms depend on your medium of expression, whether it's visual fine art, musical art, bodily/performance art, literary art, or craft. More on this in the "Cautions" box on the next page.
- **The creative critic.** Do you find that you just can't help critiquing or poking fun at culture and society? Although it's not an aptitude needed to create art, there is room for diagnostic reasoning ability in the arts, namely, in roles critiquing others' art, instructing others on how to improve their art or craft, and making art that satirizes or comments on the state of the world. Stand-up comedians are usually diagnostic-creative Maestros who love to poke fun at our cultural quirks.
- **The artisan.** Are you a sensual artistic type with a functional bent? Artisans are artists who produce functional works—often introverted Maestro spatial SF and ST with low idea flow. The master chef uses an eye for design, acute sense of taste, spatial orientation, and concentrated idea flow to craft an edible work of art. Some artisans work with wood to create artistic and functional furniture; those with a musical ear may become luthiers, who make stringed instruments. The artisan's world is a sensual one, working with their hands and heightened sensory gifts; they bask in smells, tastes, and touch as they craft their masterpieces.

CAUTIONS AND GENERAL RULES OF THUMB

- **Are you too self-critical to be an artist?** Have you tried your hand at making art but get bogged down in trying to make it too perfect? In general, lower diagnostic problem solving is a blessing in the artistic fields; high scores often produce a self-critical tendency. Artists who measure high in diagnostic reasoning often complain of a nagging inner critic that is hard to please. Making art requires practicing your craft with a less critical mind, as making mistakes and gradual progress are integral parts of your life's work. Low diagnostic talent contributes to a more tolerant mind. Of course, there have been many artists that were high diagnostic, but they usually lived a somewhat tortured life because they were rarely happy with their work.
- **Realism.** Do you prefer to create a literal interpretation of what you see, hear, and feel? For example, visual arts in the school of realism such as painting a landscape or portrait rely on natural strengths in spatial orientation, sensing, and design memory. In making accurate-to-life art, a talent for 3-D or tangible visualization and acute awareness of sensual details are major parts of the talent suite. Realism is also better suited to a steady mind with low idea flow, where concentration and attention to detail are typical of Maestros who excel in this form of art. Whether the realist creative Maestro with a literal or classical style is producing visual, musical, or performance art, the talent profile is typically the introverted Maestro SF with low idea flow. Their desire is to accurately reproduce or duplicate the original subject, rather than invent something new.
- **Interpretive art.** Do you prefer to make art that represents what you see, hear, or feel with a more personal interpretation? High idea flow artists with intuition, like Picasso, see the world metaphorically and poetically. Artists with very high idea flow are impatient with exacting details—abstract artists and impressionists use quicker strokes of paint to communicate their inner vision. If you have a very strong imagination, your art may tend toward a symbolic representation of the subject. For example, both Rodin and Dalí created spatial art with an intuitive's ability for conveying social meaning, story, and metaphor. Improvisational jazz musicians such as Miles Davis and John Coltrane were Maestro intuitives with high idea flow and musical gifts—both took jazz in new directions more than once in their lifetimes. In the dance arts, Martha Graham brought these same Maestro creative aptitudes, combined with extraordinary body kinesthetic ability; she broke all the rules and pioneered the school of modern dance. In the literary world, Mark Twain and Virginia Woolf were perfect embodiments of the introverted Maestro intuitive with high idea flow and high diagnostic reasoning.

CREATIVE AND FINE ARTS MAESTRO CAREER PATHS

The Fine Artist

- NF, NT (with spatial orientation where needed): theater acting, fiction writing, serious nonfiction writing, poetry, visual poetry, art photography (fine art, candid, documentary, photojournalism, erotic), screenwriting, script doctor, playwright (dramatist), drawing and painting, independent filmmaking, documentary filmmaking
- SF, ST (with spatial orientation and low idea flow): painting (landscape, portrait, still life), sculpture, ceramics, stained glass, furniture, printmaking, photography (landscape, portrait, sports, nature, still life, fashion, forensic)

The Musical Artist

- NF, NT (improvisational style): classical, jazz, blues, funk, country, bluegrass, folk, and progressive rock music composition and performance
- SF, ST (perform as originally transcribed): orchestral music performance, operas, and musicals

The Performance Artist

- SF, NF (with spatial orientation and high body kinesthetic intelligence): acting, stage dance, choreography, yoga, juggling, circus (Cirque du Soleil), gymnastics, acrobatics

The Creative Critic

- NT, NF (with high diagnostic reasoning and tonal memory where needed): comedy, comedy writing, social satire, political commentary, political cartoonist, comic book scriptwriter, sitcom writer (*The Simpsons*); teachers in the visual arts, music, theater, and dance; art critics and gallery owners

The Artisan

- SF, ST (with spatial orientation, low idea flow, and tonal memory where needed): furniture making, instrument making, piano tuning, executive chef, pastry chef, pottery, jewelry, gardening, makeup art, costume design
- NF, NT (with spatial orientation, high idea flow, and tonal memory where needed): film set design, film sound editing, cinematography, film special effects and animation, theater stagecraft, film scoring

Rate Yourself

How well does the Creative and Fine Arts Maestro profile describe you?

___ Nails me perfectly
___ Mostly describes me
___ Partly describes me
___ Not at all

MAESTRO APTITUDE PROFILE 4: THE SPECIALIZED KNOWLEDGE MAESTRO

Natural Talents and Traits	Profile Scores
Core Personality Type	Introverted Maestro
General Direction	All
Specific Career Path	All
Spatial-Nonspatial Orientation	Depends on situation
Diagnostic Reasoning	Low-Mid
Analytical Reasoning	Low-Mid-High

Rate of Idea Flow	Low-Mid
Visual Dexterity	High, where needed
Associative Memory	High, where needed
Number Memory	High, where needed
Design Memory	High, where needed
Manual Speed and Accuracy	High, where needed

Are you so single-mindedly passionate about a subject that you've become a walking encyclopedia on the topic? There is a fourth career area that suits Maestros—the specialized knowledge Maestro. If you've got the talents of a subject matter Maestro, you are on course to spend a lifetime mastering a deep, specific body of knowledge.

The specialized knowledge expert's key talents are introverted Maestro with low to mid-range problem solving, low idea flow, and high memories. If you've got these talents, you may be viewed as a "geek" by the Tribals, but hey, they secretly admire your genius. Your gift—to learn and retain an archive of wisdom and "know-how" in your mind—drives you to dive into the depths of your field with unrelenting curiosity. In the hidden spaces of great libraries, archives, and museums are the fulfilled, solitary specialized knowledge Maestros.

Introverted Maestro spatial and nonspatial intuitives and sensors often take one of the following career tracks in the specialized knowledge Maestro talent ballpark:

- **Information and object specialists.** If you're one of these specialized Maestros, would you be an expert with information or things? Some of these Maestros specialize in information and data fields such as library science and art history. The more spatial Maestros are usually more interested in objects and things, like gemologists, diamond cutters, and sommeliers, who can help you choose the right wine to go with your braised duck. These Maestros rely extensively on their memories. If museums and libraries feel like home territory to you, you're in the same general talent area as curators, archivists, librarians, gemologists, perfumers, docents, antiques appraisers, and art historians.
- **Craftsman and tradesman.** Do you have a knack for crafting things? Craftspeople and tradespeople are "craft and technique" specialists, using tactile hands-on knowledge to craft, build, and repair things. Shoe repair, furniture repair, jewelry repair, chefs, art restorers, and animal groomers all use specialized methods and skills to craft and repair physical objects, as do electricians, plumbers, stonemasons, and welders. If you have acute sensing perception and concentrated idea flow, this specialized Maestro niche may be in your talent area.
- **Naturalist.** Love to be out in the woods studying Mother Nature? Some knowledge maestros specialize in the natural world. Foresters, park rangers, botanists, ecologists, nature photographers, and geologists all use spatial orientation, analytical reasoning, sensing perception, and high design memory to identify, study, and understand the various natural elements, plants, animals, fish, rivers, trees, rocks, and geological terrain in their specialized fields of study.

GENERAL RULE OF THUMB

If the specialized knowledge Maestro's work involves classifying data or objects, as with librarians, curators, and bibliographers, a midrange to strong analytical reasoning talent would be needed.

SPECIALIZED KNOWLEDGE MAESTRO CAREER PATHS

The Object Specialist (Tangible to Spatial Orientation)

- SF, ST: archaeology, gemology, entomology, vintner, perfumer, sommelier, bartending, forensic odontology, forensic entomology, forensic firearms, ballistic fingerprinting, forensic geology, museum studies, museum curator, museum archivist, art conservation and restoration, color specialist, art history, antiques appraiser, master gardener (botanical gardens)

The Data Specialist (Nonspatial Orientation)

- NF, NT, SF, ST: library science, medical librarian, hospital librarian, news agency librarian, archivists, art appraiser, digital preservation, bibliography, museum docent, bioinformatics, cheminformatics, ecoinformatics, geoinformatics, neuroinformatics, health informatics, laboratory informatics, social informatics, community informatics, data mining, musicology, linguist, translator, historian

The Craftsman (Spatial Orientation)

- SF (with spatial orientation): furniture making and repair, jewelry making and repair, clothing and shoe making and repair, luthier, instrument repair, woodworking, cooking, art restoration, massage therapy, animal grooming, forensic facial reconstruction, dental technician

The Tradesman (Spatial Orientation)

- ST (with spatial orientation): carpentry, construction, plumbing, electrical, stonemasonry, appliance repair, chef/cook, cement mason, barber, hairstylist, leatherworker, line worker, locksmith, painter, plasterer, sheet metal worker, machinist, mechanic, millwright, mold maker, watchmaker, welder

The Naturalist (Tangible-Spatial Orientation)

- NF, NT, SF, ST: agricultural science, organic farming, permaculture, organic gardening, forestry, forest engineering, forest management, woodland management, horticulture, botany, ethnobotany, viticulture, conservation biology, deep ecology, sustainable living, geoarchaeology, park ranger, forest-fire fighting, search and rescue

Rate Yourself

How well does the Specialized Knowledge Maestro profile describe you?

___ Nails me perfectly
___ Mostly describes me
___ Partly describes me
___ Not at all

THE BODY KINESTHETIC AND TERRAIN NAVIGATOR APTITUDE PROFILE

Natural Talents and Traits	**Profile Scores**
Core Personality Type	All
General Direction	Primarily Spatial Sensors*
Specific Career Path	All (Spatial ST and SF are most common)
Spatial-Nonspatial Orientation	Tangible-Spatial
Diagnostic Reasoning	Low-Mid*
Analytical Reasoning	Low-Mid
Rate of Idea Flow	Low-Mid*
Design Memory	High, where needed
Body Kinesthetic	High

* Ideal score for this profile, unless noted otherwise. See career path breakouts below for more detail.

Is your body your talent? Are you always in motion, athletically graceful or enjoy being outdoors much of the day? If you were a gifted athlete from an early age, you probably have been recognized for your ability to control your body movements in sports and outdoor activities. Although each of us is packaged with varying strengths that come with our unique body type, kinesthetically gifted people stand out as exceptional in this area.

- **Athlete, outdoorsman, navigator.** If you're highly athletic, you might consider it as a component of your career. If so, you are in the same club as outdoorsmen, navigators, soldiers, law enforcement officers, heavy equipment operators, dancers, and even fashion models. People with this talent profile enjoy using their body as a primary feature of their work. You would rely extensively on spatial orientation to orient yourself in the real-world terrain, and use your sensing perception to provide an acute awareness of physical surroundings (sight, sound, smell, touch).
- **Protector.** Do you imagine yourself fighting fires, saving lives, or enforcing laws? If you have a talent for practical real-world problem solving, this may be an exciting career path to consider. Firefighters use spatial orientation to navigate their way through burning buildings, and police officers use 3-D reasoning every day on the beat.

GENERAL RULES OF THUMB

- **No "one-size-fits-all" athlete.** There is a broad spectrum of body kinesthetic talents; there is no universal or one-size-fits-all athletic type. Basketball players are tall and thin ectomorphs with sprinter muscle fibers, and sumo wrestlers are endomorphs with short legs and a low center of gravity, while football players are mesomorphs with muscles built for endurance and strength.
- **Thrill seeker?** Are you cut out for urgent problem solving? As with any critical situation where split-second decisions are made with limited information, protectors in all fields of public service benefit from diagnostic reasoning, higher idea flow, and acute visual dexterity to see details, with the cool-headed ST temperament to evaluate situations without being blinded by emotions or personal biases.
- **Never get lost in the woods?** The combination of high spatial orientation and design memory gives an ability that is highly beneficial for people who spend time navigating outdoor terrain or memorizing plays, formations, and strategies on a playing field, as well as maneuvering on the battlefield.
- **Got rhythm and flair?** A gift not typically recognized as a benefit in some sports is musical intelligence, including tonal memory and rhythm. For instance, in addition to a basketball player's athletic talent, musical abilities contribute to the graceful ballet-like dance happening between the teammates, as well as timing and elegance of body movement on the court. Fashion models combine their body intelligence with a sense of rhythm to strut gracefully down the runway.
- **Tribal team player?** Every day the local news gives us a glimpse of the amazing teamwork and skill displayed by our firefighters, police officers, and paramedics. Especially for professional firefighters in major cities, being a Tribal teammate is a way of life; they work, eat, and sleep under the same roof.
- **Diplomatic?** More often than not, police officers find themselves intervening in domestic disputes and calming the tempers of people threatening harm to one another. Talents for diplomacy and empathy are handy in these heated moments. Tribal SFs are naturals at defusing these situations and getting people to calm down. Unlike the stereotype of police being thick-skinned personality types, a great deal of diplomatic tact is needed in routine law enforcement. Animal lovers with "protector" qualities might consider a career path as an enforcer of the humane treatment of animals.

BODY KINESTHETIC AND TERRAIN NAVIGATOR CAREER PATHS

The Team Athlete (Tribal)

- ST, SF: team sports: basketball, football, baseball, soccer, rugby, volleyball

The Solo Athlete (Maestro)

- ST, SF: individual sports: golf, tennis, Olympic athletics (archery, gymnastics, cycling, track and field, fencing, swimming, diving, show jumping, shooting, table tennis, weight lifting)

The Head Coach

- ST, SF: athletic head coaching in all sports, high school level
- NT, NF: athletic head coaching in all sports, college and professional levels

The Outdoorsman

- ST, SF: ecotourism, engineering geology, environmental geology, conservation ecology, adventure education guide, wildlife management and conservation, hunting, fishing, trapping, farming, forest ranger, park ranger, search and rescue

The Navigator

- ST: bus driver, taxi driver, chauffeur, truck driver, mail and package courier, commercial airline pilot, military fighter pilot, helicopter pilot, U.S. merchant marine (midshipman)

The Protector

- SF, ST: firefighting; paramedic/EMT; federal, state, and local law enforcement; police officer; Capitol police; Secret Service agent; public safety officer; corrections officer; deputy sheriff; police chief; state trooper
- ST, NT: Combat specialty in the U.S. military (Army, Navy, Air Force, Marines, Coast Guard), National Guard, homeland security, port security, DEA field agent, FBI agent (hostage rescue team, law enforcement and critical incident units), ATF field agent, immigration and customs agent, border patrol agent, FEMA urban search and rescue task force, animal search and rescue

Heavy Equipment Operator

- ST: construction, landscaping, building demolition, mining equipment operation, manufacturing equipment operation, steel and heavy metals manufacturing, military tank operator, military and combat engineering, driller (oil rig), container ship crane operator, railroad engineer

The Model (Maestro)

- ST, SF: modeling in fashion, glamour, fitness, bikini, fine arts, hand models, acting, dancing, mime artistry

Rate Yourself

How well does the Body Kinesthetic and Terrain Navigator profile describe you?

___ Nails me perfectly
___ Mostly describes me
___ Partly describes me
___ Not at all

RESOURCES AND CONTACT INFORMATION

On the Rockport Institute Web site (www.rockportinstitute.com) you will find resources to assist you in working through this book. This includes downloadable notebooks to use with this book, other information for readers, and the world's most-used resume-writing guide, "How to Write a Masterpiece of a Resume."

You can also find out about Rockport's programs and services to help you design your future career. I strongly believe everyone committed to choosing the perfect career should go through Rockport's Career Testing Program, which measures natural talents and abilities, or a similar program from another source. If you find the process in this book difficult to do or confusing, Rockport also offers complete career design coaching programs that can guide you through your career design project.

If you find this career design method useful and want more depth about some of the concepts I've introduced, you might find it useful to get a copy of my previous book, *The Pathfinder: How to Choose or Change Your Career for a Lifetime of Satisfaction and Success.*

I also recommend that everyone going through this process get a copy of *Do What You Are: Discover the Perfect Career for You Through the Secrets of Personality Type* by Paul D. Tieger. This is the best book about work and personality type. We use this along with our own books with many of our clients.

WANT TO START A REVOLUTION?

If you are a student (or former student), don't let your school get away with the miserable career design tools they use. Every year the academic community's dim understanding of what it takes to have a career that truly fits and their lack of commitment to the quality of their students' lives cause hundreds of thousands of people to head into lives that will be unnecessarily unfulfilling and less than fully productive. Don't let them get away with this! This is an opportunity to make a huge difference in the lives of many people. What if you could convince or embarrass your school into recognizing that what they are now doing to help students choose a fitting career is a total failure? What if you could encourage them to take on career choice as a serious subject, with competent classroom courses? What if they were committed to turning the campus career center into a highly competent career design lab? Compared with the huge problems humanity and the planet are facing, this is an easy one to solve. And if this problem can be solved, the solution will provide all of us with a workforce that is more talented, more committed to excellence, and having much more fun.

ACKNOWLEDGMENTS

Anthony Spadafore, my coauthor and senior coach at Rockport Institute, for an extraordinary effort creating powerful and practical career design tools, particularly for his work in the development of the Career Finder section.

Mitra Lore, for making my life a daily miracle; Nancy Chek, for her wisdom and brilliant editing of this book; Neema Moraveji, for encouragement and support; Patti Miller, for her fine editing of Anthony's parts of this book; Rick Duff, for great ideas; Joan Sugerman, for magnificent coaching; Amanda Patten, my excellent Simon and Schuster editor; Trish Todd, who convinced me to write this; and Loretta Barrett, my amazing agent. My ancestors all the way back to Africa—thanks, guys! And special thanks to all of the many young people who were cocreators of this book.

My mentors: my mom and dad; Sam Lightnin' Hopkins; Buckminster Fuller; Werner Erhard; Randy MacNamara; I. J. "Toto" Grandes del Mazo; Dr. W. Edwards Deming; my miraculous wife, Mitra; Sam Boogandoo Lore, now in dog heaven; my wonderful clients, who taught me everything in this book.

My inspirations: John, Paul, George, and Ringo; Bob Dylan; Rembrandt; Ravi Shankar; Yeshua the carpenter; Sid Gautama.

ABOUT THE AUTHOR

Nicholas Lore is the original creator of the field of career coaching and developer of many of the leading-edge methods used in the field. He has been personally commended for excellence by two U.S. presidents. His message is that you can have a career that you love so much that you actually look forward to going to work. As the director of Rockport Institute, he has directly helped more than fourteen thousand people choose their careers, as well as hundreds of thousands of others through his writings and speaking engagements.

He has been a corporate CEO, manufacturing plant manager, entrepreneur, researcher in the field of psychology, blues singer and guitar player, organic farming pioneer, energy efficiency expert, market gardener, well driller, weave room fixer, and newspaper boy.

LEGAL NOTICE

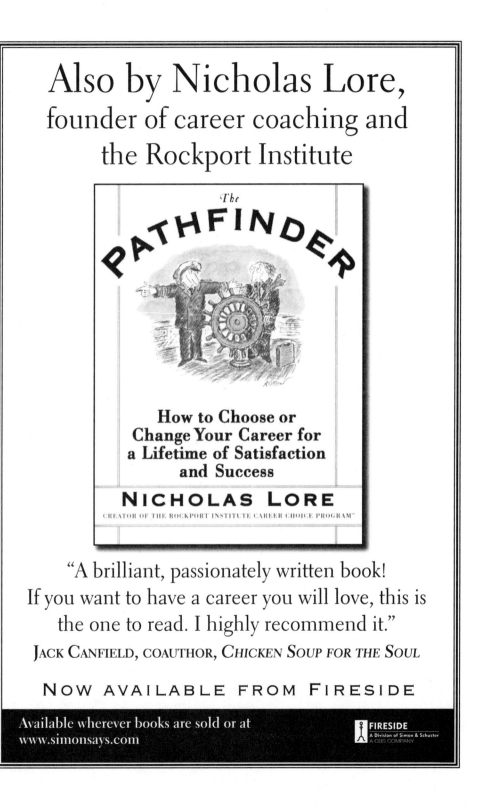